[the nest]
home
design handbook

[the nest] home
design handbook

Simple ways to
decorate, organize,
and personalize
your place

Carley Roney

and the editors of
TheNest.com

Photographs by Ellen Silverman

Clarkson Potter/Publishers
New York

All rights reserved.
Published in the United States by Clarkson Potter/Publishers,
an imprint of the Crown Publishing Group,
a division of Random House, Inc., New York.
www.crownpublishing.com
www.clarksonpotter.com

Clarkson N. Potter is a trademark and Potter with colophon
is a registered trademark of Random House, Inc.

Library of Congress Cataloging-in-Publication Data
is available on request.

ISBN 978-0-307-34191-4

Printed in Singapore

Design by Liza Aelion and Victor Thompson/The Nest

10   9   8   7   6   5   4   3   2   1

First Edition

contents

sleep

stash

resources

A design detail as simple as a vertical hand-painted wall stripe in a bold color personalizes a space.

start here

a well-decorated home looks attractive to guests, but *your* well-decorated home is an extension of your personality. Some people wake up in the morning with an instant understanding of their style. They move into a new place and know *exactly* how they are going to arrange the rooms. They know what they love and how to effortlessly pull the pieces together. And then there are the rest of us. It's not that we lack opinions or taste, we just like lots of things—and we're not always sure how to combine them. We have a sense of how stuff should work but aren't confident enough to trust our instincts, or we lack the pieces needed to complete the look. So the space just stays not quite right.

Don't give in to your doubt. A well-designed living space is as essential as the clothes you wear to work. You'll feel better, cooler, smarter, and more confident if your look is not only pulled together, but also reflects your personality. So where to begin? Tackling your whole space can be intimidating, so think of it as an adventure. Get prepared: Here are the eight things you should consider before starting your project.

1. Set a deadline and a budget. Why do home improvement projects seem to drag on endlessly? Unlike with a wedding, there's rarely a drop-dead date. So pick one, right away. Make it realistic (not next week—probably not next month, either), and stick to it. Write it on your calendar. Plan a huge housewarming party for that date and send out save-the-dates to all of your friends. It'll keep you on your toes! Even if you've lived in a place for three years, throw a celebration to say farewell to the same lackluster décor and welcome in your new living space. You also need a budget. Basic rearranging can be done without cash, but chances are you'll need to buy new bed linens or a chair or a couch. Decide right away how much you can devote to new purchases and set your sights accordingly. And keep in mind, no budget is ever big enough!

interior design cheat sheet

Want to know a little secret? There's actually a science to making a room look good. It's all about understanding (and acting on) basic design principles—overarching ideas like balance and scale. You also need to consider color, texture, light, and other specific elements, but we'll get to those later in the book. First, study up on the basic principles that will impact your space.

1 Harmony

Make sure the mood of the room is cohesive or unified. The arrangement of furniture should fit the style of your furnishings. For example, if you're going for a minimalist, modern look, don't have a cluttered corner of traditional accents. Harmony doesn't expel the chance for contrast. Using opposing elements like modern and traditional furniture can be successful when done in equal parts, like a checkerboard.

2 Rhythm

It's the repetition of elements in space and time. There's always a beginning and an end to the pattern: think of columns, or an organized grouping of photos. Symmetry, arranging elements around a center line like a fireplace, is one way to create rhythm, but it's just as rhythmic to repeat shape (for example, a circular coffee table is matched with a circular mirror) or color.

3 Scale

Scale compares the size or dimension of one thing to another. In order to properly keep a room to scale, you need to take the sizes of objects into consideration. The heights and weights of your furniture should be relative to the size of your room. A giant sofa in a tiny living room won't look right; neither will tiny nightstands next to a king-size bed. This also relates to the proportion of objects: The shade of a lamp has to be in proportion to the base.

4 Emphasis

Every room needs a focal point—the area that draws your eye. Whether it's an existing focal point (say an exposed brick wall) or a chosen one (a great patterned armchair), you need to emphasize the area around it so that everything else leads the eye to the focal point. You can also use emphasis to divert the eye from an existing focal point (an ugly fireplace) by placing hot colors or small and visually interesting items away from the area.

5 Balance

Similar to establishing harmony, balance is all about arranging furniture in a way that's pleasing to the eye. Centering certainly does the trick (think of how you hang paintings), but it's more about evenly distributing the visual weight of furniture so that no one piece overwhelms another. You need to arrange the elements of the room to provide an equilibrium: You wouldn't put an entertainment unit next to an ornate fireplace. Rather, if you have a large piece at one end of the room (the fireplace), you need to balance it out with another visually weighty piece at the other end (the entertainment unit).

2. Pick a room. Prioritize your time and resources. This book starts with the most public areas of your home leading to the most private, but if you'd rather begin by creating a calming oasis in the bedroom, go for it. Of course, some things will need to be done throughout your home, like cleaning up and appropriately categorizing everything, but working on one room at a time and following through until the last pillow is in place will help you avoid the feeling of having a hundred incomplete projects under way.

3. Find your style and make a statement. Unless you have a home with an open floor plan, each room can make a boldly different statement. Use your personality. If you live to cook and entertain, fill your kitchen with cheerful colors and artwork. More the traditional type? Start with a formal dining room conducive to serious conversation. And if you'd like them both, that's okay, too!

4. Get on the same page. The space you inhabit is not only yours, it's shared with cohabitants. What are your ideas? What are theirs? Put your inspiration on paper. Choose the colors and styles of specific items you want, and create a design inspiration sheet. You don't have to hammer out all the details right away. Focus on two things: color and spirit.

5. Get up to speed. Learn the basics when it comes to design. This book is all about understanding décor. You'll find secrets that stylists and designers use every day, and once you know why you like certain styles and ideas, you'll be able to project them onto your own stuff.

6. Throw it out. If you're moving into a new space, it's almost easier if you start with nothing. This is especially important if you're combining two sets of stuff. If you can't bear to part with an item, label it and store it in the basement or in a closet. Compromise is important here, too. If you veto an item your cohabitant loves because it won't fit into the decorating scheme, use it in a different room.

7. Shop wisely. Don't buy anything until you really know what you want, and never feel pressure to fill a space. Sparse spaces can be lovely if done right. Know what to invest in. Think of the bed, the couch, and shelves as staples, and the rest as accents.

8. Enjoy the process. Even if you make a bad decision (those bloodred walls may have seemed like a good idea on paper . . .), know that all things design are reversible. Granted, if you're tearing down walls or retiling a kitchen, you should probably think it through, but that garish set of pillows that you swore matched something in your space can be covered in under ten minutes. It's not life or death—it's home décor.

live

In this Spanish-style home's living room, an informed decision was made to make the fireplace the focal point. The placement of furniture around the hearth creates a cozy environment for conversation and allows the modern flourishes to feel friendly.

The wood-framed glass panes of the door tie the entryway to the adjacent living room's wood floors and brown couch. A quirky white terra-cotta horse is a whimsical touch.

t he living room is your most public area. It's where you meet and greet company and lounge and watch TV with friends, and it's also where you do most of your entertaining, which includes serving food and, yes, even drinks.

As such it is center stage for your personal design sensibilities. Creating the ultimate "live"-able space means combining comfort and flexibility with an imaginative design. Your living room's décor must serve a dual purpose of both welcoming outsiders and providing a private and personal space for you. You want a floor plan and furnishings that are sensibly stylish, comfortable, and adaptable to your well–rounded and often unpredictable lifestyle.

This space will also need to be personalized through decorative display. You showcase your talents, interests, history, and possibly your future in the living room. The items you put on view give people a glimpse of your style and a sense of who you are.

The L-shaped couch and facing armchairs make the marble coffee table the focal point of the room.

living room basics

Every room needs a focal point, something that grabs your eye and holds your attention. Maybe it's a bay window, a piece of artwork, a sofa, or a TV. Whatever you decide, make sure to organize your space around it. Keep this central focus in mind when it comes time to design a new living room, or even just update the one you have. Begin to group your other elements, such as chairs, lighting, and accessories, around your focal point.

Casting Your Couch

Consider how you will utilize this space. Will your friends be lounging in the room when they are over? Many of the activities that take place in this room involve sitting, so the best place to begin is with the main seating surface: the couch.

Couch style and size are obvious considerations. Do you want your couch to be the star of the show or recede from the spotlight? You can build more versatility into your living space by keeping your couch neutral. That doesn't have to mean beige or brown, though those colors—plus black, gray, blue, and shades of white—are classic. A hit of color is great; just avoid wild patterns that dictate design a little too much.

Look for traditional shapes such as those with simple squared-off arms, basic cushions (that you can flip over if you and Merlot don't mix well), and nickel-plated tubular steel legs or sedate skirts; nothing too far out for the foundation of the room.

In this rectangular
living room, an armless
sofa is the perfect
space-saving solution.
A trio of recycled
wooden coffee tables
balances the long but
narrow space.

Your couch will have a ripple effect on the rest of the room. A good rule: Be bolder with smaller furniture items, such as end tables, accent chairs, and scatter rugs, which can be upgraded more often than your couch.

If your couch is more "interior design magazine" (think a French provincial–style sofa updated with funky fuchsia fabric and gilded legs), then it will be a focal point, so counteract it with some milder pieces—knowing that updating the overall look of the room will not be as easy or economical.

Seating Yourself

What about all the other seating? In its simplest form, you need a side chair. We like the idea of a pair that complements your couch's look but isn't necessarily part of a "set." Beyond that, some convertible seating such as stools and ottomans is ideal.

The size of your sofa will dictate the size of the rest of your seating. A big couch demands larger pieces to keep your scale intact. If you supersize your sofa, don't pair it with spindly chairs and a dinky coffee table.

In a larger space, you might have a reading nook—an extra chair with a strategically placed task light and a small table—often near a window for natural light. If you have room for two armchairs, position them angled toward each other to create a more conversational grouping. This offshoot of the living room can be a spot for a couple to perch during a party, or can be drawn into the living area as extra seating for guests during a more intimate event.

TOP: The living room is a great place for pieces of furniture that might not have another home. This china cabinet gets new use as shelves for books, magazines, and display.

ABOVE: A stack of sturdy coffee table books makes an unexpected side table.

living room layouts

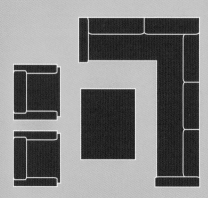

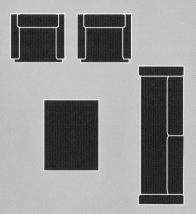

U-Shaped Plan
- Great for mismatched pieces such as an armchair, an ottoman, and a couch
- Creates better traffic flow because furniture is placed farther away
- Tends to feel more formal

L-Shaped Plan
- Great for sectional furniture
- Feels cozy
- Works when hosting many guests

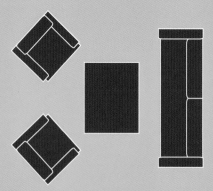

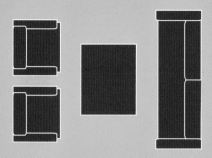

Diagonal Plan
- Great for square spaces because it takes the "edge" away
- Works well with lots of guests
- Can seem off-kilter if the furniture doesn't have consistent shape

Facing Plan
- Great for conversation
- Can feel formal or cozy depending on accents
- Is limiting in terms of expanding seating

The glass top of this Noguchi coffee table makes the L-shaped layout appear bigger.

A chair in the corner of a room can create a very private space. Personalize Eero's egg chair by layering pillows in contrasting textures.

five famous chairs

Barcelona Chair
Mies van der Rohe
1929

Womb Chair
Eero Saarinen
1948

Diamond Chair
Harry Bertoia
1952

Eames Lounger and Ottoman
Charles and Ray Eames
1956

Panton Chair
Verner Panton
1960

Two modern microfiber chairs in powder blue placed away from the couch create a conversation corner.

The clean shape of a contemporary canvas-upholstered wing chair accented with a graphic pillow and rug updates an early-twentieth-century brownstone's interior.

armchairs and sofas
shapes and terms

Sectional
A sofa made in sections that push up against each other and usually have ends with arms. Add or take away seating easily.

Love Seat
A small sofa or sofa sleeper designed for two people (smooching optional).

Settee
An early form of the modern sofa. Originally a long, ornately carved eighteenth-century seat or bench with a high back, open arms, and four to six legs.

Banquette
A fully upholstered bench or settee made to fit into a particular space. Often seen in restaurants.

Camelback
A sofa characterized by a large central hump on the back.

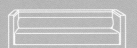

Deacon's Bench
Traditionally used in a church, the bench seen in some older homes is narrow and not comfortable.

Chaise Longue
French for "long chair"; basically a small couch with a chair back and one or two arms. Made famous in the boudoir, but modern versions are often in the living room.

Bergère
A French-style upholstered armchair with a wooden frame.

Slipper Chair
An upholstered chair with slender proportions and no arms. Comfortable and takes up less space than a regular upholstered chair.

Fiddleback Chair
A chair splat or back center shaped like a violin.

Wing Chair
An upholstered armchair that's on legs with a high back and wings along the sides.

Barrel Chair
Shaped to look like the original version made from half of a wine barrel. The back may be upholstered. Seat has a loose cushion.

Natural elements like plants, branches, and pillows with botanical prints give this space an airy and comfy feel.

Surface Savvy

Everyone needs a place to put things down, right? Coffee tables are essential to tie a seating arrangement together. Sit down and try out the distance to your coffee table, making sure you don't have to lean too far forward to reach drinks, and try to leave 1 to 3 feet of leg room between the table and the seat.

There is no ideal coffee table height. It's personal preference, though one that's about 21 inches high is easier to dine on. Remember that a coffee table that's too much higher than the seat of the couch will look out of place. Keep end tables around the same height (about 24 inches) and depth (usually 15 inches) as the arms of the sofa or chair next to it. A couple of inches above or below is fine, but end tables that are, say, 5 inches higher or lower will be awkward for guests to use while seated.

Material is important to keep in mind. Transparent tables or those made of glass or acrylic can make a tight space look and feel bigger. Heavy materials can make a space seem quite serious, particularly when items surrounding the table are lighter in hue or material type.

This coffee table is perfectly positioned from the couch in distance and height.

simple space solutions

Create zones
Give each area of the space a purpose. Place two chairs facing away from a fireplace to allow the area to multitask.

Define the space
Area rugs are a classic choice for defining space, but large plants or shelves work, too.

Transition flooring
If budget allows, using tile or stone in certain areas of your space can make the space more intimate.

Group your furniture
Too many stand-alone objects cause the space to look jumbled and messy. Aim to arrange at least two pieces together: an end table next to a sofa or a tall floor lamp next to a chair.

Style similarly
Use accent pieces like pillows and window treatments in similar colors and styles to give the space a cohesive feel without being too matchy.

This massive loft space gets sectioned off beautifully with a U-shaped setup. Unified accents pull the room together. Pillows in mandarin orange and a porcelain vase filled with pumpkin-colored blooms give the room a styled look without appearing overdone.

This mix of mid-century modern furniture grouped around a circular table is a unique take on a facing layout. Pattern and texture keep the Le Corbusier cushion basket furnishings from looking too stiff.

A palette of greens—from apple to emerald—is a chic way to tie a room together like the living room in this ranch-style home. A portrait of the household pet puts a unique stamp on the space.

GOOD DOG

styling your living space

Once you've mapped out your layout, it's time to channel your inner stylist to add a personal touch to the place. Living with color is not just about painting the walls your favorite blue hue, but also about really considering how different shades in the same family will interact with one another. Start with one dominant color and then build onto it with other tones within that palette. Remember, color should be personal and should be more than a shade that surrounds you. It should be something that excites you or soothes your senses. Without the intricate details of color, lighting, texture, and unique objects, your living room could be the setup in any department store. Time to take it up a notch.

Warm Up Your Space

The way most people add color is through accessories such as pillows, throws, lamps, and rugs. Obviously, palette is a personal choice, but when it comes to living rooms, your strategy should be to shoot for both chic and cozy. Aim to keep these accents inexpensive so you can change your style with the seasons (or any other time you feel the need).

Limit yourself to four colors, with one being a neutral, and add one pattern. That doesn't mean you're stuck with a toile or floral pattern à la Grandma. It can be graphic or abstract or just something at an unusual scale. Pattern can even come from a photograph of your favorite shoe printed on fabric. Think multiples of pillows. Throws placed strategically on anything from an ottoman to the back of the couch work well. Just don't over-throw it. One or two per room is plenty.

And don't forget about your walls! Artwork is the most quirky, individual way to add a personal touch to your living area. Mirrors can also be used like artwork to bring dimension and brightness to a room and make a small space appear larger. Frames of any type can be unobtrusive and uniform or a decorative element all on their own. Wall art should be the final step in styling your space; hang pictures only once you've determined a layout and all of the furniture is in place. We have said that design rules are meant to be broken, but in the case of hanging pictures, disregarding this rule can be risky (and involve spackle). There is little margin for error—art placed too high or low, too close together or too far apart, will look off-kilter and detract from the room's wow factor. For more on displaying art, see "The Art of Arranging" on page 41.

Textures and Patterns

True, texture is often tactile, but it far surpasses the idea of something rough or smooth. It has to do with forming a relationship between layers. Texture adds depth to a space. And there are so many elements that you can use to accomplish this in your room. Lay a soft and fluffy shag rug over wall-to-wall carpeting. Paint two walls of a room a light shade of blue and wallpaper the others with a chocolate lattice print. Hang a hand-knit chunky throw blanket over an oversized tweed armchair. These different textures and materials add a certain twist that has already been initiated by color. Believe it or not, it will take your room to an elevated level.

The retro pattern of this hand-painted mural ties it to the vintage chair and three-drawer table.

The variety of carefully selected items in this couple's room lends it an eclectic charm. Ochre yellow–washed walls add a warm backdrop for the black-and-white graphic printed chair, bright floral pillows, and Spanish bull horns.

FISHMAN & TOBIN

MFRS. OF

BOYS SUITS

5TH FLOOR

blending styles

Good design is about combining styles that work for everyone in the house.

• Color. If you love a color that the other inhabitant hates, then you need to learn to compromise by adding accessories in that hue.

• Pattern. Go graphic with stripes and dots instead of florals.

• Furniture. Merging large pieces of furniture can be tricky. Try using slipcovers or a coat of paint you both can live with.

• Art. Unify individual pieces by putting them in coordinating frames.

• Collectibles. These are perfect for personalizing—not taking over—a space.

Lacy wall stickers create an interesting and dynamic mural. They're also a good way to introduce fresh color that speaks to a blended style.

Mix in heirloom pieces like an ornate table and a tapestry pillow to personalize and style the room. The Bert Stern photo is a standout focal point.

Add Some Oxygen

Plants have an instant charm that brings life to your room. They're also a wallet-friendly way to add style to your space. Always get rid of the original planters and repot the plants in pretty ceramic, glass, or resin pots, or hide them inside vessels you already have—baskets, bronze buckets—that fit in with the colors and textures of the room.

Odd numbers of plants work best. Try a grouping of three different plants with contrasting leaves, size, and height, placing the tallest at the rear. For a more modern look, use three of the same plant in a triangle or evenly spaced in a row. The right scale and arrangement are essential; just remember to keep all plants off coffee tables or from obstructing views.

Untie the Tube

You have a giant TV. So what? You'll just have to work a little harder to make your 50-inch monster fit into the room. Decorate around the TV. Flat-panels and projection TVs, while massive, have really saved many a design snob from hari-kari. Their ability to recede into a room can free you to innovate with your living room. A hinged arm replaces a TV cart—which all seem to be so offensively ugly. If you have the benefit of a flattie, don't hate it, embrace it. Try to position your TV so it's not the first thing you see when you walk into the room.

Some books and an African violet plant perched next to it immediately warm up the TV area. Or, store the DVD collection in designer albums you won't be embarrassed to leave out. When it comes to all the components, neatly stack them and make sure all wires are tucked behind. Even better, find a receptacle to put them in. It is possible to keep your decorative charm *and* keep up with the latest technology.

easy living room updates

Change a lamp shade
A shade in a different color, material, or shape will instantly give your room a new glow.

Change your pillows
Adding or swapping out throw pillows can make tired furniture look new again. Try changing them seasonally.

Try a slipcover
Slipcover your furniture. It's like buying a new couch without the commitment (or the hefty price tag!).

Add a rug
Since the floor is 30 percent of what you see in a room, change it up by adding a colorful rug.

Rethink your walls
Add molding to bare walls, or paint them. For even less commitment, paint one wall a bold color and add a focal point, like a funky clock.

Switch out photos
Swap out black-and-white photos for colored candids to get a totally different feel on your mantel. Replace snapshots from past holidays for a seasonal quick fix.

This spacious loft incorporates structural beams into a built-in shelving unit that nestles a flat-screen TV. Natural wood elements keep the space from looking too sterile.

This sun-drenched den can handle soft brown walls. White accents such as this rug and cube bookshelf mirror the window's white panes and add brightness after dark.

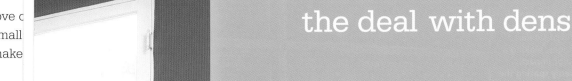

the deal with dens

love c
small
make

Be Sr
Symm
of ima
the m
effect
items

The
An as
size fr
your l
group
pieces
the fu
small
Add e
enoug

Pla
two th
item i
the fu

Live in it
A den cries for total comfort. Since it's a room for watching, lounging, and playing, it can be more relaxed than the formal living room.

Make it fun
Use it as a space to entertain company, and fill the room with board games and other fun details.

Furnish it
In terms of essentials, the den is similar to your living room: a cluster of seating, some surfaces, and light. Design-wise, consider the den the living room's casual cousin.

Style the space
This is a great place to experiment with color. Paint the walls a bold, exciting hue. Display random collections or memorabilia that doesn't seem to have a home anywhere else.

Store your stuff
Shelves, attractive bins, baskets—they all work well in this space. Since you'll probably be storing a lot of stuff in this room, consider ottomans, which can also serve as a hidden storage space and provide extra seating!

Add some seating
Aim to keep this a versatile space equipped to entertain two or ten. For a crowd, toss some oversized pillows on the floor for additional seating.

Think extras
You wouldn't dream of putting an extra fridge in your living room, but a mini in the den with diet sodas and beer chilling doesn't sound too bad, right? What about splurging on a wet bar? With running water at hand, you can entertain in this room without dashing to the kitchen.

how big should your TV be?

32" — 7' from sofa

36" — 8' from sofa

42" — 10' from sofa

50" — 12' from sofa

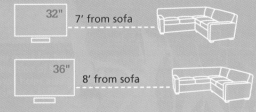

These adorable bird images carefully cut from a calendar make a great display. Four square frames lean on a shelf instead of being hung to allow art swaps without ruining the walls.

easy art ideas

Cut up a book
Use an old illustrated book and break the spine so you can get the whole page. Use an X-Acto knife to trim the pieces to the size you need. Surround each print with a mat to make it look special.

Stretch a canvas
Buy fabric stretchers and a cool piece of fabric (bright, bold prints look great). Stretch the fabric over the frame for an inexpensive large piece.

Blow up an image
Group some scraps of paper of the same color together or take a close-up photo of an object. Keep in mind the photo will need to have a minimum resolution of 1600 x 1200 pixels. Put it in a frame with a border of at least 2 inches.

Frame a collection
Take something relatively flat such as cigar labels or matchbooks and place them in floating frames. A single frame with multiple items or several frames with single items work equally well.

stretch fabulous fabric

toolbox

iron
fabric
4 fabric stretchers
rubber hammer
staple gun

how to

1. Iron fabric and set aside.

2. Lay out stretchers. Do this on the floor and tap corners together with a rubber hammer.

3. Roll your fabric design down. Then put the frame on top of it.

4. Cut to size. Leave enough fabric to staple down to the frame.

5. Begin stapling. Start in the center on any side and use about three staples (2 inches apart) in each direction.

6. Pull the fabric. Make it as taut as you can (ask for help).

7. Move to the opposite edge. Repeat for all sides.

8. Fold at the corners. Fold the edges and staple one on top of the other. Cut off extra fabric.

photo hanging layouts

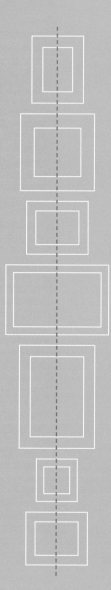

Inside the Lines
Tape out a rectangular area that you'd like your photos to fill, and arrange them loosely within the borders of the box. This is an easy way to decorate an oddly shaped or narrow space.

Line Them Up
Arrange all of your photos along a vertical line. This works well in a space with high ceilings or a very vertical structure like a beam.

Above and Below
Using a vertical line, arrange groups of photos above and below the line. Aim to cover about the same area above and below to avoid a top- or bottom-heavy arrangement.

The two walls of this library get two layouts—inside the line and above and below—creating a dynamic display. The red walls make the primarily black-and-white images pop.

Turn a wall into a family album.
Staggered wall shelves holding framed
photos and memorabilia from family
members personalize the living area.

Create a visual reminder of your latest vacation. Add a color that works with your images (blue is great for travel).

Combine Art Objects

Bring together art and objects as a grouping. The thing to remember is to make sure scale and color complement each other.

For example, create an easy and appealing arrangement by displaying all black-and-white photographs together. But when it comes to the more vibrant prints, group them based on similar colors or themes. Unify the grouping by purchasing frames of similar size, color, and thickness. If you decide to mat, make sure to match the style as well. Mixing silver-plated frames with modern wooden ones will only pull the eye away from the artwork itself. Feel free to let your eclectic style flourish, and to show off your appreciation for abstract art and impressionism without limiting your room to being called "modern." With artwork it's easy to combine different periods of time, styles, and elements of design when you find similarities among them. Challenge yourself to do the unexpected.

The perfect arrangement is all about showcasing like objects with like. Even if they're different shapes and colors, the collection is unified by theme. Sports memorabilia can be displayed in a creative corner setup (LEFT). Seashells and nautical prints make a delicate mantel display (BELOW).

creative display ideas

Stack it
Arrange items in stackable cubes. Play around with different shapes.

Group it
Display in groups of three. Try one photo and two three-dimensional objects.

Frame it
Use double-glass frames. They're especially great for items like comic books.

Put it on the wall
Use a corner shelf set up high in an unexpected place, like a hallway.

Color coordinate
Add an invigorating punch to a solid white bookcase by covering your collection of mismatched novels in pretty patterns or one solid color paper.

1. Display items in odd-numbered arrangements. Groups of three and five create a modern look.

2. Combine objects of the same color. A hodgepodge of red items brings a striking focus onto a shelf.

3. Arrange like objects with like. Even if they're different shapes and colors, the collection is unified.

4. Place in pairs. Two crystal candlesticks on one side of your mantel looks less rigid than one on each side.

Cube shelves create more storage (and display) than an ordinary entryway table would.

Group a bunch of favorite jars and vases together to make a refreshing display. Stand modern-style jars in varying shapes in a straight line and fill with bamboo shoots and botanicals.

arranging basics

Centered

This common arrangement is known for its clean, classic look. The tallest object should be placed in the center and evenly surrounded on both sides. Try a tall decorative vase in between a collection of evenly stacked books.

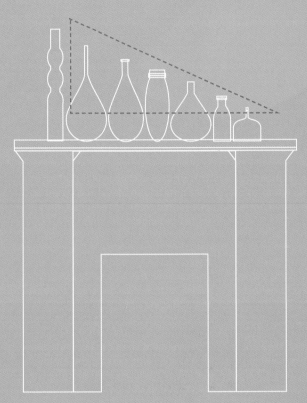

Triangular

When in doubt, arrange objects in a triangular shape. This works well with objects on top of the mantel. Start with your tallest object on one side and arrange the rest tallest to shortest. Triangles work when hanging objects on the wall, too. Hang one above the other two to create a collection.

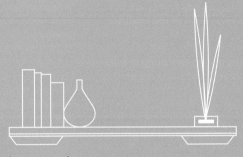

Asymmetric

This arrangement is more modern, featuring objects of different heights and/or widths. Placing them on opposing sides of the mantel draws attention to their different shapes.

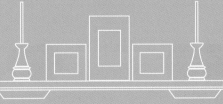

Symmetric

This arrangement places objects of equal height on the outside, with smaller items in the middle. Create this formal look by using two tall candlesticks on the edges and layering framed photographs in the middle.

101 color

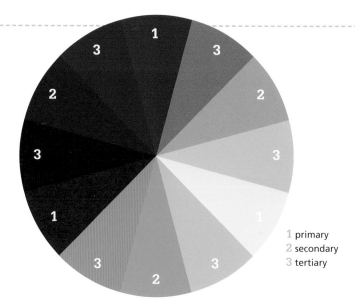

1 primary
2 secondary
3 tertiary

basic principles

Primary colors
Blue, red, and yellow. Each is completely pure; when combined, they are the basis for every color in the spectrum.

Secondary colors
Created by mixing two primary colors, orange, green, and violet are on this team.

Tertiary colors
Made by combining either all three primary colors or one primary and one secondary. There are six tertiary colors: orange-red, orange-yellow, yellow-green, blue-green, blue-violet, and red-violet.

Color wheel
A way of explaining the relationship between colors and why certain colors work better together. A useful decorating tool.

Complementary
Contrasting colors make up this scheme—those that sit directly across from each other on the color wheel (like blue and orange).

Neutral colors
These hues are colors, too! They are created when you mix two complementary colors together. Taupe, beige, and gray are just the beginning.

color schemes

Monotone
This scheme uses one color but doesn't vary tints and shades and is based on one muted color, for example, gray, white, or beige.

Analogous
Based on the bordering colors on the color wheel, this scheme features a wider variety of colors, some contrasting and some not.

Monochromatic
This scheme is composed of variations of a single color, making the entire room a feature, since no specific object stands out.

White and Red
Pair a neutral tone with an energizing bright red in activity zones, like kitchens and family rooms.

Salmon and White
A calming and balancing combination. These relaxing hues suit living rooms and dining rooms well.

Light Yellow and Gray
This combo teams up for an urban feel. Charcoal gives the yellow a golden glow. Good for dining rooms.

White and Cream
Neutrals stand strong paired together. Lighting can change their tints, too. Ideal for bedrooms and baths.

warm and cool

Warm colors—shades of yellow, red, orange, beige, and cream—stand out to the eye and act as energy boosters. (Think of the vivid colors of a sunset.) They're stimulating, exciting, and fiery, and are perfect for social spaces like living rooms, dining rooms, and kitchens to promote conversation.

Cool colors—the blues, blue-greens, grays, and violets on the spectrum—are soothing at their core (just like a clear sky or a calm sea). Because of their focusing power, cool colors are best for quiet spaces like bedrooms, offices, nurseries, and bathrooms. These shades are ideal for promoting deep and pensive thought.

change your space

Make it feel larger
Paint the walls a cool color. Hues like blue and green aren't as embracing and evoke distance.

Make it seem smaller
Choose a dark, warm color; they are inviting, and help to enclose the space. Matte finishes minimize reflection.

Make it taller
Paint the ceiling a lighter color than the walls. Consider painting vertical stripes on the walls to give the illusion of height.

Lower the ceiling
Paint the ceiling a darker shade than the rest of the room. A horizontal element like a chair rail on the walls will keep the ceiling from feeling so high.

Transition better
Use color to create a smooth flow. For example, paint one room blue and then use that shade as an accent in the next room.

Maximize impact
Apply the 60-30-10 rule. The largest area of the room (usually the walls) gets 60 percent of the color. Rugs and window treatments get 30 percent. Accents like lamps get the remaining 10 percent.

Mocha and Baby Blue
Mixing light and dark is a modern approach to color. This match is perfect for dining rooms or dens.

Cream and Taupe
Neutrals are fresh and versatile. This blending gives a clean, crisp look. A smart choice for living rooms.

Periwinkle and White
Refreshing and soothing together, these colors create a restful, refreshing ambience. Try them in baths and bedrooms.

Baby Blue and Berry
A surprising, yet cozy, combo. The blue plays off the deep rosy shade for a warm touch in dining rooms or dens.

eat

This Danish modern table and chairs are perfect for an open floor plan—elegant enough to say "dining room" but sufficiently sleek and functional to fit the adjacent kitchen.

While a traditional credenza/breakfront combo is normally set closer together, the nearly 3-foot separation here allows the pieces to serve as a sculptural element—and keeps the credenza top clear for a collection of white pottery.

the eating areas of your home should serve up function, style, and plenty of storage. Over the years, the kitchen and dining space has evolved from a formal cooking-and-eating zone to the multi-tasking hub of the home. Your kitchen, in particular, is destined to become a center of daily activity whether you're prepping your meals, grabbing a midnight snack, chatting on your cell while you empty the dishwasher, hanging with friends, or paying your bills. The space needs to feel right, no matter what kind of business you are attending to. If you're a gourmet, you need your most invaluable utensils within reach; if you are a take-out junkie, you'll want a deep drawer near the phone for menus.

When it comes to dining rooms, your challenge is a bit different. Your dining room is essentially a blank canvas just waiting for you to create a masterpiece. Unfortunately, buying furniture for it isn't always at the top of the to-do list. Your strategy here should be to have a final image in your mind and work toward that goal over time.

Vintage high-back stools make a kitchen island the perfect place for casual entertaining and are far less formal than a traditional dining set. An organic-wood bowl creates continuity with other natural elements in the open space.

Frosted glass cabinets give a small kitchen a more spacious and modern look.

A one-sided kitchen with plenty of open storage is a great option for small spaces. If you lack a convenient setup, try installing shelves in strategic spots.

kitchen ingredients

Professionals think of the kitchen as divided into a number of zones, each devoted to a particular function. Understanding these areas and organizing them to be as easy to use as possible is a perfect way to begin your revamp.

Prep School

In your food prep zone, where you are task-focused, good light is essential (see "Everything Is Illuminated" on page 71). Keep knives, cutting boards, and prep bowls nearby. Knife blocks take up precious counter space, but it is safer and more convenient to use one than to store sharp knives in drawers. (If you are crunched for space, consider a magnetic knife bar that attaches to the wall.) Make sure a portion of the counter between your prep station and the fridge is kept clear for pulling out ingredients.

Baking is often done in a separate zone as it requires enough space for pulling out that KitchenAid mixer and for rolling dough. An island is the ideal place for this activity. Place all related items like mixing bowls, measuring cups, and sifters in a drawer nearby.

Hot Food Station

At your cooking station, you need easy access to the tools you use when the burners are blazing. When your hands are greasy or garlicky, you don't want to dig around in drawers and cabinets. Pots and pans need to be nearby, but it is the items you need instantly as you are cooking that you should devote your precious counter space to. Keep your most basic seasonings—such as olive oil, garlic powder, salt, and pepper—handy by the stove as well. Storing them on a shelf is fine, but a small tray that you can quickly wash will keep you from the hassles of constant cleanup. Pot holders need to be within easy reach of the stove, too.

Keep the majority of your cookware, bowls, and utensils hidden from the grease and dust that inevitably develop in a well-used kitchen. Deep drawers are the best place for pots and pans. Pick three pans that you use almost daily (a large frying pan, a deep saucepan, and a pasta pot) and place them within easy reach. Place colanders near the front of the cabinet for quick access while cooking. Rarely used specialty items like the asparagus steamer, the fondue pot, and the Belgian waffle iron, can be stored farther back. Fluted bowls in a multicolor assortment look chic stacked and displayed on open upper shelves.

Come Clean

Even if it functions well, the sink area can make your kitchen look unclean really easily. Sponges get dingy fast, dish brushes rust and hold onto food particles, and the dishwashing liquid itself is often an eyesore. Remove pot holders from the counter-top. It may be more practical to keep your soap and sponges out, but keeping them hidden from view makes the whole kitchen look tidier. Invest in a stainless-steel refillable soap dispenser that blends with your sink, or for an extra pop of color, fill a clear acrylic pump with bright dishwashing liquid. Get a wire basket that attaches with suction cups to the inside of your sink to keep your sponge out of sight, and throw sponges away frequently.

BELOW: A simple collection of utensils—spoons, a spatula, tongs, and a ladle—should be near the stove in an upright container. Don't pack in so many that they stick together, which defeats the purpose of keeping them convenient.

OPPOSITE: Take your cue from restaurants, which often keep dishes and bowls above the cooktop and dish towels next to the sink.

counter tips

• **Ideally, your dishwasher is located next to the sink to avoid drips as you load it after rinsing.**

• **Even if your main garbage can is elsewhere, keep a small bin under the sink, or use a bowl or a bag to capture the plate remains and dispose of them in a single trip.**

• **Keep several dish towels near the counter for placing larger pots and serving pieces to drip-dry; or in a small space, try a wall-mounted dish rack that drains into the sink.**

• **Keep your often-used plates, glasses, and serving pieces within reach of the sink. Open shelves allow you to stack frequently used pieces.**

kitchen layouts

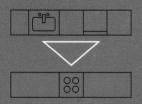

Galley

Built between parallel walls, a galley or corridor kitchen allows you to move from one workstation to another. The sink and fridge sit on one wall and the range is centered between them on the opposite wall. There should be at least 48 inches between facing counters.

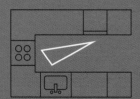

U-shaped

Perhaps the most desirable kitchen design, it accommodates the work triangle, and has endless design possibilities in a good-size rectangular room. The U-shaped layout features a fridge, a sink, and a range, each on its own wall. There should be 5 to 10 feet between facing counters.

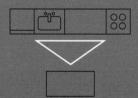

Island

This is the focal point for a large open kitchen. It also provides extra storage and added counter space. In a two-cook kitchen, the island often has its own sink and/or cooktop, wine rack, or fridge. Surrounding the island with stools creates a casual breakfast counter.

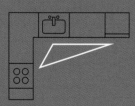

L-shaped

This shape is ideal for long, narrow spaces. It requires two adjacent walls and resemble the letter L. There's space for a dining table or an island; the latter serves as a divider between rooms and provides additional surface, seating, and storage space.

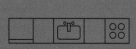

One Wall

Suited for urban studios and smaller homes, the one-wall kitchen makes good use of tight quarters by placing everything against a single wall. Enclosed versions are tight spaces with no work triangle. The sink is in the center, flanked on either side by the fridge and range with about 4 feet of counter between them.

work triangles

Most kitchens operate on some version of the time-honored work triangle, which keeps the cook only a few steps away from the three major appliances: the refrigerator, sink, and range.

The goal is to place each of these high-function points (where you retrieve, wash, and cook the food) no more than a simple pivot away from another to optimize access and work flow.

Visualize your setup by making a sketch of your kitchen's layout.

Mark the three points of the triangle—fridge, sink, and stove—and then draw lines linking the center of each in that order.

This triangle should measure no more than 26 feet total. No single leg of the triangle should be shorter than 4 feet or longer than 9 feet. If the appliances are too far apart or too close together, you compromise efficiency.

Do the best with what you've got, but think of ways to improve workflow.

Certain things are best kept outside the work triangle, such as the beverage center and the wine fridge. This helps keep traffic from impeding the cook's workflow.

eat-in kitchen options

Which setup suits your space?

• **Traditional Table** (below). Set up at least 3½ feet from the counter so one person has room to get up. A good plan for areas serving as a second entryway in your home.

• **Pub Table.** A tall, circular table with a smaller circumference— ideal for tight spaces.

• **Island** (above right). Standard size is 3 feet high and 25 inches deep; eating areas on islands should be dropped to 30 inches. When buying stools, check heights— counter stools are lower than bar stools (and they give 8 to 14 inches of legroom).

• **Corner Nook** (above left). Try a built-in nook featuring banquette-style seating attached to a wall for a more intimate feeling.

Storage Solutions

Are your everyday dining items scattered throughout the kitchen? Are the bowls over the sink, the dishes next to the fridge, and the utensils in the drawer above the trash? This won't work; prioritize according to use. Organize plates and bowls of different sizes in separate piles to avoid having to lift items to get to others. Line glasses of different heights in separate rows going front to back, rather than placing the short ones in the front and the tall ones in the back. If you are running low on space, keep items that you use only for special occasions, such as oversized platters, bread baskets, and serving utensils, in a separate room. Store deep and heavy pots and pans in lower cupboards near the stove or mount your go-to saucepan on a decorative hook near the stovetop.

Food for Thought

Ingredients rarely reached for, such as baking flour or vanilla extract, should be placed on higher surfaces, above eye level. Food should ideally be kept in pantries or cupboards close to the fridge. Group like items together. Categorize seasonings, bottled ingredients, and snack foods so you at least know the general direction in which to start your hunt. Avoid wasting space with half-filled boxes of cereal and opt for clear, air-tight canisters, which take up less room and keep food fresh. Place a freestanding stacking shelf on an existing one to create two levels, creating a prime spot for canned goods. Stop searching for spices. A rack designed to fit onto the back of a door is a smart solution. A drawer also works well.

Snack Bars

The coffee station, which contains the coffeemaker and easy access to your mugs, works best placed next to the fridge, since coffee beans stored in the

kitchen storage solutions

Drawers
Similar items should stay together and close to their point of use. Store pots and pans near the stove, and plastic bags and wrap in a drawer under the counter where you often prepare leftovers or lunches.

Cabinets
Cabinets come in various shapes and sizes, so before you start arranging your dishes, take stock of your space. Keep glasses in cabinets with more spacious shelves, while plates and bowls can be easily stacked in lower spaces. Top shelves can be home to large serving pieces. Try a lazy Susan or a pull-out shelf to keep smaller items grouped.

Pantry
Learn to love canisters. They keep food fresh and make your cabinets look more decorative yet still organized. Opt for clear acrylic ones so you can see exactly what is stored inside.

Countertops
Keep a receptacle, like an oversized low bowl, for small items, so you don't have bits and pieces all over the kitchen.

office nook ideas

If you take care of bills and work in the kitchen, make a space that fits your layout:

• Set up the office area far from where the food is handled.

• Keep your best hardware out of this nook, as the kitchen is prone to grease, dirt, steam, and other elements unfriendly to electronics.

• Have access to an electrical source for plugging in a computer, task lighting, and office supplies.

• Decorate your nook. Personal add-ons (a souvenir from a recent trip, a favorite family photo) give character to this functional spot.

Pendant lights are strategically hung above the center island in this Harlem brownstone, where the heart of the couple's kitchen activity takes place. Downlights and accent fixtures create a smooth transition in the layout as you move from one area to the next.

freezer are the freshest—plus you're closer to your favorite creamer. Keep a sugar bowl (or packets of sweetener) here, as well as spoons, or stirrers if you use them.

The beverage counter, wine rack, and snack containers frequented by others are best placed out of the cook's way. A counter wine rack always looks impressive, even if it holds only two or three bottles of your current stash. An under-cabinet wineglass rack is an excellent way to take advantage of otherwise unused kitchen space, allowing you to display your favorite glasses. Install the rack straight and securely so the glasses won't slip off and break. (Still, it's probably wise to keep the good crystal stowed away in cabinets for special occasions.) Keep the glasses away from your cooking area to avoid grease and to reduce the potential for accidents.

Everything Is Illuminated

Whenever you're handling quickly rotating blades and 12-inch knives, you definitely want to be able to see what you're doing. Recessed downlights are an efficient means of providing overall illumination in a room. Pendants brighten up a central island, anchoring the spot while enhancing its presence. Under-cabinet fixtures focus streams of light onto the countertop, to aid in technical tasks like chopping and mincing, where extra lighting is helpful.

Not planning to rewire your entire kitchen? Focus on point-of-use lighting and self-install a plug-in under-cabinet light. These are usually inexpensive and can also be discreet.

styling your kitchen

While functionality should be your foremost concern in the kitchen, you can't let this important space suffer in a state of drab utilitarianism. Your cabinets and countertop lay the foundation for your kitchen's style and performance.

Surfaces are the bones of your kitchen, and are not easily replaced. If you are designing a kitchen from scratch, choose carefully. If you have cabinets you can't live with but can't yet replace, no worries. The objects you place in and around them can significantly shift the look of your room. Freshen up a formal, wood-centric space by displaying simple, graphic white ceramic serving pieces. If an all-white or stainless-steel kitchen feels too clinical for you, add warmth with wooden bowls or playful, colorful small appliances.

Color Me Hungry

Your kitchen palette should reflect the foods you love, and put you and your guests in an eating state of mind. Color gurus swear that shades of red and orange, and also green—the natural color of many foods—stimulate the appetite.

We say any color works, but remember that the palette you choose will determine the mood of your space. Not only do you start every day in this space, it is also a place for people to congregate, and you must add the details that contribute to making you, your family, and friends feel comfortable, energized, and well fed. There are two ways

OPPOSITE: This chic chef's kitchen with sleek industrial appliances is warmed up with charming accents. Ceramic tile walls, vintage toys displayed under the island, and three well-placed succulents establish that "lived-in" tone.

ABOVE: Think beyond standard kitchen materials to include textured glass as a backdrop to a built-in shelf. The unexpected space is perfect for keeping cookbooks close by and organized.

A coat of bright blue paint makes a fun backdrop to an otherwise all-white kitchen. Bursts of yellow accents add contrast without making the space feel overly styled. Keeping knives mounted on a magnetic strip is a good solution for having them accessible yet out of harm's way.

to approach color in the kitchen: as the main ingredient or as a garnish. The commitment-free strategy is to keep your backdrop neutral and inject color with accents. Choose shades of a single color (teal and navy) or two colors that work together (red and orange, or green and brown) as your building blocks.

Consider your appliances, dishes, wine rack, towels, clock, art, and even the fruit you keep in your fruit bowl as places to reflect your palette. Don't strive to have every item in the exact same shade; it will look like a catalog. For a touch of spunk in a muted décor, a stunning orange espresso machine and orange- and red-striped dish towels will do the trick.

Color as a backdrop makes a bolder statement. Paint the open wall space a hot hue. (It's okay to

go a bit more intense in the kitchen since most of the actual wall space is given over to the cabinetry and it won't seem too overwhelming.)

Tiles in vibrant shades will give a nice kick of color to the backsplash. If you have open shelving or glass doors, paint or wallpaper the inside back wall, so color can peek out from behind the plates. For a more dramatic change, paint the cabinets themselves, but remember: Lighter hues make a small space appear larger, but darker ones can make the same space feel cramped.

Darker tones do offer a sense of coziness and warmth, but save them for the (rare) humongous kitchen. When buying paint for your kitchen, choose a durable finish: semigloss for walls and high gloss for cabinets and trim; you want that spaghetti sauce splatter to wipe off easily.

Adding a tile back-splash was the ideal way for this Harlem, New York, couple to add some color and texture to their predominantly modern and monochromatic kitchen design.

Use open shelving to add character to a space. Display fun items like vintage signs and incomplete sets of glasses and bowls. The bright pops of red in interesting shapes make a functional space a visual point of interest as well.

kitchen display ideas

Figure out your needs
Start by placing everyday items on your countertop. Arrange these items first. If they're always out in the open, you won't have to store them every day.

Color coordinate
Match the colors of your dishes and serving pieces with the overall room décor and store them on open or glass-front shelves for cohesiveness.

Artfully arrange
Display a pretty set of nesting bowls on a shelf, from largest to smallest. Added bonus: You won't have to pull the heavy stack down from the shelf each time you need a bowl.

Put it on the wall
Hang a set of gourmet saucepans near the stove, and a set of like-handled knives on a magnetic strip mounted above the counter.

Work in your everyday items
Choose stylish daily appliances that match your decorating scheme (a retro toaster or a funky red coffeemaker). Group them together in one area of your countertop.

Display your collections
Organize kitchen-related collections like salt and pepper shakers or vintage utensils together by type—and within reach of where you'll need them.

The gourmet sauce-pans scream "this is where we cook" in a graphic way. Just keep them well scrubbed!

Reinvent a bare
kitchen column with
a timeless collection
of your favorite wall
clocks. Create a focal
point by choosing
to hang the more
traditional-looking
one in the center of
the trio.

Go Graphic

The everyday, utilitarian items in your kitchen can also define your décor. The appealing shapes of a set of chrome retro appliances—blender, juicer, and mixer—can make a nice collection on a top shelf or on top of the cabinets. They are out of the way and save your precious cabinet space. Invest in stylish daily appliances—coffeemaker, toaster—to create a designer look. Take advantage of their structural quality and the myriad hues in which they're available. Accent colors in bold reds and aqua blues or even rich browns can give a simple color palette the jolt it needs.

Get Personal

You can put your personal stamp on the space by hanging a giant wooden letter representing your last name or, more subtly, by arranging a shelf to display an amazing collection of tea boxes from your last trip to China. Your food-related proclivities—a shiny copper paella pan—or even your taste, in the form of a collection of chili pepper jars, can make a space feel less prefab.

For the walls, opt for unexpected black-and-white photos of desert landscapes, your niece's artwork framed in shadow boxes, bold vintage fruit-box labels, or your collection of 1950s tangerine-hued glassware.

Feel free to have fun: Keep a Polaroid camera in the kitchen and snap a photo of every visitor holding a fruit or vegetable. Pin them up on a bulletin board as a conversation piece. Other easy ideas in this vein are a big rectangle of magnetic refrigerator poetry, a wall of blackboard paint with a weekly drawing in chalk, or even a map of the world with pushpins marking all the stops you've made or places you plan to visit.

easy kitchen updates

Switch out a light
Replace the dull ceiling fixture that came with the place with a sassy chandelier that will become an instant conversation piece.

Install a dimmer
Soften the light over a dining table or an island and create a mood.

Upgrade appliances
No rules state that the toaster and the blender need to match the rest of the kitchen—or even each other. Tangerine, seafoam green, or whatever color you are in the mood for gives a fast and fresh face-lift.

Buy yourself flowers
Or better yet, pick them fresh. Nothing brings life into a space like a bold bouquet of fragrant blooms in an interestingly shaped vessel.

Bring in extra storage
Purchase a small mobile island or a freestanding rack to match your décor—you get storage and a new work surface.

Add a runner
Kitchen floors get the shaft. Consider laying down new laminate tiles or getting a runner to brighten up below.

Cabinets could cost slightly more than half the budget for your kitchen. Stock cabinets cost from $60 to $200 per linear foot, depending on the quality of the material. Custom cabinet work—only really required if you have unusual spatial needs—will increase your budget exponentially.

cabinets

Smooth Panel
Also called Slab. It's flat, and looks like a simple, smooth slab of wood. Clean lines, no decorative detail.

Recessed Panel
Also called Flat. A flat panel is affixed inside what looks like a simple picture frame.

Mitered Panel
The most detailed door style. Layers of wood look like molding.

Beadboard Panel
Vertical seams on the recessed panel create a more casual feel.

Raised Panel
A detailed door with layers of wood embellishment. The inside panel is raised.

Curved Panel
The top portion of this raised panel curves in 0a gentle arch.

countertop materials

Granite
Natural stone with a coarse grain and crystalline texture that is thick, durable, and virtually maintenance-free.

Paper composite
Made of recycled paper (or pulp obtained from sustainable managed forests) and coated in water-based acrylic resin. Examples: PaperStone and Richlite.

Butcher block
Strips of solid maple, white oak, or beech that have been fused together. It has a warm, rustic look and can double as a cutting board.

Recycled glass
Aggregate of recycled, often postindustrial, glass tiles or chips. Examples: EnviroSLAB and IceStone.

Soapstone
Soft, easily carved stone that's generally dark gray and contains talc, which gives it the feel of dry soap.

Marble
Metamorphic rock with a swirled, clouded pattern. Comes in a range of colors.

dining room basics

When it comes to the dining room, the sky's the limit. The dining room has evolved into a multi-functional space for enjoying meals, engaging in all-night conversation, and even paying bills. The room's style should make a statement about you while providing comfort to all; and its stored items should be as easily accessed on a daily basis as they are during a formal dinner party for six.

The very words *dining room* conjure up the notion of hosting. Your dining room should be able to assume the role of a space for gathering and entertaining, though not necessarily in a stereo-typical, 1950s kind of way. The dining room has shed its formal trappings; it's equally at home with a silver candelabra as it is with eco-friendly place mats. The basics remain the same: a table and chairs and decent lighting with dimmers. Beyond that, it's all a matter of the space you have to work with and how you'll make it your own.

Table Talk

Naturally, a dining room couldn't do its job without an eating surface. A table that seats eight to twelve is optimal. The top priority is that the table fits comfortably within the room's parameters and affords those seated free range of movement. The table will have about as much presence in the room as a nine-hundred-pound gorilla, so choose one you love that can also grow along with your address book.

OPPOSITE: A wooden table can take on a totally different look when paired with leather-upholstered nailhead chairs, Lucite lamps, and a sleek industrial chandelier with dangling bulbs. Stately chic.

ABOVE: Using place mats and a runner shows off the natural wood of the table, giving character to the space. Bud vases, name cards, and candles add a fresh twist to a formal setup.

Diminutive Arne
Jacobsen chairs set
along the sides of
this table give diners
elbow room, while
bigger, comfier seats
placed at the heads
provide balance by
better fitting the
scale of the room.

If you entertain regularly, consider drop-leaf tables, which can expand to fit a not-so-little guest list. Consider a simple, less ornate, table—a wise choice if you like to update the décor with tablecloths and place settings tailored to the occasion or season. Oversized round tables are conducive to conversation but may not be expandable, and they require more space.

Whether your table is wood or another material such as a lacquer, steel, or glass, make sure you know the care instructions. Wood tables stain easily, and while you might want to show off the grain, a stain may force you to cover it. Glass is easy to clean—and it has to be, with all the fingerprints it'll get; same with stainless.

Have a Seat

When choosing chairs to complement your table, think of comfort and style first. Some people believe all chairs should match and wouldn't have it any other way; others advocate a mix-and-match strategy.

As with fashion items, tables and chairs are now sold as separates, so you have the choice of picking the combo you see in the catalog or showroom or making your own groupings. A collection of entirely unrelated chairs will make your dining space feel more whimsical and vintage, but aim for at least one unifying element—chairs that all come from the same time period or share a color scheme or style of backs. Pair a modern table in dark walnut with chairs of a similar streamlined design, but in a light ash. Pull brightly painted metal chairs up to a rustic farmhouse table. These choices will add character and a casual yet comfortable air to the gathering room.

If an entirely mix-and-match scheme is too wacky for you, why not use a different style for your host and hostess chairs (also known as captain's chairs), which are found at the heads of the table. A nice touch without going over the top, this still adds personality and creates a less uniform-looking setup.

Upholstered chairs add color and texture and a critical dose of comfort for long evenings spent lingering at the table. They can be covered in a range of fabrics and materials from trendy microfiber to formal damask. The simple lines of these chairs make them work with most décors.

Washable slipcovers are a time-saver and also easy to swap out to change your color scheme. And if sewing isn't in your skill set, in many cases you can pop off the upholstered seat cushions and staple on fresh, modern fabric for a whole new look with little effort. Just be sure to choose a durable, forgiving fabric such as microfiber or leather; spills do happen.

Resting Places and Storage

Once the table and chairs are in place, figure out your dining room's storage capacity. Measure the space again and look for credenzas and china cabinets that can house the fine silverware, linens, china, and crystal you won't be using in the kitchen. These are the supporting players to the star dining table. Avoid overfilling the room with furniture, a common mistake for first-time dining designers. The last thing you want is for a good-size room to feel cramped.

Get creative with dining room furniture. A dresser is a great, unexpected addition, and the extra drawer space is perfect for storing china set aside for special occasions. An old kitchen cabinet gets new life as a credenza. A console table provides a useful surface for serving or displaying, but the lightness of the piece keeps your room from looking heavy. A bookshelf can easily transform into a unit for showcasing oversized dishes, platters, and teapots.

side storage

Built-in cabinets
Extra storage that blends into the room is better (and easier) than a freestanding new piece. Some built-ins can even extend the whole length of a wall, without looking too large.

Sideboard
Also called a credenza or buffet, this waist-high cabinet is used to store dishes, glassware, linens, and other items.

Breakfront
A piece of furniture whose front extends out farther than the sides.

Console table
A long, narrow table, usually without shelves below; primarily a spot for display. It can be kept against a wall in a dining room and used for buffet service.

Hutch
An enclosed cupboard, often glass-fronted, that sits above a base (such as a credenza) or mounts to the wall.

China cabinet
A cabinet with a glass front, traditionally kept in the dining room and used for storage and to showcase a fine china collection.

Show off your eclectic style by pairing a light wooden table with a set of Breuer chairs and accessories in white lacquer. Built-in bookshelves in the dining room are a bright idea! Avid readers will be all over the notion of books being as valuable as crystal.

furniture 101

wood furniture buying tips

Look for quality wood
Wood comes in two varieties based on the plant species it comes from—hardwood and softwood. Hardwood is typically stronger and more expensive, and includes ash, cherry, maple, oak, teak, walnut, and mahogany. Softwood—like cedar, fir, and pine—is less expensive and more dent-prone.

Check the joints
You might not see them, but the joints of any interlocking piece of furniture (that is, couch arms, table legs, drawer corners) should be double- or triple-doweled, corner blocked, glued, and high-pressure stapled for support. Always double-check and ask a salesperson if you aren't sure.

Open drawers, close doors
A high-quality drawer will feel weighty and solid, yet slide with ease. Check the condition of the glides and stops. The drawer interior should be smooth and sanded. Doors should feel substantial to the touch, but swing without squeaking or rubbing. Above all, they should be properly aligned when shut.

Look for dust panels
They're not integral to the foundation of your wood furniture, but a high-quality piece should have these partitions between drawers that keep dust (obviously) and varmints from invading the drawer space.

Stay level
Since most homes have variations in the floor level, large pieces of wood furniture, like entertainment centers, dressers, and armoires, should have leveling devices in the base to provide better balance. Otherwise, you might end up with doors sticking or drawers not sliding open.

Check the bells and whistles
Read the product card and investigate the specific features of your piece: Do the table leaves fit with ease? Is there a hole for cords in the entertainment center? Do the interior lights work? Is the switch easy to find? Make sure what's promised to you is what's delivered.

Regency
Nineteenth century, French. Identified by elegant lines and an introduction of brass work.

Shaker
Around the time of the American Civil War. Clean modern lines best represented by the ladder-back chair.

Victorian
Nineteenth century, English. Exaggerated curves and carvings as well as rich woods like mahogany and walnut.

Arts and Crafts
Late nineteenth, early twentieth century, European. Promotes hand craftsmanship with simple oak, and hammered copper.

Be hard on hardware

Make sure all hardware is secure and strong: The hinges should handle the load of the door, there should not be rough edges on the hardware, and the latches under the table leaves should function properly.

Inspect the finish

Wood furniture should feel smooth to the touch (unless it's distressed). Inspect the finish from different angles: The finish should be clear and uniform in color, with no visible lines, dark spots, dents, or bubbles.

Support the shelves

Long shelves should have center supports to prevent them from buckling. Gently lean on them to check the strength. If the shelves are adjustable, can they shift with ease? Is the hardware provided of high quality?

Push it around

The piece should feel sturdy when rocked. If you get lots of movement (more than the typical give), there's a flaw in the construction.

wood glossary

Ash
Creamy light wood finish; perfect for furniture and trim; does not stain well.

Birch
Fine grained, usually light brown in color; suitable for furniture and trim; stains well, easily simulating pricier woods.

Cherry
Reddish-brown and warp-resistant; great for furniture and trim.

Ebony
A dark wood that makes a fabulous statement as a table or a sideboard.

Mahogany
Reddish- to golden-brown; tends to be expensive but is excellent for furniture and paneling.

Maple
Blond in color; super-strong wood with a fine texture and an even grain. You've seen it in bowling alleys.

Oak
Ranges from reddish tan to grayish tan; good for furniture, trim, and paneling.

Pine
White pine is soft enough to dent. Yellow pine is the stronger version, with a streaky grain.

Walnut
Chocolate brown to nearly black; strong but expensive; great for furniture and paneling.

Mission
Early twentieth century, American. U.S. answer to Arts and Crafts. Crude, over-sized furniture like the pieces found in Spanish missions.

Art Deco
1920s, renaissance. Strong geometric lines, exotic woods, and mirrored or chrome details.

Scandinavian
First half of twentieth century (aka Gustavian). Commonly made from blond woods; features smooth designs and small bursts of color.

Mid-Century Modern
Designed by Eero Saarinen in 1956. Also called the Tulip chair. Smooth lines and curves give a space-age feel.

This room decked out in classic black and white suggests a respect for tradition, but geometric patterns, whimsical light fixtures, organically shaped tableware, and off-the-beaten path wall art are playfully modern touches in this home.

decorating for dining

No longer is the dining room reserved for formal dinners and holiday feasts. Think about how you plan to use the area and then decide on the theme. Formal entertainers may prefer darker, more dramatic colors for walls, decadent chandeliers, wainscoting, and a glass cabinet to display fine china. The more casual option would be white or bright colors on walls (maybe even wallpaper in a graphic pattern), cherrywood or lacquer-finish furniture, and track lighting. Forget that floral centerpiece; informal settings may feature collectibles or an assortment of votive candles.

Work Your Furniture

The table is to the dining room as the sofa is to the living room. Pretty important. The color of the wood in the dining table is, more often than not, the anchor of the room. But you can play off that with other elements such as carpet, curtains, and tabletop décor. Choose surfaces in a style that coordinates with your table—don't pair a maple sideboard with an inlaid table. The materials don't need to match exactly, but they should carry a similar weight in the room.

Many china cabinets feature glass-front hutches for displaying tableware. The surface of a credenza is a great display spot. Try a symmetrical arrangement by flanking the sideboard with a pair of lamps, or add creative, distinctly personal

Unlike the ultra-chic black-and-white setup at left, this nouveau rustic table with its steel legs and organic wood top suggests a more classic design sensibility.

touches such as framed illustrations of your pets, or a sophisticated 1950s pottery collection.

Light Right

You can definitely live with an overhead light on a dimmer, but the perfect lighting scheme combines accent with ambient (both natural and artificial) illumination. Try a hip chandelier hung so that the bottom is about 30 inches above the table's surface, and set it on a dimmer switch to avoid an off-putting glare.

Candle versions are elegant and moody while electric models are often glamorous and create a sense of opulence in a small room. Install wall sconces for an elegant touch, or a row of blown-glass pendants for a handcrafted look. Place two small table lamps on the sideboard on three-way switches to create low, ambient light when you want to use only candlelight on the table.

There are several types of overhead lamps. A chandelier is a fixture with branching arms. Use clear bulbs to enhance sparkle. A pendant gives off both task and general lighting. It uses shades or globes to avoid glare. Pendants should be hung about 30 inches above the tabletop and be about 12 inches narrower than the table on all sides. Another option is to aim downlights at the table to reduce an unpleasant glare.

A combination of chandelier and downlight—two downlights placed 2 feet from either side of the chandelier—will provide even lighting. To highlight items displayed in your china cabinet or on a buffet, use a halogen lamp. Its brightness will add sparkle and project attention onto the showcased items.

Light sources can serve a decorative function. This classic dining area uses a Lucite lamp and a combo of tall candles and low votives for the table's centerpiece. This is a great setup for illuminating the table while filling in the shadows.

This Manhattan town house gets a great deal of sunlight from the oversized windows. Fluorescent can lighting is energy-efficient yet stylish.

A one-of-a-kind table pairs well with a
mix of leather armchairs and stools.
The eclectic amber vases are dramatic in
scale yet create a harmonious balance
with the brown palette.

Tie in Textures

Texture in the form of window treatments, rugs, and linens softens your space. Window treatments vary with taste. You can't go wrong with simple sheers or roll-up shades that let the daylight in but allow artificial mood light to take center stage when night falls.

A sizable rug can anchor the room and add both visual and underfoot texture. Choose materials such as jute or hand-knotted cotton that wash easily and can withstand chairs being dragged back and forth across their surface.

If you have a hard floor, and you choose an area rug, make sure that when the chairs are pulled back to accommodate guests while seated, the entire chair rests on the area rug. You never want to have the back legs on the hard surface and the front legs on the rug. To make sure chairs won't fall off an area rug, measure the width of your table and add 4 feet. Your rug should be at least this wide. Dining rooms tend to be quite geometric, so experiment with different rug shapes such as oval and round.

Add Some Character

The dining room has a reputation of needing to feel formal, but don't let this sense of decorum leave your space dour or dry. Add some personality with the objects you display. Fill one wall with old family photos, place your glass bird collection on the mantel, or mount your grandmother's china in a graphic pattern above the sideboard. Embrace color; don't feel trapped by a neutral palette. Create a unique ambiance with walls in a bright shade of aqua, burnt orange, or even a warm chocolate. And always place an eye-catching object in the center of the dining table—a dramatic bowl, a Buddha, a stack of small books—even when you're not using it.

table shapes

Rectangular
The most traditional shape for a dining room table.
36" x 72"; seats 6
36" x 84"; seats 8
36" x 96"; seats 10

Oval
Similar to a rectangular table in the amount of seats it accommodates and space it takes up.
44" x 66"; seats 6
76" x 46"; seats 8

Round
A circular table is most conducive to socializing but tends to require more room.
48"–60" diameter; seats 4 to 6
72" diameter; seats 8

touch if your china pattern is simple. You can have chargers for different occasions—bamboo for your dinner parties, and gold-rimmed bone china for your parents' fortieth wedding anniversary.

There are several practical matters to consider when setting the table. For sufficient elbow room, place settings should be spaced at least 12 inches from one another. Follow the proper arrangement for formal and casual place settings—you would be surprised at the number of people who notice.

Use only silverware that is required for the meal (no soup, no soupspoons!). Place left-handed pals on appropriate corners so they won't bump another guest. If multiple wines will be served, multiple glasses should be set, all to the right of the water glass, in the order they will be needed.

Find Your Center

Unless you are serving family style, the table will look empty without a strong element in the center. A floral centerpiece is the classic choice. Make sure to choose either a very low or a very high and narrow centerpiece that won't force diners to crane their necks in an effort to interact. Stay away from highly fragrant flowers like Easter lilies that will conflict with the flavor of the food.

Objects can also be a part of a centerpiece. Three of your favorite vases grouped together, a collection of candlesticks of varying heights and widths, or even a favorite bamboo bowl filled with colorful pieces of fruit can add a punch of personality in an unexpected way. Incorporate gourds on Thanksgiving, brightly colored Christmas balls over the holidays, and when hosting a birthday party, framed photos of the honored guest. Keep candlelight soft and either above or below eye level. A combination of tall candles and low votives illuminates the table and fills in shadows. Plus, it's super flattering!

classic ways to set a table

CASUAL

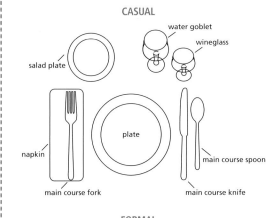

water goblet
wineglass
salad plate
plate
napkin
main course spoon
main course fork
main course knife

FORMAL

champagne flute
water goblet
dessert spoon and fork
wineglass
bread plate and knife
plate
napkin
soupspoon
appetizer or salad fork
main course fork
main course knife
appetizer or salad knife

A tablecloth dresses up a hand-me-down table. When choosing the linen, measure the width and length (or diameter) of the surface. Add 4 to 6 inches of drop on every side. If you find yourself with too much fabric, just make sure it falls at either end of the table—not on your guests' laps!

Wood cabinet doors and a collection of colorful glass warm up the functional look of a streamlined metal wet bar.

glasses glossary

Cordial Glasses
Similar to shot glasses, for special liqueurs at cocktail hour or after dinner.

Double Old-fashioned Glasses
Short tumblers that hold straight alcohol such as scotch or vodka.

Highballs
Tall, narrow glasses for mixed drinks like rum and Cokes, vodka tonics, or screwdrivers.

Iced-Tea Glasses
A bit smaller than highball glasses; can be used for any iced beverage.

Margarita Glasses
Full rims spread around a wide, bubblelike bowl.

Martini Glasses
V-shaped beauties; the most elegant of pieces.

Port Glasses
Used for dessert wines; look like small wineglasses and have tapered bowls.

Snifters
Bulging bowls allow for optimal swirling of brandy or cognac.

building your bar

If you entertain regularly, a bar is a key ingredient in turning your living space into a sophisticated party space. A well-stocked bar (liquor, mixers, garnishes, glasses, and tools) not only helps you host impromptu cocktails, but also adds a stylish vibe to your place.

For those most serious about their libations, a built-in wet bar is the ideal. A mini kitchen–style setup complete with running water, a refrigerator, and extensive storage for all shapes and sizes of cocktail glasses can be built along a wall in the kitchen or off the dining or living rooms.

The styling of this area needs to be driven by a theme or a color palette. A bar built into the living room should echo the wood most prevalent in that space. The colors and patterns—of decanters, cocktail napkins, serving trays—should also coordinate with the space the bar inhabits.

The Options
Construction isn't required to set up an attractive serving area for cocktails. If you have a sideboard or a buffet, utilize this practical place to keep all your glasses, liquor, and mixers. A bar cart—easily parked in the corner until the party begins—is perfect if the fun travels from kitchen to dining room to den over the course of the evening. Even an interesting tray holding the three most common liquors and a couple of glasses can serve as your makeshift bar.

bar checklist

Tools
- [ ] Bottle opener
- [ ] Can opener
- [ ] Corkscrew
- [ ] Stirring rod
- [ ] Bar strainer
- [ ] Jigger
- [ ] Cocktail muddler
- [ ] Citrus squeezer
- [ ] Cutting board
- [ ] Sharp paring knife
- [ ] Ice bucket
- [ ] Tongs
- [ ] Coasters
- [ ] Cocktail napkins
- [ ] Bottle sealers
- [ ] Swizzle sticks
- [ ] Straws

Garnishes
- [ ] Maraschino cherries
- [ ] Green olives
- [ ] Fruit (lemons, limes, oranges, raspberries)

Liquor
- [ ] Vodka
- [ ] Gin
- [ ] Scotch
- [ ] Tequila
- [ ] Blended whiskey
- [ ] Vermouth
- [ ] Cognac

Mixers
- [ ] Club soda
- [ ] Tonic water
- [ ] Cola
- [ ] Juices (lime, orange, and cranberry)

Extras
If you have more in mind than rounds of martinis, keep on hand an ice crusher, a blender (for frozen drinks), an ice chipper or pick, an ice scoop, and a vegetable peeler (for fruit peels).

Aficionado Confidential

If your passion is for wine, focus your attention on creating a nice display—and suitable conditions—for storing and decanting your collection. Wine you drink every day can sit on a coordinated wine rack in the kitchen away from heat and direct sunlight.

For the more serious bottles, you need a refrigerator. House a basic industrial-style cooler in the kitchen or pantry. They are reasonably priced and widely available. Consider a wine cellar designed to look like a beautiful mahogany cabinet that can sit in a hallway or act as a console in your dining space. If you are building or renovating a wet bar, perhaps you want wine and spirits to come together in one space. You can install a wine refrigerator in your drink zone. Note that high-end bottles of whiskey often require storage conditions similar to those of wine.

Personalizing Your Bar

Beyond the basics, you will certainly want to add touches of personality to your bar. One way to accomplish this is to integrate collections of related items like vintage ashtrays, designer barware such as jiggers in various materials, or even the shot glass collection you've put together.

Don't forget to have a house drink to serve. Stock the ingredients so you're always ready to mix. It's as simple as twisting tradition by modifying a classic like the margarita to include an orange flavor. Or use a trendy ingredient like designer soda. To ensure the greatest crowd-pleasing cocktail you can, don't go too wild with the type of liquor you choose as a base. Have cranberry juice or other flavors on hand to mix up some fave concoctions, and add a little punch to a cocktail. Remember those nondrinkers too by always having chilled soft drinks or sparkling water available.

Barware is stored in the room where most of the entertaining is done. Glasses and bottles are showcased in this open-faced armoire.

sleep

In lieu of a head-board, think about paneling a wall with wood. A 4-inch-deep ledge secured at least 3 feet above the pillows keeps head banging to a minimum while allowing for a personalized space.

Put a personal stamp on a bedroom by letting vintage vases serve as stylish jewelry storage.

Your bedroom should be the ultimate sanctuary, a calming, comforting, soothing space, closely tied to who you are on the most intimate level. It's the place you escape to at the end of each day to curl up with a book, chat on the phone, surf the Web, or perhaps engage in something less G-rated. But instead of this being a relaxing haven, without care, it can turn into the exact opposite.

Despite the fact that we spend about a third of our lives in this 30-or-so-square-foot area, it is often the room most overlooked and last to be decorated. Why? Probably because it is that place that other people respect as being your personal zone and, for obvious reasons, rarely step foot into. Your hideaway transforms into a home for furniture odds and ends, bare walls, and even unpacked boxes! This seems silly when you think of all the activities that take place there beyond the hours of sleep.

bed frame styles

Canopy
A bed with a draped fabric cover supported by a four-poster frame.

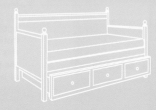

Day
A bed made to look like a sofa; it usually holds a twin mattress and has a headboard and footboard that simulate arms, and a sideboard that simulates the back of a sofa.

Four-poster
An old-fashioned bed characterized by four tall posts, one in each corner.

Platform
A bed with a horizontal surface elevated a foot or more above the ground by legs or framing; it often lacks a footboard and headboard.

Sleigh
A nineteenth-century design featuring a scrolled headboard and footboard that resembles the shape of a sleigh.

Trundle
A low bed that is usually on casters and stored by sliding under another bed.

mattress sizes

California king
Measures 72 x 84 inches and was originally available on the West Coast (though most major retailers will ship nationwide).

King
Typically 76 x 80 inches. Because of its generous width, be sure to measure doorways and hallways before attempting to navigate a king mattress through your home.

Queen
At 60 x 80 inches, it's the most popular size, probably because it straddles the line between conserving space and allowing occupants enough room to sleep comfortably.

Full
Also known as a double, this 54 x 75-inch bed is a great space saver, but leaves each person with just over 2 feet of personal space.

Twin
Usually 39 x 75 inches. Consider outfitting a guest bedroom with a pair of twin beds, which can offer more flexibility than a full or a queen.

This guest room gets great light from the high window. Adding a sheer gives the room a welcoming feel; dark shades would weigh it down and mask the natural light.

This room (ABOVE and RIGHT) is warm, inviting, and well thought out, thanks to the details woven throughout. A dark finish was selected for the bed frame and desk. Accents such as the robin's-egg blue sheets and area rug work well with the orange throw pillows placed strategically on the bed and corner chair.

The bed is the largest piece of furniture—and therefore the natural starting point for decorating. The darkness of this sleigh bed allows you to go both light and dark with linens and a rug.

Linens can add texture to simple, staid décor. A pop of periwinkle on a floral bed-spread and bamboo-printed pillowcases can make the bed the room's focal point.

bedding basics

materials

Chenille
A nubby cotton or synthetic fabric made with slubbed yarn, often used for blankets and throws.

Damask
A glamorous textile with a Jacquard-woven, tone-on-tone pattern. It may be silk, satin, twill, or sateen.

Dupioni silk
An elegant silk yarn reeled from two cocoons in which the silk is intertwined, giving it an uneven, decorative texture. Often sold in vibrant jewel tones.

Egyptian cotton
Thanks to extra-long fibers that can be woven into the finest possible thread, this is the strongest and most luxurious cotton available. Egyptian cotton sheets are so soft, they feel silken to the touch.

Flannel
A plain- or twill-woven wool, cotton, or synthetic brushed fabric that provides extra softness and warmth.

Jersey
A stretchy, plain-woven cotton fabric (think T-shirt material) used for casual sheets and pillowcases.

Matelassé
From the French word for "cushioned," this luxurious, often Jacquard-woven coverlet material has an embossed pattern that looks like a quilted weave.

Merino wool
A thick, durable fleece gathered from merino sheep, which are known for their high-quality wool yarn. Makes for a warm, resilient blanket fabric.

Percale
A closely woven, crisp cotton fabric with a high thread count, it's a standard sheet and pillowcase material.

Pima cotton
A lush fabric made from extra-long staple (ELS) cotton, usually grown in Australia, Southwest America, and Peru. Often used for high-end sheets and duvet covers.

Sateen
A smooth, high-sheen, glossy cotton fabric that is a decadent option for sheets, pillowcases, and more.

Supima
A licensed trademark used to promote textiles and fabrics made of 100 percent American Pima cotton. The name is an abbreviation for "Superior Pima."

pillow glossary

Bolster
A cylindrical accent pillow.

Boudoir
A small accent pillow.

Euro
At 26 x 26 inches, this decorative square pillow is larger than a standard pillow.

King-Size
Longer than a standard pillow by 10 inches, and best for king- and California-size beds.

Standard
This most commonly used pillow measures 20 x 26 inches.

Get creative with your headboard—no one says it needs to be attached to the bed! Mount chocolate brown and spring moss green canvas squares in a grid formation.

easy bedroom updates

Add new linens
Since your bed takes up much of the surface area of your bedroom, changing your bedspread and sheets will dramatically change the feel of the room. Or, for a more subtle, seasonal touch, change the throw pillows on your bed—an airy cotton eyelet fabric is beautiful for summer and is easily replaced by a heavy corduroy pillow come October.

Change up the art
Instead of black-and-white photos, try a watercolor in muted tones. If you're ready for a change but don't want to stop admiring your favorite piece, move it to another room. High-impact headboards are an easy and inexpensive addition to bare wall space.

Paint one wall
For a quick pick-me-up, paint just one wall of your room. Select the wall and color with care because this will immediately turn into the focal point of the space. Here's your opportunity to go bolder while not interfering with the overall flow and balance of the room.

Go ahead and hang a beaded curtain behind your bed to add a high-impact texture to the sleek black-and-white décor.

window treatments

length glossary

Apron-length
Hangs from the top of the window to the bottom of the apron (or the bottom of the windowsill). Good for tieback curtains, so that the curtains fall at the sill when tied back.

Café
Starts in the middle of the window and falls to the bottom of the pane just above the sill. Usually it is simply hooked or gathered and hung on a rod attached to the inner window frame, just above the lower pane. These curtains look casual and country, providing privacy while allowing light to stream in from the top.

Full-length
Hangs from the top of the window to barely touching the floor. Best for tall rooms and well-proportioned windows that you wish to draw attention to.

Puddled
Hangs from the top of the window to about a foot or more past the floor so that the fabric "puddles" on the floor. The look is even more striking and eye-grabbing than full-length. Tip: Be sure to leave a generous amount of excess fabric so that the style looks deliberate and not accidental.

Sash
Falls to the exact length of the inner windowpane, and is mounted inside the frame with brackets or a rod. The look is very basic and simple. When tied in the middle, the look is more done-up and the curtains are called hourglass curtains.

Sill-length
Hangs from the top of the window to barely touching the windowsill. Best for small windows, and rooms with low ceilings.

shades and blinds

Roller Shade
Simply a panel of fabric rolled around a tension rod that can be lowered or raised to any position on the window.

Roman Shade
When pulled up, the fabric folds into broad, horizontal pleats; hangs flat like a roller shade when down.

Honeycomb Blind
Also called cellular shades. Made of two layers of pleated fabric, giving the effect of venetian blinds. Allows light to filter through but offers temperature insulation, too.

drapes vs. curtains

Drapes
Operate mechanically on a traverse rod. The rod includes a track or a slide, which each drape hangs from. (A double traverse rod will get you two separate sets of drapes, such as one lightweight and another heavier curtain, which can operate independently.) A one-way traverse only allows the curtain to move to one side.

Curtains
Hang from rings on a curtain rod or pole. Rods come in a number of lengths, widths, and designs. For café or sash curtains that need to fit the window perfectly, your best bet is to find a spring tension rod or a sash rod, which is designed to adjust and fit inside any window.

Adjusting the light
source in your bed-
room is important.
Hanging tailored pleat
drapery with sheers is
a perfect combo.

Paint one wall a rich java brown, making it the room's focal point. Linens in white add a delicate touch while working with the frame of the mirror, the bedside table, and the lamp. Laying a neutral-tone jute rug creates a smooth transition when living with dark and light shades.

guest rooms

styling tips

The room should be neutral enough that your guests don't feel as if they are intruding on your personal space.
• Pick a soothing guest room palette; stick to different shades of a single color, like a sky blue wall, a turquoise lamp, and a comforter of washed denim.
• Try a room bathed in pure, placid white. Work splashes of color in with a bold throw or a vibrant nightstand.
• Start with a comfortable bed. Ascertain who your most frequent visitors are (your best friend and her husband? your niece?) to determine the size of the bed. A full-size bed is a safe bet—it's large enough for two but not too large for one.

• Layer the bed with linens and keep extra blankets at the foot of the bed, just in case.
• A nightstand or other surface is essential for small personal items like jewelry, books, or plane tickets.
• Don't clutter the space, but don't hesitate to display family photos, vacation pictures, or collections.
• Incorporate space-saving hidden storage like a chest or a storage ottoman to keep all the guest supplies such as extra linens hidden until they arrive.
• Consider shades or curtains to allow for privacy.

guest room checklist

☐ Lamp
☐ Books/magazines
☐ Alarm clock
☐ Pen and notepad
☐ Local guidebook
☐ Two soft pillows
☐ Two firm pillows
☐ Extra blankets
☐ Waffle-weave robes
☐ Water
☐ Flowers
☐ Toothbrush and toothpaste
☐ Soap, shampoo, and conditioner
☐ Towel, face towel, and washcloth
☐ Tissues

hosting tips

Prep the space
An inviting guest room is one in which amenities are at the ready (don't let guests have to awkwardly ask for extra towels or toilet paper).
   Provide a set of travel-size toiletries to the bathroom so your guests will feel at home—even if they forgot an item. Don't forget to add at least one special touch like hand cream in the bedroom—start the bottle so it won't be intimidating to use.

Host a tour
Let guests know where everything is by hosting a house tour when they arrive. Hit all the important spots like the bathroom, where glasses and paper towels are in the kitchen, and the like. Warn guests of quirks like plumbing issues or a loose stair rail.

Give some space
Clear out some space in a nearby closet or chest of drawers, or even leave a chair in the room so your guests have a place to put their stuff.

Give your shower that charming bed-and-breakfast feel with the classic oval curtain ring that is a perfect fit for a built-in tub.

stand up to moist conditions. Keep away from the shower and sink to avoid water damage. Ventilate the bathroom after showering to ensure there is no moisture buildup. Place a dehumidifier next to the toilet bowl or under the furniture as an added security measure.

Storage Solutions

Many of the fixtures in this room are non-negotiable, so careful planning is required for creative storage solutions you can access easily. The last thing you want is to be standing there dripping and unable to reach bath towels in a jiffy.

Built-in vanities with doors or drawers (or both) are the most obvious solutions, but don't stop there. Tuck freestanding cabinets into corners and leave at least 2 feet in front of them to allow for the swinging of doors and pulling of drawers.

Baskets and pails beneath the sink are a great storage idea, but leave at least 2 feet of clearance between the top of the basket and the bottom of the sink so you won't have to pull the vessel out too far in order to access towels. Shelves and racks, both freestanding and built-in, create excellent exposed storage.

Think double duty. Weave storage ideas throughout all the rooms of your home. A trusty wine rack is just as impressive when it is stocked with towels and a bottle of bubble bath on the bathroom floor.

bathroom storage ideas

Go inside
Wicker or metal baskets are a great place to store extra linens, toilet paper, and magazines. For storage in areas closer to the tub or shower, choose bins with lids to keep the moisture out.

Go on top
Add wall shelves on an untiled wall. In tight spaces, narrow shelves can hold canisters of cotton balls, hair accessories, and decorative soaps.

Go deeper
If you have the square footage for deeper shelves, stack extra towels on them. Choose towels that work with your color scheme since they'll be in full view—towels are a great way to add some color to a neutral space.

Go high
Add a shelf above a bathtub for showcasing small decorative items or pretty bottles of bubble bath.

stash

SELECTIONS FROM THE LILIANE AND DAVID M. STEWART COLLECTION

DESIGN 1935-1965
WHAT MODERN WAS
LE MUSÉE DES ARTS DÉCORATIFS DE MONTRÉAL
ABRAMS

MODERN GLAMOUR
KELLY WEARSTLER

COUNTRY HOUSES

CHURCH IN AS
THE COUNTRY HOUSES OF LOS ANGELES
STUDIO VISTA WHITNEY

ANDY GOLD

FURNITURE DESIGN
modern ch
Nina Börnsen-Holtmann
THE ART OF STAR W

AMEGAY

FORT BRACE & COMPANY

ecorating
harper & row

Dover 0-486-23357-X

usanna
artsch

Taschen

HELDERMAN/CAULKINS	HANUKKAH TRIVIA
GREIVE	The Blue Day Book
bad hair	james innes-smith & henrietta webb

1000 chairs
Charlotte & Peter Fiell
TASCHEN

KITES David Pelham   ISBN # 14

HISTORY AND DESTINY OF THE JEWS by Josef Kastein   GARDEN CITY PUBLISHING CO.

A PLACE TO STAY   Sheehan & Cassidy

flowers for the table   CHRONICLE BOOKS

Bonham Introduction to Dog Agility   ISBN 0-7641-1439-5 BARRON'S

HIDEAWAYS   Flammarion

NTAIN HOUSES

HENDERSON/BALDWIN 2x4 Projects for Outdoor Living

DEVIL'S WORKSHOP 25 Years of Jersey Devil Architecture SUSAN PIEDMONT-PALLADINO and MARK ALDEN BRANCH

CHIHULY: FORM FROM FIRE

ISSEY MIYAKE
weekend utopia modern living in the Hamptons

THE RED BALLOON
BY A. LAMORISSE

McLARIN
garden

EVA ZEISEL, Designer for Industry

PHOTOGRAPHS BY IRVING PENN

even the most beautifully decorated homes require spaces that are defined solely by their function, such as storage or work areas. Their primary purpose is utilitarian. These spaces are the most hidden from view and the most challenging to decorate, so they usually end up last on the list. From your entryway to your office, from closets to the forgotten corner of the laundry room, making the best use of all of your space ensures productivity. The design goal with these spaces should be first and foremost to make them highly functional—organized, easy to use, practical—and then easy on the eye.

Wrangling all of the stuff—particularly in rooms like offices, entries, or laundry rooms—is a challenge, but it is not impossible. Put a little extra effort into not wasting the hall closet by stuffing it with rolls of wrapping paper, folding chairs, and the vacuum cleaner you hardly ever use.

The entryway is a perfect place for a fun piece of furniture, like this bureau with unique drawer pulls. Extra cabinets will come in handy for concealing unattractive containers. The table-top provides plenty of space for a key and mail drop-off tray.

engaging entries

Whether it's a formal entryway or a back door mudroom, the space that welcomes people to your home also serves as a catchall for the daily necessities you drop off as you enter your house. Set an inviting tone in this area, but also utilize the space with practicality and functionality in mind. Let a small table, a console, or a shelf assume this role. Ideally, you should give yourself 4 feet of room to walk, so if you've got space, consoles and other furniture should be no wider than 18 inches. Apartment dwellers faced with only 3 feet should opt for a small shelf or an 8-inch table.

Storing Your Stuff

Outerwear should be your first consideration. There are tons of options that are great for quickly hanging coats and jackets, from nickel-plated coat racks to vintage wooden pegs. Think about how much wall space you have before deciding. Pegs should be mounted 6 to 8 inches apart. Invest in decorative baskets for storing hats, mittens, and scarves, which are sufficiently attractive to stay out even in warm weather. And if you are lucky enough to have tons of extra room, a coat rack makes a charming addition. A bench or a chair is a practical idea for guests who sit to put on or remove shoes. If your space permits, pick a bench with a flip-top seat that provides even more storage hidden beneath the cushion.

Maximize your space. Devote one cubbyhole to everyday items like bags and sunglasses. Use a bowl as a decorative spot for keys to keep clutter off the surface and to avoid frantic searches.

Trendy animal-print rugs create a fashionable but not fussy effect. Choose one in a rectangular shape so it doesn't look like an animal hide you hauled back from a safari.

Lighting

You'll want to set the right mood, so don't forget about lighting, especially since most entryways don't have windows. Pendant lighting, either flush with the ceiling or in the form of recessed can lights, with fifty-watt halogen bulbs on a dimmer should suffice. A chandelier adds a designer touch. If you don't have high ceilings, consider pin-spot lighting for illuminating hanging artwork. Tip: Narrow halls can look wider if you use sconces that project light up and down the wall on both sides.

Organizing

Chic baskets or ceramic bowls can be decorative yet functional for stashing keys, PDAs, cell phones, and mail. Have one receptacle for each type of item you drop. Color-coded containers are helpful for sorting and will make identifying items easy when you are rushing out the door. A wire rack is perfect for bundling newspapers awaiting recycling pickup day. A message or bulletin board in the foyer is a handy place to tack to-do lists, birthday reminders, invitations, and schedules.

Flooring

Since this part of the home gets the most traffic, an entryway's flooring needs to be durable. Think hardwood or stone, not carpet. It should also be easy to clean. If you want a little bit of softness underfoot, a durable runner or area rug is your best bet; just be sure the corners lay flat so when the door opens your visitors don't trip. A washable doormat keeps you from tracking in mud. Leave rain- or snow-soaked accessories outdoors or designate a semi-hidden spot inside your entryway for them. Cubbyholes beneath a console work well for shoes, and a tall galvanized planter will catch your umbrella's drip and still look nice.

Adding a vibrant
piece of art like this
oversized fabric will
create a dominant
color scheme in a
busy entryway.

This settee greets guests as they enter this Philadelphia home. The antique piece was reupholstered in this charming orange and ivory toile fabric.

150

• Display a favorite print or piece of art. If you are not into collecting, an oversized mirror is inexpensive and will make the space look bigger and add drama to a bare and neutral area.

• Bold hues are warm and inviting. Paint the walls a deep rust, red, green, or teal, depending on the colors in the rest of your home. Use gloss paint, which is easier to clean.

• A little plant life eases the transition from outside in. If you have a large entryway, try a tall tree. If your space is small, a plant on the table or a bowl of fresh flowers works just as well.

• Embrace a sense of balance by arranging furniture in clean, sleek lines to give positive energy flow to the space.

OPPOSITE: This workstation is ideal for extra side storage without scrimping on legroom. Add labels to containers for a fast and foolproof search method.

ABOVE: Bright colored folders are a must-have for differentiating files (green for bank statements) so that you know where to go without having to strain your eyes to read all the little labels.

work spaces

A desk is the centerpiece of any office, and it is the first piece of furniture you should finalize. A traditional desk is 30 inches high, while computer tables are typically 26 inches. This difference becomes important if you plan to put filing cabinets under your desk, because many sit slightly over 26 inches.

Large, freestanding work surfaces suit more spacious home offices. They allow room underneath for a trash can, a newspaper bin, or a computer tower, and often have coordinating rolling files that fit well below the desk.

If you're worried about not having enough space to conceal wires (or a little creative clutter!), try a kneehole desk. These typically come with built-in drawers on the left and right, making them a compact, though heavy, option. If you don't have room for a traditional desk, play around with what you have. A small table and a hutch can easily be converted to a workspace in a kitchen corner or a living room nook.

Pick Your Chair

Though the desk will be the focal point of your office, if you plan to spend more than two hours a day there, the most significant purchase you make should be an ergonomic desk chair. Admittedly, most desk chairs are pretty ugly. If that really bugs you and you use your office a lot, suck it up and cover the back of the chair with a throw; form is

less important than function here. Choose a chair on casters with lumbar support, adjustable height, and front-and-back tilt. Just know that if your office area has anything but wood floors or woven carpet, wheels will smash the fibers.

Five-star bases are the most stable. Removable and breathable seat covers are smart if you eat and drink at your desk or have a pet who likes to curl up on your chair.

Leave at least 3 feet between your chair and the wall or other pieces of furniture for easy access and mobility. Visit stores to "test" chairs, even if you plan on buying online—what looks best in a photo may not be the most comfortable piece of furniture. Add a lumbar support pillow for stress-relieving back support.

Make Sure You Can See

Good lighting reduces eye strain, fatigue, potential headaches, and even bad posture. If you primarily use a computer in your work area, position your desk so that there is no glare on the screen from overhead and existing light sources. Remember that natural light at certain times of the day can cause images to become washed out and put a strain on your eyes. Shades are the easiest solution.

Though overall lighting in the room is important, task lighting illuminates your workspace and is great for crafting and detail-oriented projects. Ceiling lights can cause a distracting glare, but if you can't control them, try positioning yourself between rows of lights rather than directly underneath them. The best options for adding light include an adjustable desk lamp with a flexible arm, wall- or ceiling-mounted styles, or a traditional table lamp that casts light over your entire workspace. Test different locations and bulb wattage until you find a setup that works for you.

ABOVE: A makeshift home office is simple to set up in a spare corner of a room. The one above has an extra-long table fit for two. Add a curtain over the window to diffuse light.

RIGHT: A modern shelving unit provides extra space for stowing items and also doubles as a table.

A black-and-white office space gets an invigorating jolt of color with stylish red storage boxes. Store photos, CDs, and unattractive wires that are best kept concealed.

155

This Manhattan apartment boasts a streamlined workstation complete with an overhead
shelving unit in a matching white. The ample
overhead storage is ideal for binders and
books. Add a curtain or decorative fabric as
an attractive solution for avoiding unneces-
sary visual distractions.

Tackle Your Technology

Most likely, your desk is home to a computer, if not a printer, a router, a scanner, cameras, and various other gadgets. Flat-screen monitors are ideal for small spaces, since they take up barely any desktop space. Computer towers should be placed underneath the desk. Gather wires together with plastic twist ties or cord clips and tape them to the bottom of your desk. Label each cord on both the source and outlet ends to avoid cord confusion when you need to move an item. Go wireless whenever possible!

Surge-protection strips safeguard your electronics from short but strong bursts of high voltage. These jolts can potentially ruin electronics, so avoid basic strips that only provide extra outlets.

Store Wisely

The more accessible your files, the more you'll use them. Standard file cabinets offer letter- and legal-size drawers, plus bonus surface space. (We like legal-size files to accommodate oversized documents.)

Specialized drawer inserts are available so you can transform any ordinary chest or box into office storage. Rolling file carts and plastic hanging-file crates from the office-supply store are less expensive options. To store selective file groupings that you'll need to carry with you, try a leather tote with handles.

Once a year, you should plan to do a total sweep of your office to clear out any unimportant files and paperwork, making sure to shred financial or other sensitive material. If you keep super-important files like your stock certificates or marriage license at home (as opposed to in a safety-deposit box at the bank), invest in a fireproof filing cabinet. In the event of an emergency, you'll know your important files are safe.

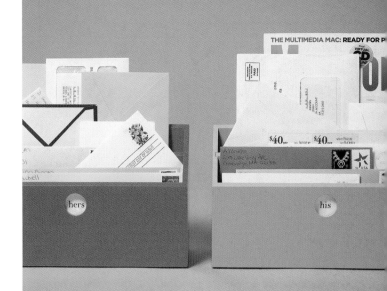

organize the mail

Designate a spot
Choose a place where it's easy to toss the mail: a desk in the kitchen, a drawer near the entryway. Devise a good system using trays, baskets, or file holders, and label each for different categories, from "bills" to "things to file." Make sure to clean out the files regularly. If you tend to ignore the mail, keep it in open containers. It'll force you to deal.

Sort mail over the trash
You'll get rid of all of the junk right away, and won't waste time sorting through a larger pile later. Then divide it into appropriate categories. Set aside a time to go through the stack, and put it on your calendar.

Some mail is optional
Besides bills and correspondence from companies you do business with, you don't need much else. Put catalogs and magazines in a place where you like to read, and store them in a vertical organizer, not a pile.

Reduce the amount of mail that comes
Choose paperless billing whenever you can and pay your bills online. Opt out of catalog mailings and sign up for e-mail notifications of new products and specials from your favorite stores.

Shape a corner nook into a full-fledged crafting station with sewing machine and supplies, natural and task lighting, and an inspiration board for posting fave fabrics and swatches.

LEFT: A makeup kit doubles as a craft supply organizer.

BELOW: Store craft supplies in an open-faced unit with separate compartments for easy access.

BOTTOM: Hobby meets display when yarn is arranged in a pretty bowl with related props.

craft space ideas

• Store basic work items like scissors, glue, needles, et cetera, in a box in one place close to your work surface.

• Have a place with compartments, like a professional makeup kit, to keep everything organized.

• Keep a laptop nearby for last-minute Web checks of directions or answers to questions.

• Empty shoe boxes can hold markers, colored pencils, and other writing tools.

• Stash a cordless handheld vacuum in a drawer so that messes can be cleared instantly.

• Hang a clear pocket organizer to hold paints, brushes, and other supplies. This way you can see what's inside and wash it if spills should occur.

• A standing paper towel holder can also keep ribbon and twine tidy and untangled.

• Use clear glass jars for storing opened cans of paint and label appropriately.

lighting 101

types of light

Ambient
The overall lighting of a room, from the sun's rays streaming through a bay window to an overhead fixture providing its primary glow.

Accent
The complementary component, from artificial sources like lamps and picture lights, or from natural ones such as candles and fireplaces.

Task
Light in its most functional form: direct illumination for a particular task, such as dicing vegetables.

Use combinations of these three lights in every room. In the living room, try overhead light in the middle of the ceiling, several reading lamps, and candlelight to create a soft mood.

types of bulbs

Incandescent
The most popular at home, its glow is flattering both to the skin and to furnishings within the room.

Halogen
The whitest of all light, thus a great choice for utilitarian task lighting. Good for the kitchen or home office.

Fluorescent
More energy-efficient than other types, compact fluorescent bulbs are rising in popularity and fit into most light sources. They tend to give off unflattering light.

High–intensity discharge
Also called HID bulbs, they have a longer life and provide more light per watt than others. Primarily for outdoor use.

placing lights

Ceiling
A center fixture, or a series of evenly spaced recessed downlights (which look like built-in cans), is a classic means of achieving ambient light. Balance the scheme with accent and task illumination by affixing a track of adjustable spotlights or picture lights to the ceiling.

Tabletop and floors
Disperse lamps throughout the room to supplement ambient lighting; consider three-way versions for different times of day and a range of moods.

Chandelier
A branched light fixture suspended from the ceiling that holds multiple bulbs.

Pendant
Lights suspended from the ceiling by chain or pipe.

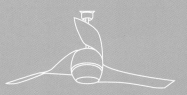

Ceiling Fan
The light is incorporated into a ceiling fan.

10

Acknowledgments

This book is a team effort of truly talented people. Among them are:

John Cronan, technical editor, corrected many errors, added many tips and notes, and greatly improved the book. John is also a good friend and an author in his own right. Thanks, John!

Lisa McCoy, copy editor, added to the readability and understandability of the book while always being a joy to work with. Thanks, Lisa!

Valerie Perry, indexer, who adds so much to the usability of the book, and does so quickly and with much thought. Thanks, Valerie!

Jody McKenzie and **Smita Rajan**, project supervisor and project manager, greased the wheels and straightened the track to make a smooth production process. Thanks, Jody and Smita!

Roger Stewart, sponsoring editor, believed in us enough to sell the series and continues to stand behind us as we go through the third edition. Thanks, Roger!

Nancy, Lee, Stuart, and **Craig**, friends and island neighbors, who do a lot to support our writing efforts. Thanks, Nancy, Lee, Stuart, and Craig!

Introduction

QuickSteps books are recipe books for computer users. They answer the question "how do I..." by providing a quick set of steps to accomplish the most common tasks with a particular operating system or application.

The sets of steps are the central focus of the book. QuickSteps sidebars show how to quickly perform many small functions or tasks that support the primary functions. Notes, Tips, and Cautions augment the steps, and are presented in a separate column so as not to interrupt the flow of the steps. The introductions are minimal, and other narrative is kept brief. Numerous full-color illustrations and figures, many with callouts, support the steps.

QuickSteps books are organized by function and the tasks needed to perform that function. Each function is a chapter. Each task, or "How To," contains the steps needed for accomplishing the function, along with the relevant Notes, Tips, Cautions, and screenshots. You can easily find the tasks you want to perform through:

- The table of contents, which lists the functional areas (chapters) and tasks in the order they are presented

- A How To list of tasks on the opening page of each chapter

- The index, which provides an alphabetical list of the terms that are used to describe the functions and tasks

- Color-coded tabs for each chapter or functional area, with an index to the tabs in the Contents at a Glance (just before the table of contents)

Conventions Used
in This Book

Windows 7 QuickSteps uses several conventions designed to make the book easier for you to follow. Among these are:

- A or a in the table of contents or the How To list in each chapter references a QuickSteps or QuickFacts sidebar in a chapter.

- **Bold type** is used for words on the screen that you are to do something with, like "...click the **File** menu, and click **Save As**."

- *Italic type* is used for a word or phrase that is being defined or otherwise deserves special emphasis.

- <u>Underlined type</u> is used for text that you are to type from the keyboard.

- SMALL CAPITAL LETTERS are used for keys on the keyboard, such as ENTER and SHIFT.

- When you are expected to enter a command, you are told to press the key(s). If you are to enter text or numbers, you are told to type them.

Chapter 1
Stepping into Windows 7

Windows 7 as an *operating system* performs *the* central role in managing what a computer does and how it is done. An operating system provides the interface between you and the computer hardware: It lets you store a file, print a document, connect to the Internet, or transfer information over a local area network (LAN) without knowing anything about how the hardware works.

This chapter explains how to start and/or log on to Windows 7; how to use its screens, windows, menus, and dialog boxes; and how to shut it down. You will also learn how to get help and discover some ways to have fun with Windows.

Start Windows

To start Windows, you need to turn on the computer. Sometimes, that is all you need to do. If, when you turn on the computer, you see a screen similar to Figure 1-1, you have started Windows. In many cases, in addition to turning on the computer, you also need to log on.

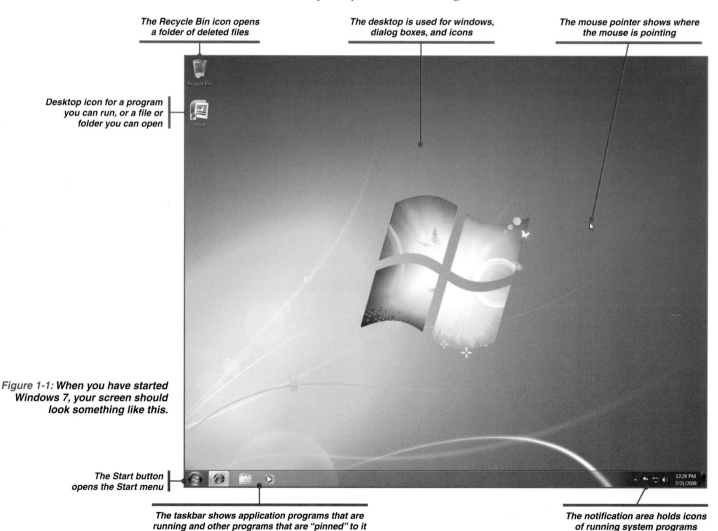

The Recycle Bin icon opens a folder of deleted files

The desktop is used for windows, dialog boxes, and icons

The mouse pointer shows where the mouse is pointing

Desktop icon for a program you can run, or a file or folder you can open

Figure 1-1: **When you have started Windows 7, your screen should look something like this.**

The Start button opens the Start menu

The taskbar shows application programs that are running and other programs that are "pinned" to it

The notification area holds icons of running system programs

Q UICKSTEPS

USING THE MOUSE

HIGHLIGHT AN OBJECT ON THE SCREEN

Highlight an *object* (a button, an icon, a border, etc.) on the screen by pointing to it. *Point* at an object on the screen by moving the mouse until the tip of the pointer is on top of the object.

SELECT AN OBJECT ON THE SCREEN

Select an object on the screen by clicking it. *Click* means to point at an object you want to select and quickly press and release the left mouse button.

OPEN AN OBJECT OR START A PROGRAM

Open an object or start a program by double-clicking it. *Double-click* means to point at an object you want to select and press and release the mouse button twice in rapid succession.

OPEN A CONTEXT MENU FOR AN OBJECT

Open a context menu, which allows you to do things specific to an object, by right-clicking it. *Right-click* means to point at an object you want to select and quickly press and release the right mouse button.

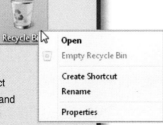

Continued . . .

Log On to Windows

If, when you start Windows, you see a Log On screen on which you can click one of several users, click your name or that of the default user and, if requested, enter your password. Windows will log you on to the system. If someone else, such as a system administrator, installed Windows 7 on your computer, he or she should have given you a user name and password, if one is needed. If you purchased a computer with Windows 7 installed on it or upgraded to Windows 7, a default user is shown on the logon page. As you will see in Chapter 8, you can change and add users if you wish.

Use the Mouse

A *mouse* is any pointing device—including trackballs, pointing sticks, and graphic tablets—with two or more buttons. This book assumes you are using a two-button mouse. Moving the mouse moves the pointer on the screen. You *select* an object on the screen by moving the pointer so that it is on top of the object and then pressing the left button on the mouse.

You can control the mouse with either your left or right hand; therefore, the buttons may be switched. (See Chapter 2 to switch the buttons.) This book assumes you are using your right hand to control the mouse and that the left mouse button is "the mouse button." The right button is always called the "right mouse button." If you switch the buttons, you must change your interpretation of these phrases.

Use the Screen

The Windows 7 screen can hold windows and other objects. In its simplest form, shown in Figure 1-1, you see a background scene, a bar at the bottom with a button on the left and the time and date on the right, and some icons in the upper-left area.

QUICKSTEPS

USING THE MOUSE *(Continued)*

MOVE AN OBJECT ON THE SCREEN

Move an object on the screen by dragging it. *Drag* means to point at an object you want to move, then press and hold the mouse button while moving the mouse. You will drag the object as you move the mouse. When the object is where you want it, release the mouse button.

QUICKSTEPS

USING THE NOTIFICATION AREA

The *notification area* on the right of the taskbar contains the icons of special programs and system features, as well as the time and date.

SHOW HIDDEN ICONS

Click the up arrow to see the icons of hidden programs, and then click any you wish to open.

OPEN A SYSTEM FEATURE

Click one of the icons in the middle to open a system feature.

SET THE TIME AND DATE

Click the time and date area to see a calendar and an analog clock, then click **Change Date And Time Settings** (see related Note).

SHOW THE DESKTOP

On the far right of the taskbar is an unmarked rectangular area, which, if you click it, will minimize all open windows and dialog boxes and display the desktop. Clicking it again restores all open windows and dialog boxes. Simply moving the mouse over (also known as *to mouse over*) this button temporarily clears from the screen all open windows and dialog boxes until you move the mouse away.

The parts of a screen are:

- The **desktop**, which takes up most of the screen.
- The **Start button** in the lower-left corner, which opens the Start menu.
- The **taskbar** across the bottom, which identifies programs that are running or "pinned" to it.
- The **notification area** in the lower-right area, which holds icons of running system programs.
- The **Show Desktop** button, at the rightmost of the taskbar, minimizes all open windows so you can see the desktop.
- **Desktop icons**, which can be in any number and anywhere on the desktop, are in the upper-left corner of Figure 1-1. Desktop icons are used to start programs or open files or folders.
- The **mouse pointer**, which can be anywhere on the screen.

USE THE DESKTOP

The *desktop* is the entire screen, except for the bar at the bottom. Windows, dialog boxes, and icons, such as the Recycle Bin, are displayed on the desktop. You can store *shortcuts*, which are icons for your favorite programs, on the desktop (see Chapter 2). You can drag windows, dialog boxes, files, and icons around the desktop. Double-click an icon on the desktop to open it.

USE THE START BUTTON

The *Start button,* located on the left of the taskbar, opens the Start menu when clicked. This provides you with primary access to the programs, utilities, and settings that are available in Windows.

USE THE TASKBAR

The *taskbar* at the bottom of the screen contains the active *tasks*, which are icons and titles of the programs that are running on the computer or folders that are open. The taskbar also holds the Start button on the left and the notification area and Show Desktop button on the right. Click a program on the taskbar to open it.

NOTE

NOTE

Your taskbar may have more or fewer objects than those shown in the illustration.

NOTE

If you are connected to the Internet, you should never need to set your time and date, even when changing to or from daylight saving time (summertime in Europe), because Windows automatically synchronizes your computer's time with a local time server.

NOTE

The icons you have in the notification area will depend on the programs and processes you have running and the system features you have available. The icons shown here include system messages, which access the Action Center ; Network, which accesses the Network And Sharing Center ; and Speakers, which allows you to control the sound from your computer . In a laptop or notebook computer, you probably have two additional icons: Power and Wireless .

Programs "pinned" to the taskbar · Show Desktop button

Start button · Active programs or open folders · Notification area

USE A DESKTOP ICON

A *desktop icon* represents a program or folder that can be started or opened and moved about the screen. The Recycle Bin is a desktop icon for a folder that contains all of the files that have been deleted since the Recycle Bin was last emptied. Double-click a desktop icon to open or start what it refers to.

USE THE MOUSE POINTER

The *mouse pointer,* or simply the *pointer* or *mouse,* shows where the mouse is pointing. Move the mouse to move the pointer.

Open the Start Menu

To open the Start menu:

1. Point at the **Start** button by moving the pointer so that it is over the Start button. You will see that the button changes color. When this happens, the button is said to be selected or *highlighted.*

2. Press and release the left mouse button (given that your mouse buttons have not been switched) while the pointer is on the Start button. The Start menu will open, as you can see in Figure 1-2.

Use the Start Menu

The Start menu contains icons for programs and folders, as well as access to control functions and other menus, as shown in Figure 1-2. The most important menu item is All Programs, which opens a menu within the Start menu of all your programs. The buttons in the lower-right corner—Shut Down and session-ending choices—are important control functions discussed later in this chapter. The text box in the lower-left corner allows you to enter criteria and search the

NOTE

The two steps describing how to open the Start menu can be replaced with the two words "click **Start**." You can also open the Start menu by pressing the Windows Flag key  on your keyboard, if you have that key, or by pressing both the **CTRL** and **ESC** keys together (**CTRL+ESC**). In the rest of this book, you will see the phrase "click **Start**." This means open the Start menu using any technique you wish.

NOTE

Depending on the edition of Windows 7 you have (Starter, Home Basic, Home Premium, Professional, Enterprise, or Ultimate), your Start menu may be slightly different from the one shown here for Windows 7 Ultimate edition.

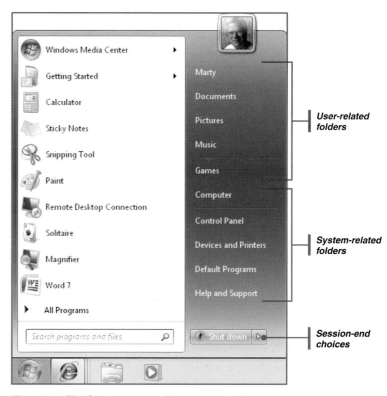

Figure 1-2: The Start menu provides access to the programs, utilities, and settings in Windows.

files and folders on the computer or the Internet for those that contain a match. All other options on the menu open folders or start programs, or both. The eight lower icons on the left change to reflect the programs you have used most recently (which are probably different from those shown here). In most cases, these are the programs that Windows 7 initially displays.

The remaining icons in the Start menu fall into two categories: user-related folders and system-related folders, programs, and options.

OPEN USER-RELATED FOLDERS

The top five options on the right in Figure 1-2 (including the user's name at the top) are used to access folders related to the user who is logged on. These options start the Windows Explorer program and display the folder identified. Clicking the user's name opens a folder containing the user's libraries (with four subsidiary folders), as well as other features, as shown here. Windows Explorer will be discussed later in this chapter and again in Chapter 3.

OPEN SYSTEM-RELATED FOLDERS

The remaining five icons in the bottom-right area of the Start menu (see Figure 1-2) help you manage your computer and its resources or get help. The function of each is as follows:

- **Computer** starts the Windows Explorer program and displays disk storage devices on the computer. From this point you can open any disk, folder, and file that is available to you on your computer and the network to which you are connected.

- **Control Panel** provides access to many of the settings that govern how Windows and the computer operate. This allows you to customize much of Windows and to locate and solve problems. The Control Panel is discussed primarily in Chapter 2.

- **Devices And Printers** allows you to check the status of and change the settings on the hardware devices and printers in or connected to your computer.

- **Default Programs** allows you to associate a program with a file type and automatically start that program when you double-click that type of file.

- **Help And Support** opens a window from which you can search for information on how to use Windows 7. It includes a tutorial and a troubleshooting guide. Help is discussed in more detail later in this chapter.

Your computer's manufacturer may have added an icon that connects you to the manufacturer's Internet Help center.

NOTE

If you are looking for Internet-accessing programs on the Start menu, you'll see how to add them in Chapter 4.

QUICKSTEPS

STARTING A PROGRAM

The method for starting a program depends on where the program icon is located. Here are the alternatives:

ON THE DESKTOP

Double-click the program icon, or "shortcut," on the desktop.

ON THE START MENU

Click the program icon on the Start menu.

A PINNED ICON ON THE TASKBAR

Click the program icon on the taskbar.

IN THE NOTIFICATION AREA

Click the program icon in the notification area.

ON THE ALL PROGRAMS MENU

1. Click **Start**.

2. Click **All Programs**.

3. Click the relevant folder or folders.

4. Click the program icon, as shown in Figure 1-3.

USING THE RUN COMMAND

1. Click **Start** and click **All Programs**.

2. Click **Accessories** and then click **Run**.

3. Type the path and program name, and press **ENTER** or click **OK**.

TIP

In Chapter 3 you will see how to start programs with Windows Explorer.

Figure 1-3: All Programs on the Start menu may lead you through several folders before you find the program you want.

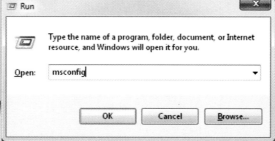

Use a Window

When you start a program or open a folder, the program or folder appears in a "window" on your screen, as shown with the Windows Explorer window in Figure 1-4.

The window in Figure 1-4 has a number of features that are referred to in the remainder of this book. Not all windows have all of the features shown in the figure, and some windows have features unique to them.

- The **title bar** is used to drag the window around the screen, and may contain the name of the program or folder in the window (the Windows Explorer window in Windows 7 does not contain a name in the title bar).

- The **address bar** displays the complete address of what is being displayed in the subject pane. In Figure 1-4, this is the Ch01 folder, in the QuickSteps-Win 7 folder, on drive C of the Marty2 computer in the local network.

- The **toolbar** contains tools related to the contents of the window. Click a tool to use it. The toolbar is always displayed.

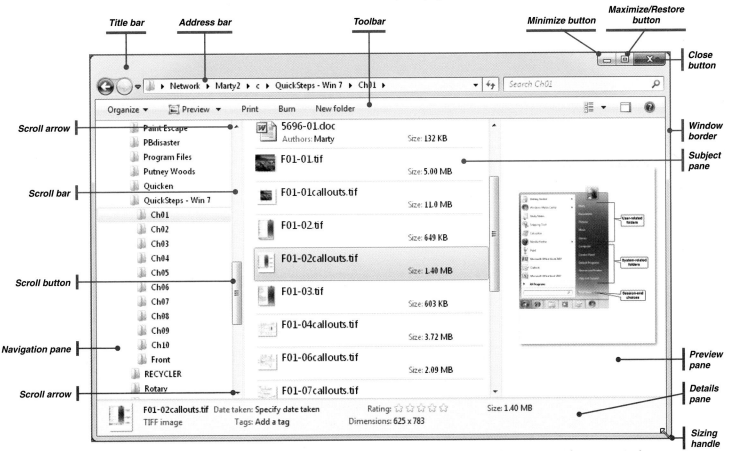

Figure 1-4: The Windows Explorer window has a number of different features that allow you to perform many tasks.

- The **Minimize button** decreases the size of the window so that you see it only as a task on the taskbar.

- The **Maximize/Restore button** increases the size of the window so that it fills the screen. When the screen is maximized, this button becomes the **Restore button**, which, when clicked, returns the screen to its previous size.

- The **Close button** shuts down and closes the program, folder, or file in the window.

- The **window border** separates the window from the desktop, and can be used to size the window horizontally or vertically by dragging the horizontal or vertical border, respectively.

- The **sizing handle** in each corner of the window allows it to be sized diagonally, increasing or decreasing the window's height and width when you drag a handle.

- The **preview pane** displays the object selected in the subject pane. For example, in Figure 1-4, the navigation pane points to a particular folder whose files of screenshots are shown in the subject pane, where one particular file is selected and displayed in the preview pane. By default, the preview pane is turned off.

- The **details pane** displays detailed information about the object that is selected in the subject pane. The details pane is turned on by default.

- The **subject pane** displays the principal subject of the window, such as files, folders, programs, documents, or images. The subject pane is always on.

- The **navigation pane** provides links to the most commonly used folders related to the user who is logged on, as well as an optional hierarchical list of disks and folders on the computer. The navigation pane is turned on by default.

- **Scroll arrows**, when clicked, move the window contents in small increments in the direction of the arrow.

- The **scroll button** can be dragged in either direction to move the contents accordingly.

- The **scroll bar** allows you to move the contents of the pane within the window so that you can see information that wasn't displayed. Clicking the scroll bar itself moves the contents in larger increments.

Use a Menu

A *menu* provides a way of selecting an action, such as turning on the preview pane, as shown in Figure 1-5. To use a menu in an open window:

1. Click the menu name on the menu bar.

CHANGING THE WINDOW LAYOUT

The window shown in Figure 1-4 has all of its panes turned on. By default, the preview pane is not visible. You can turn these panes on and turn other panes off.

TURN ON PANES

Click **Organize** on the toolbar, click **Layout**, and click **Preview Pane** (see Figure 1-5).

TURN OFF PANES

Click **Organize** on the toolbar, click **Layout**, and click **Details Pane** or **Navigation Pane**.

TURN ON CLASSIC MENUS

If you miss the menus that were in Windows Explorer in earlier versions of Windows, you can turn them on.

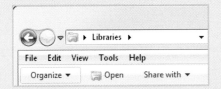

Click **Organize** on the toolbar, click **Layout**, and click **Menu Bar**.

There are several ways to distinguish a dialog box from a window. The purpose of a window is to display information, while the purpose of a dialog box is to gather information. Dialog boxes cannot be sized and do not have a control menu icon, a menu bar, or Minimize and Maximize buttons.

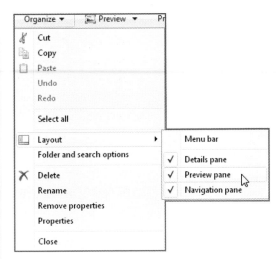

Figure 1-5: *By default, menus are not available in Windows Explorer, but you can turn them on if you wish.*

2. Move the pointer to the option you want.

3. Click the option you want.

Use a Dialog Box

Dialog boxes gather information. A *dialog box* uses a common set of controls to accomplish its purpose. Figures 1-6 and 1-7 show two frequently used dialog boxes with many of the controls often seen.

The common controls in dialog boxes are used in the following ways:

- The **title bar** contains the name of the dialog box and is used to drag the box around the desktop.

- **Tabs** let you select from among several pages in a dialog box.

- A **drop-down list box** displays a list from which you can choose one item that will be displayed when the list is closed.

- A **list box** (not shown) lets you select one or more items from a list; it may include a scroll bar.

- **Option buttons**, also called radio buttons, let you select one among mutually exclusive options.

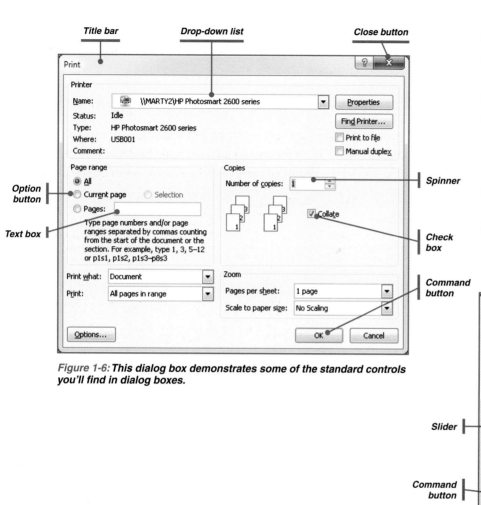

Figure 1-6: *This dialog box demonstrates some of the standard controls you'll find in dialog boxes.*

- **Check boxes** let you turn features on or off.
- A **preview area** shows you the effect of the changes you make (not shown).
- A **text box** lets you enter and edit text.
- **Command buttons** perform functions such as closing the dialog box and accepting any changes (the OK button), or closing the dialog box and ignoring the changes (the Cancel button).
- A **spinner** lets you select from a sequential series of numbers.
- A **slider** lets you select from several values.

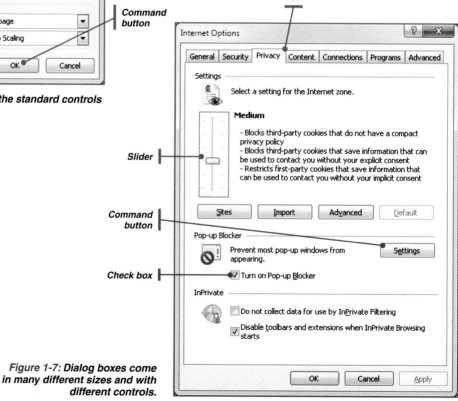

Figure 1-7: *Dialog boxes come in many different sizes and with different controls.*

You will have a great many opportunities to use dialog boxes. For the most part, you can try dialog boxes and see what happens; if you don't like the outcome, you can come back and reverse the setting.

Navigate the Windows Desktop

When multiple windows are open, and possibly a dialog box or two, navigating among them and displaying the one(s) you want could be difficult. Figure 1-8, for example, shows such a situation. Earlier versions of Windows tried to address

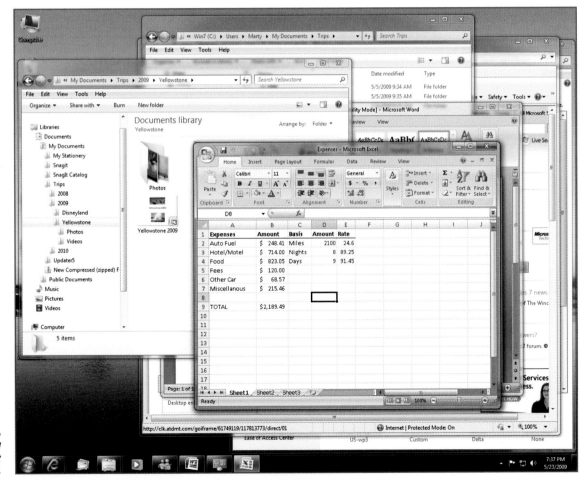

Figure 1-8: A screen can become cluttered with windows and dialog boxes, making it difficult to find what you want.

this, but Windows 7 has added a number of features to handle it elegantly, including:

- **Aero Peek** to see what's hidden on the screen
- **Aero Shake** to minimize other open windows
- **Aero Snaps** to resize and position windows
- **Jump Lists** to see recent files and program options
- **Taskbar Previews** to see what is open in a program

AERO PEEK

Aero Peek allows you to see what's hidden on the desktop behind all the open windows. You can do this on a temporary (or "peek") basis or a more long-lasting one.

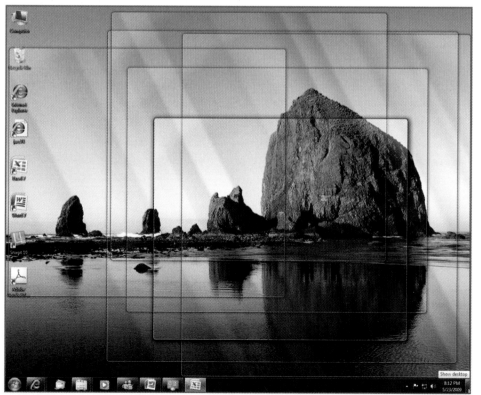

Figure 1-9: **With Aero Peek, all open windows become transparent.**

- **Temporarily peek** at the desktop:

  Move the mouse pointer to ("mouse over") the Show Desktop area on the far right of the taskbar. All the open windows will become transparent ("glass") frames, as you can see in Figure 1-9.

- **Return** to the original desktop after a temporary peek:

  Move the mouse pointer away from the Show Desktop area. All the open windows will reappear, as shown in Figure 1-8.

- **Hide** all open windows so you can see and work on the desktop:

  Click in the Show Desktop area on the far right of the taskbar. All the open windows will be hidden, and you can move the mouse around the entire desktop.

- **Unhide** all open windows and return to the original desktop:

  Click in the Show Desktop area on the far right of the taskbar. All the open windows will be returned to their original position.

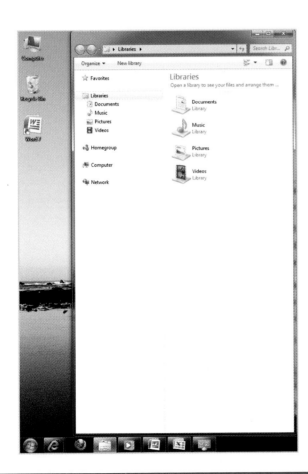

AERO SHAKE

Aero Shake allows you to minimize all open windows except for the one you are "shaking." To "shake" a window:

Point to the title bar of the window you want to remain open. Press and hold the mouse button while moving the mouse rapidly to the left and then to the right, as if you were shaking it.

–Or–

Press and hold the Windows Flag key while pressing **HOME**.

To return the minimized windows to their original size and position, repeat the same steps.

AERO SNAPS

Aero Snaps "snap" a window to various parts of the screen, a function similar to the Maximize/Restore button (which can still be used) on the title bar of a selected, floating (not already maximized) window, with some useful additions.

- **Maximize** a floating window:

  Point within the title bar of the window, not on its edge, and drag it to the top of the screen. The window will be maximized to fill the screen.

  –Or–

  Press and hold the Windows Flag key while pressing **UP ARROW**.

- **Restore** a maximized window (independent of how it was maximized):

  Double-click the title bar.

  –Or–

  Press and hold the Windows Flag key while pressing **DOWN ARROW**.

- **Vertically maximize** a floating window while not spreading it out horizontally, as shown on the left.

  Point to the top or bottom edge of a window, and drag it to the corresponding edge of the screen. The window will be vertically maximized.

  –Or–

  Press and hold the Windows Flag key while pressing **SHIFT+UP ARROW**.

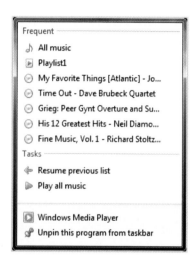

- **Left-align** a floating window and have it occupy 50 percent of the screen:

  Point to the title bar of a window, and drag it to the corresponding edge of the screen. When the mouse pointer reaches the edge of the screen, the window will fill the left 50 percent of the screen.

  –Or–

  Press and hold the Windows Flag key while pressing **LEFT ARROW**.

- **Right-align** a floating window and have it occupy 50 percent of the screen:

  Point at the title bar of a window, and drag it to the corresponding edge of the screen. When the mouse pointer reaches the edge of the screen, the window will fill the right 50 percent of the screen.

  –Or–

  Press and hold the Windows Flag key while pressing **RIGHT ARROW**.

- **Restore** a window that is filling 50 percent of the screen:

  Double-click the title bar twice.

  –Or–

  Press and hold the Windows Flag key while pressing the key opposite to the one used to enlarge it.

  –Or–

  Point at the title bar of a window, and drag it down and away from the window edge it was aligned to.

JUMP LISTS

Jump lists are a context or pop-up menu for application icons on the taskbar or the Start menu, as shown above to the left. When you right-click a program icon on either the Start menu or taskbar, a menu will appear containing a list of recent files or web pages, as well as options to close the application, pin or unpin it from the Start menu or taskbar, and open the application with a blank file or web page.

TASKBAR PREVIEWS

Taskbar previews are a miniature image, or thumbnail, of an open window attached to a taskbar icon. When you mouse over an icon on the taskbar,

a thumbnail of the open window or windows related to that icon will temporarily appear, as shown here. If you then move the mouse to the thumbnail, a temporary full-sized image will appear (see Figure 1-10). When you move the mouse off the thumbnail or the icon, the corresponding image will disappear. Open a window by clicking its thumbnail. Close a window by clicking the **Close** button on the thumbnail.

TIP

Look at the icons on the taskbar in Figure 1-10. It is obvious by its bright highlight that the Windows Explorer icon is selected and the one displaying the thumbnails. You can also tell that the Windows Live Mail and Windows Media Player icons (the two following Windows Explorer), by their lack of any highlight and border, do not have any open windows, while all the remaining program icons, which are highlighted, do have open windows.

Figure 1-10: The natural instinct is to move the mouse from the thumbnail to the temporary larger window to open it, but that causes both images to disappear. You must click the thumbnail.

NOTE

In the illustration shown here of the lower-right area of the Start menu there is an exclamation mark in a shield on the Shut Down button. This tells you that when you shut down, updates will be installed and then the computer will be shut down.

NOTE

The function of the Shut Down button can be changed to any of the other session-end options (see Chapter 5).

TIP

There are two distinct schools of thought on whether you should use Sleep or Shut Down when you leave the computer for any length of time. There are two primary considerations: security and power usage. Older computers used less power running in Sleep mode than the power consumed during shutting down and starting up. New computers have reduced the power consumed during these events, so it is now a toss-up. From a security standpoint, there is no security like having your computer completely turned off. A computer is also fairly secure in Sleep mode, but it is theoretically possible for a hacker to awaken it. The choice becomes a matter of preference. I turn my computers off; my wife leaves hers on.

End Your Windows Session

You can end your Windows session in several ways, depending on what you want to do. All of these can be found on the Start menu.

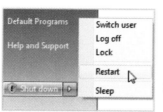

1. Click **Start**. Note in the lower-right area of the Start menu there is a button marked Shut Down and a right-pointing arrow which opens a menu of options that are in addition to Shut Down.

2. Click either **Shut Down** or the right-arrow, and click the option you want.

The meanings of the various options are:

- **Shut Down** closes all active programs and network connections and logs off all users so that no information is lost, and then turns off the computer (if it is done automatically) or tells you when it is safe for you to turn it off. When you start up the computer, you must reload your programs and data and reestablish your network connection to get back to where you were when you shut down.

- **Switch User** leaves all active programs, network connections, and your user account active but hidden while you let another person use the computer.

- **Log Off** closes all active programs, network connections, and your user account but leaves Windows 7 and the computer running so another person can log on.

- **Lock** leaves all active programs, network connections, and your user account active but displays the Welcome screen, where you must click your user icon and potentially enter a password, if you have established one, to resume using the computer.

- **Restart** closes all active programs, network connections, and logs off all users so that no information is lost. Windows is then shut down and restarted. This is usually done when there is a problem that restarting Windows will fix or to complete setting up some programs.

- **Sleep** leaves all active programs, network connections, and your user account active and in memory, but also saves the state of everything on disk. Your computer is then put into a low power state that allows you to quickly resume working exactly where you were when you left. In a desktop computer, it is left running in this low power state for as long as you wish. In a mobile computer (laptops, notebooks, netbooks, and tablet PCs), after three hours or if the battery is low, your session is again saved to disk and the computer is turned off.

UICKSTEPS

HAVING FUN WITH WINDOWS

Windows 7 has a number of games besides FreeCell. The following sections explain how to play three more.

PLAY HEARTS

Hearts is a card game that can be played by as many as four people on the network.

Games menu:
- Games
- Chess Titans
- FreeCell
- Games Explorer
- Hearts
- Internet Backgammon
- Internet Checkers
- Internet Spades
- Mahjong Titans
- Minesweeper
- More Games from Microsoft
- Purble Place
- Solitaire
- Spider Solitaire

1. Click **Start**, click **All Programs**, click **Games**, and click **Hearts**. The game board will appear. By default, you will have three simulated opponents.

2. Click three cards you want to give away, and click the arrow to give your cards to the person in the direction of the arrow.

The objective is to have the lowest score by *not* taking tricks with hearts or the queen of spades in them *unless* you can take all such tricks. You take a trick by playing the highest card in the suit led for that trick. You begin the game by passing three cards from your hand to another player. You want to pass your highest hearts and spades. The person with the two of clubs leads. You must follow suit if you can. If you can't, you may throw away your high hearts or spades or any other card. Whoever takes a trick plays the first card for the next trick. Play continues until all cards have been played. At the end of a game, one point is assessed for each heart in the tricks you took plus 13 points for the queen of spades. If you get all the hearts plus the queen of spades, you get zero points and all other players get 26 points.

Continued . . .

RESUME FROM SLEEP

There are several ways to resume operation after a computer has been put into Sleep mode, which depend on your type of computer, how it was put to sleep, and how long it has been sleeping. A computer can be put into Sleep mode either by your action on the Start menu or as the result of the computer not being used for a period of time, which is controlled in the Power Options (see Chapter 5). The ways to resume include:

- Press any key on your keyboard. This works with most desktop computers and mobile computers that have only been asleep a short time.

- Quickly press the power button on your computer. This works with most recent computers of all types. Holding down the computer's power button will, in most cases, either fully turn off the computer or cause it to restart (shut fully down and then restart).

- Open the top. This works with most mobile computers.

Get Help

Windows 7 Help provides both built-in documentation and online assistance that you can use to learn how to work with Windows 7. For example, to use Help to start a program:

1. Click **Start** and click **Help And Support**. The Windows Help And Support window, like the one shown in Figure 1-11, opens.

2. In the Search Help text box, type start a program. A number of options related to starting a program will be displayed.

3. Click the **Close** button to close the Help And Support window.

Play FreeCell

There are a number of games you can play in Windows 7. Probably the most addictive of them all is FreeCell, which is a solitaire-like card game. To start playing:

1. Click **Start**, click **All Programs**, click **Games**, and click **FreeCell**. The game board will be displayed, and a new hand will be dealt.

QUICKSTEPS

HAVING FUN WITH WINDOWS
(Continued)

PLAY MINESWEEPER

Minesweeper is a game of chance in which you try to accumulate points by not encountering mines.

1. Click **Start**, click **All Programs**, click **Games**, and click **Minesweeper**. The first time you play, you are asked to click the level of difficulty you want to use. The game board will then appear.

2. The object is to find the mines hidden in the squares without clicking one. Click a square. You will see one or more squares showing numbers or blanks or a mine. The number tells you how many mines are contained in the eight surrounding squares. Mark the suspected mines with the right mouse button. Clicking a mine ends the game.

3. After a game has ended, to restart the game, click **Restart This Game**; to start a new game, click **Play Again**; or click **Exit**.

PLAY SOLITAIRE

Solitaire is a game of chance and strategy. The object of the game is to end up with the deck of cards arranged sequentially in suits from ace to king.

1. Click **Start**, click **All Programs**, click **Games**, and click **Solitaire**. The game board is displayed.

   You will see a row of seven stacks of cards; all are face-down except the top card. You move the cards between the stacks to create columns

   Continued . . .

Figure 1-11: The Windows 7 Help and Support window provides you with several options for getting help.

The objective is to get the complete set of cards in each of the four suits in order from ace to king in the home cells in the upper-right area. You can temporarily place up to four cards in the free cells in the upper-left area. You can also temporarily place a card on the next highest card of the opposite color in the stacks at the bottom.

2. To move a card, click it and then click where you want it to go. If it is not a legal move, you will be told that. If you get an empty column at the bottom, you can build your own sequence in it.

QUICKSTEPS

HAVING FUN WITH WINDOWS

(Continued)

of alternating suits, exposing the hidden cards so you can eventually move them to the empty cells. In the upper-left area of the board is another turned-down stack of cards, which you can click and move to a proper place on one of the seven stacks. In the upper-right area are four empty cells, where you will place the suits, beginning with the aces.

2. Start a new game by clicking **Game** and clicking **New Game**.

The secret is to think several moves in the future and never fill up the free cells without having a way to empty them. The game is lost if you have no moves left and haven't moved all the cards to the home cells. Figure 1-12 shows a game that was played for a few minutes and is all but won. The queen of diamonds is the only card left to move. When all your cards are in order, they will be moved to the home cells automatically and you will be told you won.

3. When you are done playing, click **Close** and then click **Yes** to "resign" from the game if you did not finish it.

*Figure 1-12: **A great many people spend a lot of time playing FreeCell.***

TIP

FreeCell has two neat features. You can undo your moves (on the Game menu click **Undo** or press **CTRL+Z**) and get a hint (on the Game menu, click **Hint** or press **CTRL+H**).

Chapter 2
Customizing Windows 7

Windows 7 has many features that can be customized. You can keep the default Windows 7 setup or you can change the display, Start menu, taskbar, and sounds. You can also rearrange the desktop and enable accessibility options.

Change the Look of Windows 7

An important aspect of Windows that leads to your enjoyment and efficient use of it is how it looks. Windows 7 provides significant flexibility in this area. You can change how the screen looks, including the desktop, the Start menu, and the taskbar.

Use the Personalization Window

Much of what you see on the Windows 7 screen is controlled by the Personalization window. Open it to make many of the changes in this chapter.

(Several of the features controlled in the Personalization window, such as sounds and the mouse pointer, are discussed on their own later in this chapter.)

1. With Windows 7 running and displayed on your computer, right-click a blank area of the desktop. The desktop *context menu* is displayed.

2. Click **Personalize**. The Personalization window opens, as shown in Figure 2-1.

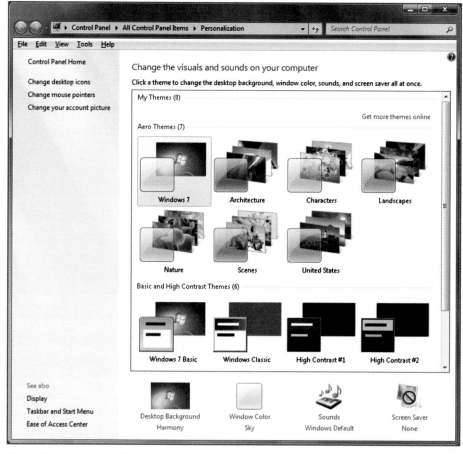

Figure 2-1: The Personalization window lets you change the appearance of Windows 7.

CHANGE THE DESKTOP THEMES AND COLORS

You can use any picture, color, or pattern you want for your desktop background. Windows 7 comes with a number of alternatives. From the Personalization window:

1. Drag the scroll bar on the right and review the themes that are available with Windows 7 (or click **Get More Themes Online** to view Microsoft's online library). Click the theme you want to use. With each theme you can select a desktop background and a window color, as well as the sounds used and a screen server.

2. Click **Desktop Background**. Click the **Picture Location** down arrow, and select a source of pictures (see Figure 2-2), or click **Browse** and navigate to a location on your computer where you have a picture you want to use (Chapter 3 explains how to navigate on your computer). Click **OK**, and click the picture or pictures desired.

3. Click **Save Changes** to close the Desktop Background window.

4. At the top of the themes list, click **Save Theme** to save any changes to or to save a new theme.

5. In the Save Theme As dialog box, name the theme, and click **Save**.

CHANGE THE RESOLUTION AND TEXT SIZE

Depending on your computer and monitor, you can display Windows 7 with various resolutions and text sizes. You can select the text and object size in the Display window and then go on to adjust the resolution. From the Personalization window:

1. Click **Display**. The Display window will appear, as shown in Figure 2-3.

2. Click the text and object size you want to use, and click **Apply**.

3. Click **Adjust Resolution**. If you have more than one display device, click **Identify**. The display's number appears on each screen. In the Display drop-down list, click the display whose resolution you want to change.

Figure 2-2: Selecting a background picture causes it to be instantly displayed as your background.

The Advanced Settings link at the right of the Screen Resolution window will provide access to settings that are specific to your display hardware.

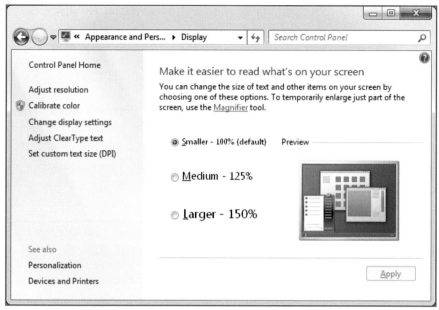

Figure 2-3: *Increasing the text and object size lets you see less of what's on the screen, but what you see is larger and possibly easier to read.*

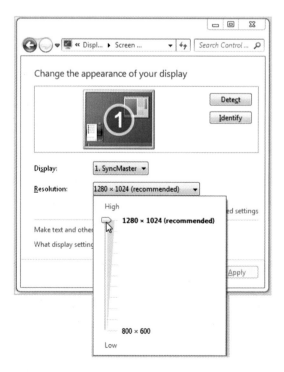

4. Click the **Resolution** drop-down arrow. Drag the slider up or down to adjust the resolution. (You can try this and if you don't like it, come back and change it.)

5. Click **Apply** to save the settings and then click the **Back** arrow in the upper-left area until you are back to the Personalization window.

ALTER THE APPEARANCE OF OBJECTS

You can alter the appearance of windows, icons, and dialog boxes, changing their shapes and colors, as well as the font used in those objects. From the Personalization window:

1. Click **Window Color** at the bottom of the window. The Window Color And Appearance window will appear.

2. Click a different color scheme, if desired; turn off transparency if you don't like looking through window borders; or change the color intensity.

3. Click **Advanced Appearance Settings** to open the old style (circa Windows XP) Window Color And Appearance dialog box, shown here. Select an object whose color and/or font you want to change, make those changes, and click **OK**. All settings made here will provide a Windows Classic look or style.

4. When you are ready, click **OK** to close the Window Color And Appearance dialog box. Then click **Save Changes** to return to the Personalization window.

PICK A NEW SCREEN SAVER

When the computer is left on but not in use, the unchanging image on the screen can be burned into the face of a cathode-ray tube (CRT) monitor. The newer, thin, flat-screen liquid crystal display (LCD) monitors are not as affected by this, but plasma displays can be. To prevent this damage, you can choose to use a *screen saver*, which constantly changes the image on the screen when the computer is not in use. Windows 7 provides a number of alternative screen savers you can use. From the Personalization window:

1. Click **Screen Saver** in the lower-right corner. The Screen Saver Settings dialog box appears.

2. Click the **Screen Saver** down arrow, and review the options in the drop-down list.

3. Click a screen saver option to see it previewed in the dialog box (see Figure 2-4).

4. Click **Preview** to see the screen saver on your full screen. Press **ESC** to return to the dialog box.

Figure 2-4: You can use your own photos with the Photos screen saver option.

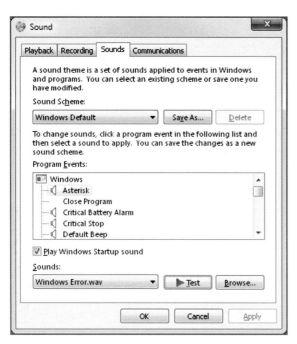

Figure 2-5: *Your sounds can be associated with various events.*

5. Click the up or down arrow on the **Wait** spinner to set the time to wait before enabling the screen saver.

6. When you have the screen saver you want, click **Settings**, if it is enabled, to see what settings are available for your screen saver. With the Photos option, you can select the folder, such as Pictures, from which to display photos.

7. When you are ready, click **OK** to close the dialog box.

SELECT THE SOUNDS WINDOWS 7 PLAYS

You can select the sounds that are played when various events occur, such as a critical stop or Windows shutdown, in the Sound dialog box. From the Personalization window:

1. Click **Sounds**. The Sound dialog box will appear, displaying the Sounds tab, as shown in Figure 2-5.

2. Click the **Sound Scheme** down arrow, and select one of the options.

3. Double-click a **Program Events** option to hear its current sound played.

4. Click the **Sounds** down arrow to select a different sound for the event. Click **Test** to hear the sound.

5. When you have made all the changes you want to the association of sounds and events, click **Save As** to save your changes as a new scheme. Type a name for the new scheme, and click **OK**.

6. When you are ready, click **OK** to close the Sound dialog box.

USE A DIFFERENT MOUSE POINTER

If it is difficult for you to see the mouse pointer, you can change how it looks and behaves in the Mouse Properties dialog box. From the Personalization window:

1. Click **Change Mouse Pointers**. The Mouse Properties dialog box will appear with the Pointers tab displayed, as shown in Figure 2-6.

2. Click the **Scheme** down arrow, and choose the scheme you want to use.

3. If you want to customize a particular mouse pointer, select that pointer, click **Browse**, locate and select the pointer you want to use, and click **Open**.

4. Click **OK** to close the Mouse Properties dialog box.

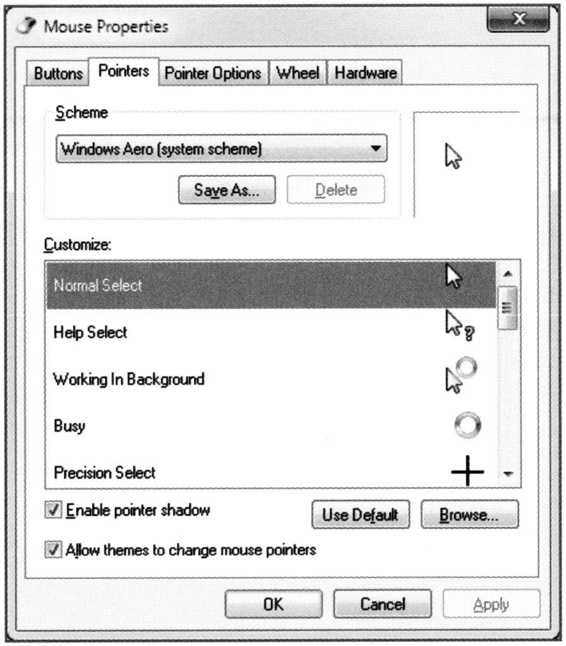

Figure 2-6: The mouse pointer should be easily seen and instantly informative for you.

Add Windows Program Icons

When you first install and start up Windows 7, you will only have a couple icons on the desktop, including the Recycle Bin, which is the only one Windows has by default. Some computer manufacturers may include additional icons. The purpose of having program icons on the desktop, called *shortcuts*, is to be able to easily start the programs by double-clicking their icons. To add Windows program icons, such as Windows Explorer and Control Panel, to the desktop and customize them:

1. Right-click a blank area of the desktop, and click **Personalize** to open the Personalization window.

2. Click **Change Desktop Icons** on the left to open the Desktop Icon Settings dialog box, shown in Figure 2-7.

3. In the Desktop Icons area, click one to five icons that you want to have on the desktop. For example, you might want icons for Computer and Control Panel. The others you might use less often, and they can be quickly accessed from the Start menu.

4. To customize a Windows program icon, click the icon and click **Change Icon**. A dialog box will appear displaying alternate icons.

5. Select the alternative you want, and click **OK**.

6. When you are satisfied with the Windows program icons you have selected and/or changed, click **OK**.

7. Click the **Close** button to close the Personalization window.

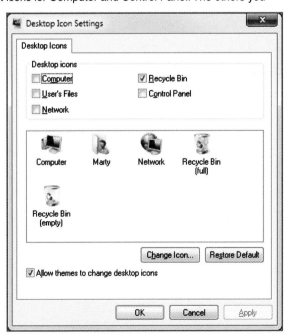

Figure 2-7: Add the icons to the desktop for the programs you use most often.

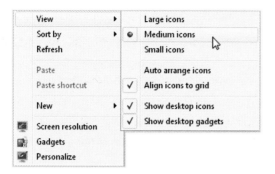

Change Desktop Icons

When you have the icons that you want on the desktop, you can change the size of the icons, their order, and their alignment through the desktop context menu:

Right-click a blank area of the desktop to open the context menu, and click View to open the View submenu.

RESIZE ICONS

Windows 7 gives you the choice of three different sizes of icons. The size you choose is a function of both the resolution you are using on your display and your personal preference. By default (the way Windows is set up when you first install and/or start it), your icons will be medium size. From the View submenu:

Click each of the sizes to see which is best for you.

Large   **Medium**   **Small**

ALIGN ICONS

You can drag desktop icons where you want them; by default, Windows 7 will align your icons to an invisible grid. If you don't like that, from the View submenu:

Click **Align To Grid** to clear the check mark and allow any arrangement on the desktop that you want.

If you should move your icons around and then change your mind, reopen the View submenu, and:

Click **Align Icons To Grid** to reselect it. Your icons will jump to the invisible grid and be aligned.

ARRANGE ICONS

By default, there is no particular order to the icons on the desktop, and you can drag them into the order that suits you. However, you can have Windows arrange and sort the icons in several ways. From the View submenu:

Click **Auto Arrange Icons**. By default, the icons will be placed in a column alphabetically by name, except that the *system* icons (Computer, Recycle Bin, Internet Explorer, User's Files, Control Panel, and Network) will be at the top.

ADDING OTHER PROGRAM ICONS TO THE DESKTOP

The method for adding other program icons, or shortcuts, to the desktop depends on where the icons are.

ADD ICONS FROM THE START MENU

Click **Start** to open the menu, and drag the icon from the menu to the desktop.

ADD ICONS FROM THE PROGRAMS MENU

1. Click **Start**, and click **All Programs**.
2. Locate and point to the icon, hold down the right mouse button, and drag the icon to the desktop. (This is called *right-drag*.)
3. Click **Copy Here**.

ADD ICONS FROM OTHER MENUS

1. Click **Start**, click **All Programs**, and open additional folders as needed.
2. Point to the icon, and right-drag the icon to the desktop.
3. Click **Copy Here**.

ADD ICONS NOT ON A MENU

1. Click **Start**, and click **Computer**.
2. In the Computer window, open the drive and folder(s) needed to locate the program (most programs are stored in their own folder within the Program Files folder on the C: drive).
3. Drag the program icon to the desktop.

NOTE

Changing the size of Start menu icons only affects the icons on the left of the Start menu. The purpose of smaller icons is to list more programs.

If you want to change the order in which Windows 7 arranges desktop icons:

1. Right-click a blank area of the desktop to open the context menu, and click **Sort By** to open that submenu.
2. Click one of the options to have the icons sorted in that manner.

RENAME DESKTOP ICONS

When you add program icons to the desktop, they may have the word "Shortcut" in their names, or they may have names that are not meaningful to you. To rename desktop icons:

1. Right-click an icon name you want to change, and click **Rename**.
2. Type the new name that you want to use, and press **ENTER**.

Change the Start Menu

The Start menu has several areas you can customize, including the size of the icons, the number of programs on it, the programs to use for the Internet and for email, and how the Start menu operates.

CHANGE WHAT IS DISPLAYED ON THE START MENU

Windows 7 gives you considerable flexibility as to what is displayed on the Start menu and how those items work.

1. Right-click **Start** and click **Properties** to open the Taskbar And Start Menu Properties dialog box.
2. With the Start Menu tab selected, click **Customize**. The Customize Start Menu dialog box will appear (see Figure 2-8).
3. Scroll through the list of links, icons, and submenus. Select the ones you want included on the Start menu and indicate how they should operate. Toward the end of the list there is an option that lets you change the size of the icons on the Start menu.
4. Use the **Number Of Recent Programs To Display** spinner to select the number displayed in the lower-left corner of the Start menu.
5. Use the **Number Of Recent Items To Display In Jump Lists** spinner to select the number displayed in jump lists (see Chapter 5).
6. To return to the original default settings, click **Use Default Settings**.
7. When you have made the changes you want, click **OK** twice.

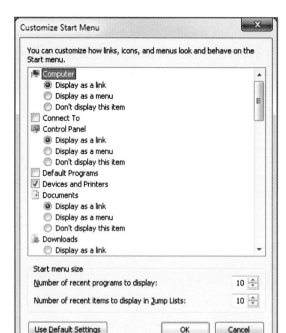

Figure 2-8: *You can customize what is displayed on the Start menu and how those items work.*

ADD PROGRAMS TO THE START MENU

You can add programs to the upper-left corner of the Start menu (where they will remain unless you remove them).

1. Click **Start**, click **All Programs**, and open the appropriate folders to display the program you want on the Start menu.

2. Right-click the program and click **Pin To Start Menu**. The program will appear on the Start menu. For example, if you want to add Internet Explorer, click **Start**, click **All Programs**, right-click **Internet Explorer**, and click **Pin To Start Menu**.

3. Click outside the Start menu to close it.

Figure 2-9 shows a changed Start menu, which you can compare with Figure 1-2 in Chapter 1.

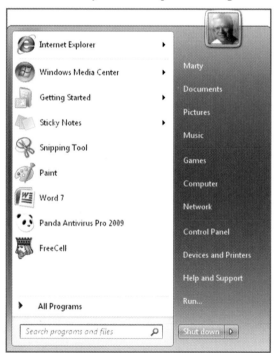

Figure 2-9: *A Start menu with changes described in this chapter.*

TIP

To remove a program on the Start menu, click **Start**, right-click the program, and if it is one you added in the upper-left corner of the menu (semi-permanent area), click **Unpin From Start Menu**. If the program you want to remove is in the lower-left corner (recently used program area), click **Remove From This List**. Then click outside the Start menu to close it.

Change the Taskbar

The taskbar at the bottom of the Windows 7 screen has four standard areas: the Start button on the left, the task list in the middle, and the notification area and the Show Desktop button on the right. In addition, there is an optional "pin-to" area next to the Start menu. You can change the taskbar by moving and sizing it and by changing its properties.

Start button   Programs currently running   Notification area and clock

Programs pinned to the taskbar   Show Desktop button

MOVE AND SIZE THE TASKBAR

You can move the taskbar to any of the four sides of the screen. Do this by dragging any empty area of the taskbar to another edge. For example, Figure 2-10 shows the taskbar moved to the right edge of the screen.

*Figure 2-10: **A taskbar can be moved to any of the four sides of the screen.***

UICKSTEPS

CHANGING TASKBAR PROPERTIES

A number of taskbar features can be changed through the Taskbar And Start Menu Properties dialog box (see Figure 2-11).

OPEN TASKBAR PROPERTIES

Right-click on an open area of the taskbar, and click **Properties**. The Taskbar And Start Menu Properties dialog box appears with the Taskbar tab selected. (Click **Apply** to test a change without closing the dialog box.)

UNLOCK THE TASKBAR

By default, the taskbar is locked. To move or resize the taskbar, it must be unlocked.

Click **Lock The Taskbar** to remove the check mark and unlock the taskbar.

HIDE THE TASKBAR

Hiding the taskbar means that it is not displayed unless you move the mouse to the edge of the screen containing the taskbar. By default, it is displayed.

Click **Auto-Hide The Taskbar** to select the check box and hide the taskbar.

USE SMALL ICONS

If you want to conserve desktop space and you have good eyesight, you can make the icons smaller, the size they were in previous versions of Windows.

Click **Use Small Icons** to add a check mark and make the icons smaller.

CUSTOMIZE TASKBAR BUTTONS

There are three choices for customizing taskbar buttons:

- Always combine similar items and hide the labels, such as program names.

Continued . . .

You can size the taskbar by dragging the inner edge (top edge when the taskbar is on the bottom) in or out. Here is a taskbar at double its normal size.

In either case, you must first unlock the taskbar. See the "Changing Taskbar Properties" QuickSteps to do this.

Permanently Pin Icons to the Taskbar

Windows 7 provides the ability to permanently "pin," or attach, frequently used program icons to the taskbar next to the Start button. Once there the icons are always visible (unless you hide the taskbar), and the related program can be started by a single click. By default Windows 7 has three icons pinned to the taskbar: Internet Explorer, Windows Explorer, and Media Player. You can pin additional icons, you can remove those that are currently pinned, and you can rearrange the current icons.

Figure 2-11: *You will use the taskbar often, so it should look and behave the way you want.*

CHANGING TASKBAR PROPERTIES

(Continued)

- Combine similar items when the taskbar is full, but display the labels.
- Never combine similar items under any circumstances, but display the labels.

Combining similar items, for example, puts all Microsoft Word documents in one icon or all Internet pages in one icon so that they take up less room on the taskbar. By default, similar items are combined.

Click the **Taskbar Buttons** down arrow, and make your choice.

USE AERO PEEK

Aero Peek allows you to see the desktop and what is under the open windows on the screen when you move the mouse to the Show Desktop button on the far right of the taskbar. This is turned on by default.

Click **Use Aero Peek** to turn off the check mark and this capability.

CLOSE TASKBAR PROPERTIES

After you've made any of these changes to the taskbar, click **OK** to enable them and close the Taskbar And Start Menu Properties dialog box.

NOTE

You can pin a file or folder to the Windows Explorer icon on the taskbar by opening Windows Explorer, navigating to the file or folder, and dragging it to the Windows Explorer icon on the taskbar.

PIN AN ICON TO THE TASKBAR

After you have used Windows 7 for a while you may find that you use a program more often than others and would like to have it more immediately available. This is what pinning to the taskbar is for. You can do that by either:

Locating the program icon in Windows Explorer, any part of the Start menu, or on the desktop, right-clicking it, and clicking **Pin To Taskbar**.

–Or–

Start the program in any of the ways described in Chapter 1. When it has started, right-click its icon on the taskbar, and click **Pin This Program To Taskbar**.

REMOVE AN ICON PINNED TO THE TASKBAR

To remove a program icon pinned to the taskbar:

Right-click the icon and click **Unpin This Program From Taskbar**.

REARRANGE ICONS PINNED TO THE TASKBAR

The icons that are pinned to the taskbar can be moved around and placed in any order.

Drag icons pinned to the taskbar to where you want them.

Change How Windows 7 Operates

How Windows 7 operates is probably more important to you than how it looks. For that reason, Windows 7 has a number of facilities that allow you to customize its operation.

QUICKSTEPS

CHANGING THE NOTIFICATION AREA

The notification area on the right of the taskbar can also be changed through the Taskbar And Start Menu Properties dialog box (see the "Changing Taskbar Properties" QuickSteps for instructions on displaying the dialog box). The notification area, which can get crowded at times, contains program icons put there by Windows and other programs. You can control which icons are displayed along with their notifications, which icons are hidden but their notifications displayed, or not there at all. To change the notification area:

Click **Customize** under Notification Area. The Notification Area Icons window will appear, as shown in Figure 2-12.

CUSTOMIZE NOTIFICATION ICONS

To customize the behavior of icons in the notification area:

Click the drop-down list opposite the icon you want to change, and select the behavior you want.

DISPLAY SYSTEM ICONS

Up to five system icons—Action Center, Network, Volume, Power (on mobile computers), and Clock—are shown in the notification area by default. You can turn them off if you wish.

1. Click **Turn System Icons On Or Off**.

2. Click the drop-down list opposite an icon name, and click **Off** to not display it.

3. When you have made the changes you want, click **OK**.

CLOSE TASKBAR PROPERTIES

After you've made any of these changes to the notification area, click **OK** to enable them and close the Notification Area Icons window. Click **OK** again to close the Taskbar And Start Menu Properties dialog box.

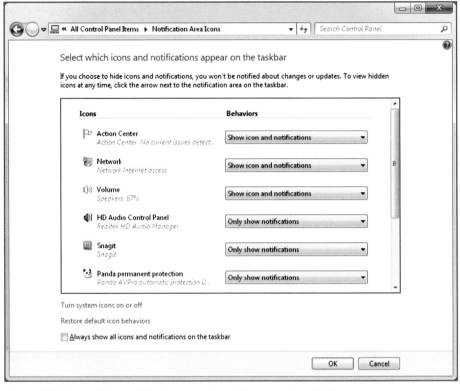

Figure 2-12: *Turn off the notification area icons that are not useful to you.*

Set and Use the Date and Time

The time and date in the lower-right corner of the screen may seem simple enough, but significant capability lies behind these simple numbers.

1. Move the mouse until your cursor is on the time in the notification area. The current day and date will appear.

Figure 2-13: Setting the date and time is normally automated using an Internet time server.

2. Click the time. The full calendar and clock appear.

3. Click **Change Date And Time Settings**. The Date And Time dialog box will appear, as shown in Figure 2-13.

4. With the Date And Time tab selected, click **Change Date And Time**. The Date And Time Settings dialog box appears.

5. Use the arrows on the calendar to change the month. Or, click the month to display the year, use the arrows to change the year, click the month, and then click a day.

6. Double-click an element of time (hour, minute, second, A.M./P.M.), and use the spinner to change the selected time element. Click **OK** to close the Date And Time Settings dialog box.

7. Click **Change Time Zone**, click the **Time Zone** down arrow, and click your time zone.

8. Click **Automatically Adjust Clock For Daylight Saving Time** if it isn't already selected and you want Windows 7 to do that. Click **OK** to close the Time Zone Settings dialog box.

9. Click the **Additional Clocks** tab to add one or two clocks with different time zones. Click **Additional Clock 1**, open the drop-down list box, and click a time zone. Enter a display name, and repeat for a second additional clock, if desired. (The additional times will appear when you point to the time in the notification area.) Click **OK** when done.

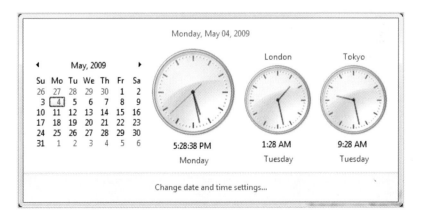

10. Click the **Internet Time** tab and see how your computer's time is currently being synchronized. If you want to change that, click **Change Settings**.

NOTE

The blue and yellow shield on the Change Date And Time button tells you that the function being selected requires administrator permission. You must be an administrator or have a password for one.

11. Click **Synchronize With An Internet Time Server** if it isn't already selected, open the drop-down list, click a time server, and click **Update Now**. Once turned on, Windows will check the time every seven days. Click **OK** to close the Internet Time Settings dialog box.

12. Click **OK** to close the Date And Time dialog box.

Change Ease-of-Access Settings

Ease-of-access settings provide alternatives to the normal way the mouse and keyboard are used, as well as some settings that make the screen more readable and sounds more understandable.

1. Right-click a blank area of the screen, click **Personalize**, and click **Ease Of Access Center** in the lower-left area. The Ease Of Access Center window will open, as shown in Figure 2-14.

   –Or–

   Press and hold the **Windows Flag** key while pressing **U**.

2. Select the options you want to use in the common tools area at the top (see the upper part of Table 2-1). You can also turn the options on or off using the keyboard shortcuts shown.

3. Click any of the blue text links in the lower part of the window to review, and possibly change, the ease-of-access settings that apply to various areas of the computer. Within links there are a number of assistive tools, shown in the lower part of Table 2-1, that can be turned on, either in these links or with the keyboard shortcuts shown.

4. When you have set up the accessibility options you want, click **Close**.

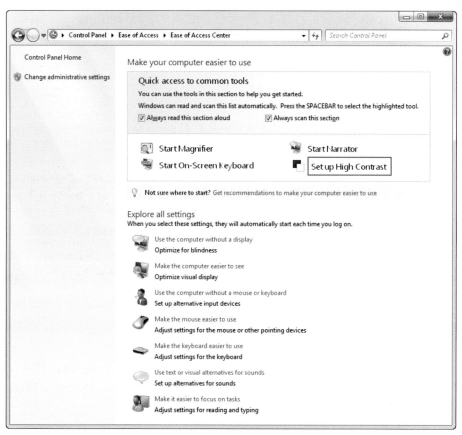

Figure 2-14: *Ease-of-access settings let you work with Windows 7 and your programs in ways that facilitate use with various physical limitations.*

TIP

You can also turn on the most common ease-of-access options from the Windows 7 logon screen by clicking the **Ease Of Access** icon in the lower-left corner of the screen.

NOTE

By default, and if you have speakers and a sound card, Windows 7 will scan and read aloud the four options in the Quick Access section.

QUICKSTEPS

USING THE CONTROL PANEL

The Control Panel is a facility for customizing many of the functions available in Windows. The individual components of the Control Panel are discussed throughout this book (several in this chapter); this section is an introduction to the Control Panel itself.

OPEN THE CONTROL PANEL

Click **Start** and click **Control Panel** on the right. The Control Panel is displayed. By default, it will be as shown in Figure 2-15. (Mobile computers will show additional hardware devices unique to them.)

Continued . . .

OPTION	DESCRIPTION	KEYBOARD SHORTCUT
Magnifier	Enlarges a part of the screen around the mouse.	
On Screen Keyboard	Displays an image of a keyboard on the screen that you can click to select the appropriate keys.	
Narrator	Reads aloud selected text on the screen.	
High Contrast	Uses high-contrast colors and special fonts to make the screen easy to use.	Press together left **SHIFT**, left **ALT**, and **PRINT SCREEN**.
Mouse Keys	Uses the numeric keypad to move the mouse around the screen.	Press together left **SHIFT** and **NUM LOCK**.
Sticky Keys	Simulates pressing a pair of keys, such as **CTRL+A**, by pressing one key at a time. The keys **SHIFT**, **CTRL**, and **ALT** "stick" down until a second key is pressed. This is interpreted as two keys pressed together.	Press either **SHIFT** key five times in succession.
Filter Keys	Enables you to press a key twice in rapid succession and have it interpreted as a single keystroke; also slows down the rate at which the key is repeated if it is held down.	Hold down the right **SHIFT** key for eight seconds.
Toggle Keys	Hear a tone when **CAPS LOCK**, **NUM LOCK**, or **SCROLL LOCK** is turned on.	Hold down the **NUM LOCK** key for five seconds.

Table 2-1: Ease-of-Access Tools

Customize the Mouse

The mouse lets you interact with the screen and point at, select, and drag objects. You also can start and stop programs and close Windows using the mouse. While you can use Windows without a mouse, it is more difficult, making it important that the mouse operates in the most comfortable way possible. Change the way the mouse works through the Control Panel Mouse component.

1. Click **Start** and click **Control Panel**.

QUICKSTEPS

USING THE CONTROL PANEL
(Continued)

SWITCH THE CONTROL PANEL VIEW

The Control Panel has three views: the default Category view, shown in Figure 2-15, which groups Control Panel functions, and Large and Small Icons views (Figure 2-16 shows Small Icons view), which show all the Control Panel components in one window.

- When in Category view, click the **View By** down arrow on the right, and click either **Large Icons** or **Small Icons**.

- When in Large or Small Icon view, click the **View By** down arrow on the right, and click **Category** to switch back to that view.

OPEN A CONTROL PANEL CATEGORY

Category view groups components into categories that must be opened to see the individual components, although some subcategories are listed.

Click a category to open a window for it, where you can either select a task you want to do or open a Control Panel component represented by an icon.

OPEN A CONTROL PANEL COMPONENT

When Category view's secondary windows are opened in the previous step, the icons for individual Control Panel component icons are displayed. In either Large or Small Icons view, these component icons are directly displayed. To open a component:

Click the component's icon.

Figure 2-15: Category view provides a hierarchy of windows that leads you to the settings you want to change.

2. In Category view, click **Hardware And Sound**, and under Devices And Printers, click **Mouse**.

   –Or–

   In Large or Small Icons view, click **Mouse**.

   Either way, the Mouse Properties dialog box will appear, as you can see in Figure 2-17.

3. If you want to use the mouse with your left hand, click **Switch Primary And Secondary Buttons**.

4. Double-click the folder in the middle-right area of the Buttons tab. If the folder opens, your double-click speed is okay. If not, drag the **Speed** slider until the folder opens when you double-click it.

5. Select the options you want to use on the **Buttons**, **Pointer Options**, **Wheel**, and **Hardware** tabs.

6. Click the **Pointers** tab. If you want to change the way the pointer looks, select a different scheme (see "Use a Different Mouse Pointer," earlier in the chapter).

7. When you have set up the mouse the way you want, click **OK**.

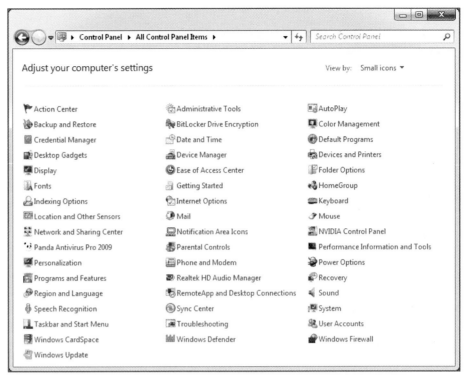

Figure 2-16: *The Control Panel's Small Icons view shows all of the components in the Control Panel.*

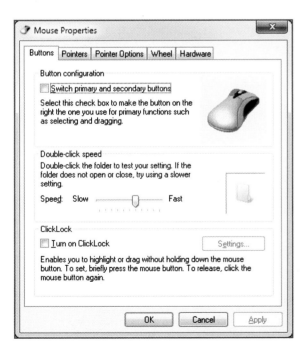

Figure 2-17: *The mouse is the primary way you operate in Windows 7.*

Customize the Keyboard

Windows requires a keyboard for manual communications (speech recognition can replace the keyboard in many instances). You can change the length of the delay before a key that is held down is repeated and the rate at which the key is repeated.

1. Click **Start** and click **Control Panel**.

2. In Category view, click **Large** or **Small Icons** view, and then click **Keyboard**. The Keyboard Properties dialog box appears.

3. Click in the text box in the middle of the dialog box, and press a character key to see how long you wait before the key is repeated and how fast the repeated character appears.

4. Drag the **Repeat Delay** slider in the direction desired, and then test the repetition again.

5. Drag the **Repeat Rate** slider in the direction desired, and then test the repetition again.

6. Drag the **Cursor Blink Rate** slider in the direction desired, and observe the blink rate.

7. When you have set up the keyboard the way you want, click **OK**.

Change Sounds

Windows 7 uses sounds to alert and entertain you. Through the Control Panel's Sound component, you can select the sound scheme you want (see Figure 2-18).

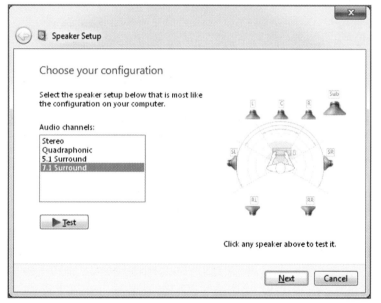

1. Click **Start** and click **Control Panel**.

2. In Category view, click **Hardware And Sound**, and then click **Sound**.

   –Or–

   In Large or Small Icons view, click **Sound**.

   In either case, the Sound dialog box appears.

3. Click **Speakers**, click **Configure** in the lower-left corner, select your configuration in the Audio Channels list, and click **Test** to test your setup. When you are ready, click **Next**.

4. Click the speakers that aren't present, and click **Next**. Click the speakers that are full-range speakers, and click **Next**. When you are done, click **Finish**.

5. Double-click **Speakers**, click the **Levels** tab, and drag the sliders in the direction desired to set the volume. Click **OK** to close the Speakers Properties dialog box.

6. Click the **Sounds** tab, and select a different sound scheme to change it, if desired (see "Select the Sounds Windows 7 Plays" earlier in the chapter).

Figure 2-18: Windows 7 can handle up to seven-speaker surround sound.

7. When you have set up the sounds the way you want, click **OK**.

Change Regional Settings

Windows 7 lets you determine how numbers, dates, currency, and time are displayed and used, as well as the languages that will be used. Choosing a

![Region and Language dialog box]

Region and Language

Formats | Location | Keyboards and Languages | Administrative

Format:

English (United States)

Date and time formats

Short date: M/d/yyyy

Long date: dddd, MMMM dd, yyyy

Short time: h:mm tt

Long time: h:mm:ss tt

First day of week: Sunday

What does the notation mean?

Examples

Short date: 5/4/2009

Long date: Monday, May 04, 2009

Short time: 10:45 PM

Long time: 10:45:41 PM

Additional settings...

Go online to learn about changing languages and regional formats

OK | Cancel | Apply

Figure 2-19: Region and language options allow Windows 7 to operate almost anywhere in the world.

CAUTION

Changing the format used for dates and times might affect other Windows programs, such as Excel.

primary language and locale sets all the other settings. You can customize these options through the Region And Language component in the Control Panel.

1. Click **Start** and click **Control Panel**.

2. In Category view, click **Clock, Language, And Region**, and then click **Region And Language**.

   –Or–

   In Large or Small Icons view, click **Region And Language**.

   In either case, the Region And Language dialog box will appear, as you can see in Figure 2-19.

3. In the Formats tab, click the **Format** drop-down list, and select the primary language and region in which the computer will be used. This changes the standards and formats that will be used by default.

4. Customize the date and time formats by clicking the down arrow associated with each setting and selecting the option that you want.

5. Click **Additional Settings** and then go to the individual tabs for numbers, currency, time, and date, and set how you want these items displayed. Click **OK** when you are done.

6. Review the Location, Keyboards And Languages, and Administrative tabs, and make any desired changes.

7. When you have set up the regional settings the way you want, click **OK**.

Manage Gadgets

The Gadgets feature displays a clock and other gadgets—initially on the right side of the screen, but they can be moved. To manage gadgets:

1. Click **Start** and click **Control Panel**.

2. In Category view, click **Appearance And Personalization**, and then click **Desktop Gadgets**.

   –Or–

   In Large or Small Icons view, click **Desktop Gadgets**.

   In either case, the Gadgets window will open.

3. Double-click the gadgets that you want displayed.

4. If you want to see more gadgets, click **Get More Gadgets Online**. Internet Explorer will open and display the gadgets that are available. Under the gadget that you want, click **Download Gadget** and then click **Download**. On the Windows Live page that appears, review the gadget, and click the **Download** button. Click **Save**, navigate to a folder in which you want the gadget stored, and click **Save** again. Close Internet Explorer, open Windows Explorer, navigate to the folder in which you stored the gadget, and double-click it. Click **Install**. The new gadget appears on your desktop

5. When you are ready, click **Close** to close the Gadgets window. Gadgets for headlines, stocks, and traffic are shown here on a desktop.

Chapter 3

Storing Information

The information on your computer—documents, email, photographs, music, and programs—is stored in *files.* So that your files are organized and more easily found, they are kept in *folders,* and folders can be placed in other folders for further organization. For example, a folder labeled "Trips," which is contained in the My Documents folder, contains separate folders for the years 2008, 2009, and 2010. The 2009 folder contains folders for Yellowstone and Disneyland. The Yellowstone folder contains folders of photos and videos, as well as files for notes and expenses. Such a set of files and folders is shown in the My Documents folder in Figure 3-1.

In this chapter you'll see how to create, use, and manage files and folders like these. The term "objects" is used to refer to any mix of files, folders, and disk drives.

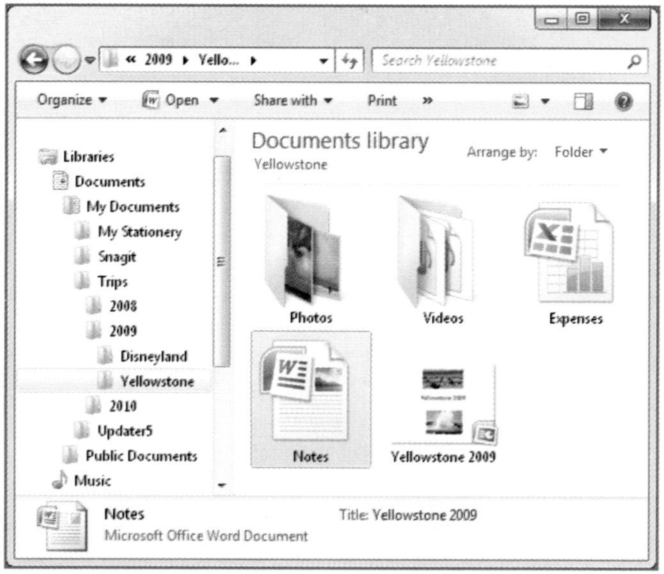

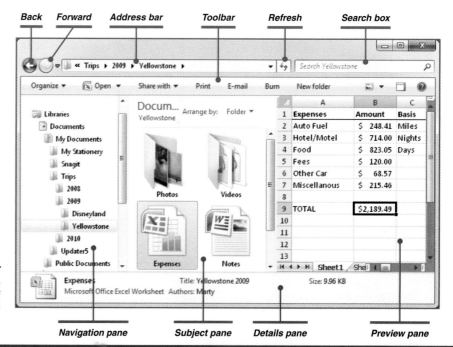

Figure 3-1: *Windows stores files in folders, which can be within other folders.*

Use the Windows File System

The tool that Windows 7 provides to locate and work with files and folders is *Windows Explorer* (often called "Explorer," not to be confused with Internet Explorer discussed in Chapter 4). Windows Explorer has a number of components and features, most of which are shown in Figure 3-2 and described in Table 3-1. Much of this chapter is spent exploring these items and how they are used.

When you open Windows Explorer, you can choose what you want it to initially display from among the choices to the right of the Start menu. These choices give you access to (from top to bottom):

- Your personal folder, which contains your documents, pictures, music, and games

- Your documents

Figure 3-2: *Windows Explorer provides the means to access files, folders, disks, and memory devices on your computer.*

AREA	FUNCTION
Back and Forward buttons	Displays an object previously shown
Address bar	Displays the location of what is being shown in the subject pane
Toolbar	Contains tools to work with objects in the subject pane
Refresh	Updates what is displayed in the address bar
Search box	Provides for the entry of text you want to search for
Preview pane	Displays the contents of the object selected in the subject pane
Details pane	Provides information about the object selected in the subject pane
Subject pane	Displays the objects stored at the address shown in the address bar
Navigation pane	Facilitates moving around among the objects you have available

Table 3-1: Windows Explorer Components

NOTE

Depending on the permissions you have and whether you are connected to a network, you may have Network on your Start menu.

- Your pictures
- Your music
- Your games
- The computer on which you are working

Open Windows Explorer

To open Windows Explorer:

1. Start your computer, if it's not running, and log on to Windows if necessary.

2. Click **Start**. The Start menu will open, and you'll see the Windows Explorer choices on the right of the menu.

3. Click your personal folder. Explorer will open and display in the subject pane the files and folders that either come standard with Windows 7 or that have been placed there by you or somebody else, as shown in Figure 3-3.

Figure 3-3: Windows 7 starts with a number of standard folders that are a part of the personal folder.

QUICKSTEPS

CHANGING THE WINDOWS EXPLORER LAYOUT

As you saw in Figure 3-2, the Windows Explorer window has several different panes that you may want to use. You can turn them on or off through the Organize menu's Layout options.

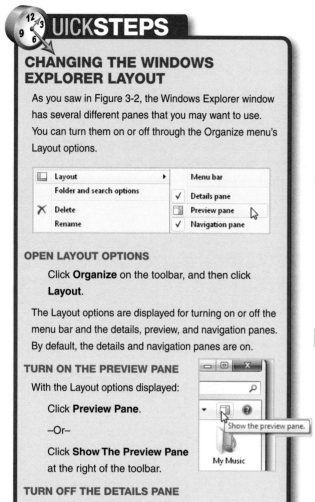

OPEN LAYOUT OPTIONS

Click **Organize** on the toolbar, and then click **Layout**.

The Layout options are displayed for turning on or off the menu bar and the details, preview, and navigation panes. By default, the details and navigation panes are on.

TURN ON THE PREVIEW PANE

With the Layout options displayed:

Click **Preview Pane**.

–Or–

Click **Show The Preview Pane** at the right of the toolbar.

TURN OFF THE DETAILS PANE

With the Layout options displayed:

Click **Details Pane**.

You can:

Click an object in the subject pane to *select* it and get information about it in the details pane, preview it in the preview pane, or use the toolbar tools with that object.

–Or–

Double-click an object in the subject pane to *open* it so that you can see and work with its contents.

Customize Windows Explorer

You can customize how Windows Explorer looks and which features are available with the toolbar.

1. If Windows Explorer is not already open, click **Start** and click your personal folder.

2. Click **Pictures** in the navigation pane, and then double-click **Sample Pictures** in the subject pane. Windows 7's sample pictures should open, as you can see in Figure 3-4.

3. Click one of the pictures. The toolbar changes to something like this:

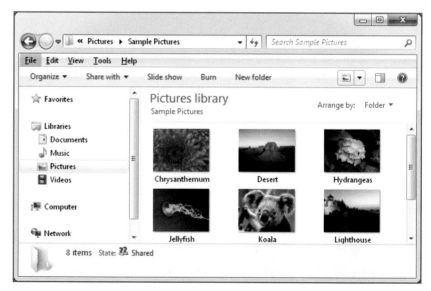

Figure 3-4: *Windows Explorer's toolbar changes to provide commands for what is selected in the subject pane.*

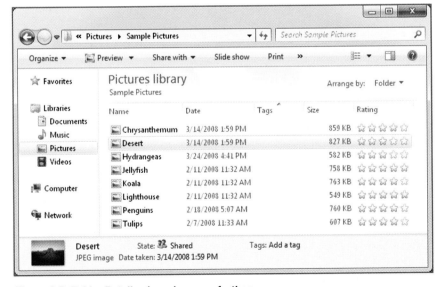

These toolbar options are specific to a picture. The selection of other types of files would have generated different options.

4. Click **Organize** to open the Organize menu. Here you can perform operations on the object you have selected using menu options such as Cut, Copy, Paste, Delete, and Rename, and perform folder-related operations with menu options such as Layout, Folder and Search Options, and Close.

5. Click the **Views** down arrow (not the Views button, which gives you another view of your folder) on the right of the toolbar. Drag the slider up and down to change first the size of the objects in your folder, and, as you continue downward, the arrangement of the objects.

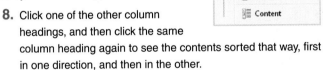

6. Click the **Views** down arrow, and click **Details**, which is shown in Figure 3-5.

7. Click **Name** at the top of the left column in the subject pane. The contents of the subject pane will be sorted alphanumerically by name. Click **Name** again, and the contents will be sorted by name in the opposite direction.

8. Click one of the other column headings, and then click the same column heading again to see the contents sorted that way, first in one direction, and then in the other.

9. Click the **Close** button in the upper-right corner of the Explorer window to close it.

Use Windows Explorer Menus

The Windows 7 Explorer does not display the menu bar by default, although earlier versions of Windows Explorer did. Most of the menu commands are available on the toolbar, but, if you prefer, you can turn on and use the menus.

1. Click **Start**, click **Pictures**, and then click **Sample Pictures** to open the Windows Explorer window and display the sample pictures.

Figure 3-5: Folder Details view gives you further information about the objects in a folder.

2. Click **Organize**, click **Layout**, and click **Menu Bar**. The Windows Explorer menu bar will appear between the address bar and the toolbar.

3. Click the **File**, **Edit**, and **View** menus, and review the available options. The toolbar's Organize and View menus in Windows 7 Explorer, along with the features of the column heading, replace many of the options in the first three menus on the menu bar. The Help menu is equivalent to the Help icon on the toolbar.

4. Click the **Tools** menu. The first three options are discussed in Chapter 9. Click **Folder And Search Options** (also available from the Organize menu). The Folder Options dialog box will appear with the General tab displayed, as shown in Figure 3-6. This allows you to:

- Open a new window for each folder you open.
- Use a single click in place of a double-click to open a window.
- If you choose single click, you can also determine whether to permanently underline an icon title, as in an Internet browser, or underline an icon only when you point at it.
- Display more or fewer folders in the navigation pane.

5. Click the **View** tab, which is shown in Figure 3-7. This gives you a number of options that determine what is displayed for the current folder and allow you to apply these changes to all folders. The default settings generally work for most people.

Figure 3-6: Folder options allow you to determine how folders look and behave.

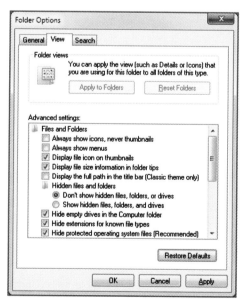

Figure 3-7: There are a number of options in the way that Explorer can display folder and file information.

6. When you are ready, click **OK** to close the Folder Options dialog box. (The Search tab will be discussed under "Search for Files and Folders" later in this chapter.)

7. If you want to turn off the menu bar, click **Organize**, click **Layout**, and click **Menu Bar**.

8. Click **Close** to close the Explorer window.

Figure 3-8: Your computer stores information in a hierarchy of disk drives and folders.

Locate and Use Files and Folders

The purpose of a file system, of course, is to locate and use the files and folders on your computer, and possibly on other computers connected to yours (accessing other computers is called *networking* and is discussed in Chapters 9 and 10). Within your computer, there is a storage hierarchy that starts with storage devices, such as disk drives, which are divided into areas called folders, each of which may be divided again into subareas called subfolders. Each of these contains files, which can be documents, pictures, music, and other data. Figure 3-1 showed folders containing subfolders and eventually containing files with information in them. Figure 3-8 shows a computer containing disk drives, which in turn contain folders. Windows Explorer contains a number of tools for locating, opening, and using disk drives, folders, and files.

Identify Storage Devices

Files and folders are stored on various physical storage devices, including disk drives, CD and DVD drives, memory cards and sticks, and Universal Serial Bus (USB) flash memory. You will have some, but not necessarily all, of the following:

- Primary floppy disk, labeled "A:"
- Primary hard disk, labeled "C:"
- CD or DVD drive, labeled "D:"
- Other storage devices, labeled "E:" and then "F:" and so on

Your primary floppy drive is always labeled "A:" (given that you still have one—most new computers don't). Your primary hard disk is always labeled "C:."

Other drives have flexible labeling. Often, the CD or DVD drive will be drive "D:," but if you have a second hard disk drive, it may be labeled "D," as you saw in Figure 3-8.

Select and Open Drives and Folders

When you open Windows Explorer and display the items in Computer, you see the disk drives and other storage devices on your computer, as well as several folders, including Program Files, Users, and Windows, as you saw in Figure 3-8. To work with these drives and folders, you must select them; to see and work with their contents, you must open them.

1. Click **Start** and click **Computer** to open Windows Explorer and display the local disk drives.

2. In the subject pane (right pane), click disk **(C:)**. Disk (C:) will be highlighted and its characteristics will be displayed in the details pane (bottom pane).

3. Double-click disk **(C:)** in any pane. Disk (C:) will open and its folders will be displayed in the subject pane.

4. Double-click **Users** to open that folder and display your folder along with a Public folder.

5. Double-click your personal folder (the folder with your name on it). The subject pane displays the files and folders in your folder. This will include Contacts, Desktop, My Documents, My Music, and others, as shown in Figure 3-9.

6. Keep double-clicking each folder to open it until you see the contents you are looking for.

Navigate Folders and Disks

Opening Windows Explorer and navigating through several folders—beginning with your hard disk—to find a file you want is fine. However, if you want to quickly go to another folder or file, you won't want to have to start with your hard disk every single time. The Windows 7 Explorer gives you three ways to do this: through the Libraries folder in the navigation pane, by using the folder tree in the navigation pane, or by using the address bar.

Figure 3-9: Double-clicking a drive or folder will open it in the subject pane.

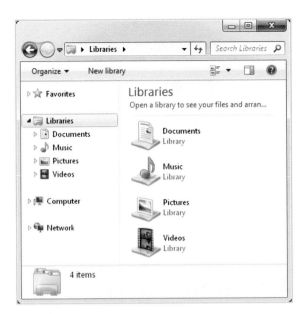

NAVIGATE USING LIBRARIES

The Windows 7 suggested way to navigate is through the Libraries folder, which contains links to the folders within your personal folder (called a "library" in this case, as shown here). By clicking a library in the navigation pane and then double-clicking folders within the subject pane, you can move around the folders and files within your personal folder. For example, given the folder structure shown in Figure 3-1, here are the steps to open the hypothetical Yellowstone folder:

1. Click **Start** and click **Documents**, which opens the Documents library within your personal Libraries folder.

2. In the navigation pane, click the right-pointing triangle or arrow opposite the Documents library to open it.

3. Still in the navigation page, click the right-pointing arrow opposite My Documents to open it.

4. If you had such a set of folders, you would repeat step 3 to open the Trips and 2009 folders, and then click the **Yellowstone** folder to open it in the subject pane.

NAVIGATE USING FOLDERS

The portion of the navigation pane starting with Computer is a folder tree that contains all the disk drives, folders, and files on your computer in a tree, or hierarchical, structure. To open the same folder structure shown in Figure 3-1 through Computer:

1. Click **Start** and click **Computer**, which opens Computer in the navigation pane, as you saw in Figure 3-8.

2. In the navigation pane, click the right-pointing arrow opposite (C:) disk drive to open it.

3. Still in the navigation page, click the right-pointing arrow opposite Users to open it.

4. Repeat step 3 to open your personal folder and then the My Documents, Trips, and 2009 folders.

5. Click the **Yellowstone** folder to open it in the subject pane.

You can see that Libraries saves a couple of steps, but at the cost of possible confusion.

TIP

It is easy to get confused with the various folders in the navigation pane. Both Favorites and Libraries are folders with *shortcuts*, or links to folders and files on your computer. (See "Create Shortcuts" later in this chapter.) The shortcuts in Libraries are links to the actual folders in the C:/Users/Personal Folder/My Documents, as you can see in "Navigate Using Folders."

TIP

The folder tree is also useful for copying and moving files and folders, as you will see in the "Copying and Moving Files and Folders" QuickSteps in this chapter.

QUICKSTEPS

RENAMING AND DELETING FILES AND FOLDERS

Sometimes, a file or folder needs to be renamed or deleted (whether it was created by you or by an application) because you may no longer need it or for any number of reasons.

RENAME A FILE OR FOLDER

With the file or folder in view but not selected, to rename it:

In the subject pane, slowly click the name twice (don't double-click), type the new name, and press **ENTER**.

–Or–

In either the navigation or subject pane, right-click the name, click **Rename**, type the new name, and press **ENTER**.

DELETE A FILE OR FOLDER TO THE RECYCLE BIN

With the file or folder in view in either the navigation or subject pane, to delete it:

Click the icon for the file or folder to select it, press **DELETE**, and click **Yes** to confirm the deletion.

–Or–

Right-click the icon, click **Delete**, and click **Yes** to confirm the deletion.

Continued . . .

NAVIGATE USING THE ADDRESS BAR

Windows 7 gives you another way to quickly navigate through your drives and folders by clicking segments of a folder address in the address bar, which looks like this:

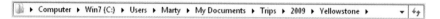

By clicking the down arrow on the far right of the address bar, you can see how this same address looked in previous versions of Windows and use the address bar as it was in the past: C:\Users\Marty\Documents\Trips\2009\Yellowstone

With Windows 7, if you click any segment of the address, you will open that level in the subject pane. If you click the arrow to the right of the segment, it displays a drop-down list of subfolders that you can jump to. By successively clicking segments and their subordinate folders, you can easily move throughout the storage space on your computer and beyond to any network you are connected to.

Create New Folders

While you could store all your files within one of the ready-made folders in Windows 7—such as Documents, Music, or Pictures—you will probably want to make your files easier to find by creating several subfolders.

For example, to create the Trips folder discussed earlier:

1. Click **Start** and click **Documents**. Make sure nothing is selected.
2. Click **New Folder** on the toolbar. A new folder will appear with its name highlighted.
3. Type the name of the folder, such as <u>Trips</u>, and press **ENTER**. Double-click your new folder to open it (you will see it's empty).

As an alternative to clicking New Folder on the toolbar, right-click the open area in the subject pane of Windows Explorer. Click **New** and click **Folder**. Type a name for the folder, and press **ENTER**.

QUICKSTEPS

RENAMING AND DELETING FILES AND FOLDERS (Continued)

RECOVER A DELETED FILE OR FOLDER

To recover a file or folder that has been deleted:

Click the **Organize** menu, and click **Undo**. This only works if you perform the undo operation immediately after the deletion.

–Or–

Double-click the **Recycle Bin** on the desktop to display the Recycle Bin. Right-click the file or folder icon, and choose **Restore**.

PERMANENTLY DELETE A FILE OR FOLDER

If you're sure you want to permanently delete a file or folder:

Click the icon to select it, press and hold **SHIFT** while pressing **DELETE**, and click **Yes** to confirm the permanent deletion.

–Or–

Right-click the icon, press and hold **SHIFT** while clicking **Delete**, and click **Yes** to confirm the permanent deletion.

TIP

To select all objects in the subject pane, click **Organize** and click **Select All**; or click any object in the subject pane, and press **CTRL+A**.

Select Multiple Files and Folders

Often, you will want to do one or more operations—such as copy, move, or delete—on several files and/or folders at the same time. To select several files or folders from the subject pane of an Explorer window:

Move the mouse pointer to the upper-left area, just outside of the top and leftmost object. Then drag the mouse to the lower-right area, just outside of the bottom and rightmost object, creating a shading across the objects, as shown in Figure 3-10.

–Or–

Click the first object, and press and hold **CTRL** while clicking the remaining objects, if the objects are noncontiguous (not adjacent to each other). If the objects are contiguous, click the first object, press and hold **SHIFT**, and click the last object.

Figure 3-10: Drag across multiple objects to select all of them.

Figure 3-11: The Recycle Bin holds deleted items so that you can recover them until you empty it.

Use the Recycle Bin

If you do a normal delete operation in Explorer or the desktop, the deleted item or items will go into the Recycle Bin. Should you change your mind about the deletion, you can reclaim an item from the Recycle Bin, as explained in the "Renaming and Deleting Files and Folders" QuickSteps earlier in this chapter.

The Recycle Bin is a special folder and it can contain both files and folders. You can open it and see its contents as you would any other folder by double-clicking its desktop icon or clicking it in the navigation pane. Figure 3-11 shows a Recycle Bin after deleting several files and folders. What makes the Recycle Bin special are the two special tasks in the toolbar:

- **Empty The Recycle Bin** permanently removes all of the contents of the Recycle Bin.

- **Restore All Items** returns all the contents to their original folders, in effect, "undeleting" all of the contents.

Obviously, there is a limit to how much the Recycle Bin can hold. You can limit the amount of space it takes so that it doesn't take over your hard disk. That and other settings are configured in the Recycle Bin's Properties dialog box.

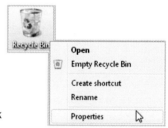

1. Right-click the **Recycle Bin** on the desktop, and click **Properties**. The Recycle Bin Properties dialog box will appear, as you can see here.

2. If you have multiple hard disks, select the drive you want to set. In any case, make sure **Custom Size** is selected, select the size, and type the number of megabytes you want to use ("3082" megabytes is 3.082 gigabytes).

3. If you don't want to use the Recycle Bin, click **Don't Move Files To The Recycle Bin**. (This is strongly discouraged since this means that files will be permanently deleted with no hope of recovery.)

4. If you don't need to see the deletion confirmation message, click that check box to deselect it. (Again this is discouraged since it tells you what is happening to the files in case it is not what you want.)

5. When you are ready, click **OK** to close the dialog box.

Create Shortcuts

A shortcut is a link to a file or folder that allows you to quickly open the file or folder from places other than where it is stored. For example, you can start a program from the desktop even though the actual program file is stored in some other folder. To create a shortcut:

1. In Windows Explorer, locate the folder or file for which you want to create a shortcut.

2. If it is a program file (one identified as an "application" or with an .exe extension), drag it to a different folder (as from a folder to the desktop).

3. If it is any other file or folder, hold down the right mouse button while dragging the file or folder to a different folder, release the right mouse button, and then click **Create Shortcuts Here**.

–Or–

1. In Windows Explorer, open the folder in which you want to create a shortcut.

2. Right-click a blank area in the subject pane of the folder, click **New**, and click **Shortcut**.

3. In the dialog box that appears, click **Browse**, and use the folder tree to locate and select the file or folder for which you want to make a shortcut.

4. Click **OK**, and click **Next**. Type a name for the shortcut, and click **Finish**.

Search for Files and Folders

With large and, possibly several, hard disks, it is often difficult to find files and folders on a system. Windows Explorer's Search feature addresses that problem.

1. Click **Start** and notice the blinking cursor in the Search Programs And Files text box at the bottom of the menu.

COPYING AND MOVING FILES AND FOLDERS

Copying and moving files and folders are similar actions, and can be done with the mouse alone, with the mouse and a menu, and with the keyboard.

COPY WITH THE MOUSE

To copy with the mouse, hold down **CTRL** while dragging any file or folder from one folder to another on the same disk drive, or drag a file or folder from one disk drive to another.

MOVE NON-PROGRAM FILES ON THE SAME DISK WITH THE MOUSE

Move non-program files from one folder to another on the same disk with the mouse by dragging the file or folder.

MOVE NON-PROGRAM FILES TO ANOTHER DISK WITH THE MOUSE

Move non-program files to another disk by holding down **SHIFT** while dragging them.

MOVE PROGRAM FILES WITH THE MOUSE

Move program files to another folder or disk by holding down **SHIFT** while dragging them.

COPY AND MOVE WITH THE MOUSE AND A MENU

To copy and move with a mouse and a menu, hold down the right mouse button while dragging the file or folder. When you release the right mouse button, a context menu opens and allows you to choose whether to copy, move, or create a shortcut (see "Create Shortcuts" in this chapter).

> Copy here
> Move here
> Create shortcuts here
> Cancel

Continued . . .

2. Type all or part of the folder name, file name, or keyword or phrase in a file in the Search box. As you type, Windows 7 will start locating files and folders that match your criteria and display them in the top of the Start menu.

   Initially, the search will be of all indexed files (Windows 7, by default, will index your files and folders automatically) and will show all results.

3. If you see the file or folder you are searching for, click it and it will be displayed in Windows Explorer (if a folder) or in the program that created it (if a file).

4. If you want to see more results, click **See More Results** at the bottom of the menu. Windows Explorer will open. Review the list in the subject pane; if you see the file or folder you want, click it to open it.

5. If you still are not finding what you want, scroll the subject pane to the bottom and you'll see some additional options, as shown in Figure 3-12.

6. In the Search Again In options, you can choose one of three specific places to search, or click Customize to select one or more other places to search.

7. To filter the search results, click in the search text box in the upper-right corner of the Windows Explorer window. Four options will appear that let you filter the search results by the kind of file, the date it was modified, the type or size of the file, or the file name (the last only appears if you select one of the other options).

8. To change search options, click **Organize** in the toolbar, and click **Folder And Search Options**. The Folder Options dialog box will appear. Click the **Search** tab. Make any change to the settings that you want, and click **OK**.

QUICKSTEPS

COPYING AND MOVING FILES AND FOLDERS *(Continued)*

COPY AND MOVE WITH THE KEYBOARD

Copying and moving with the keyboard is done with three sets of keys:

- **CTRL+C** ("Copy") copies the selected item to the Windows Clipboard.
- **CTRL+X** ("Cut") moves the selected item to the Windows Clipboard, deleting it from its original location.
- **CTRL+V** ("Paste") copies the current contents of the Windows Clipboard to the currently open folder. You can repeatedly paste the same Clipboard contents to any additional folders you want to copy to by opening them and pressing **CTRL+V** again.

To copy a file or folder from one folder to another using the keyboard:

1. In Windows Explorer, open the disk and folder containing the file or folder to be copied.

2. Select the file or folder, and press **CTRL+C** to copy the file or folder to the Clipboard.

3. Open the disk and folder that is to be the destination of the copied item.

4. Press **CTRL+V** to paste the file or folder into the destination folder.

TIP

You can also use the Cut, Copy, and Paste commands in the object's context menu (by right-clicking the object) or from the Organize menu in Windows Explorer.

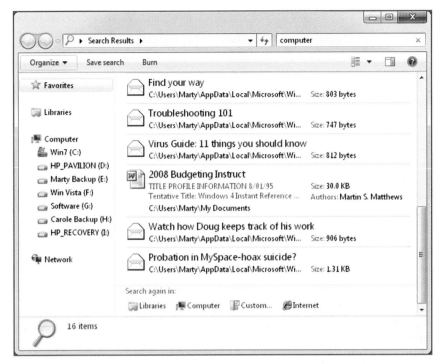

Figure 3-12: You may need to refine your search criteria to get only the files you are looking for.

9. If you want to save the search, click **Save Search** on the toolbar, select the folder in which you want to store the file, type the file name, and click **Save**. If you don't select another folder, saved searches are available in the Searches folder by default. Saved searches also appear under Favorites in the navigation pane.

10. When you are done, close Windows Explorer.

Create Files

Files are usually created by applications or by copying existing files; however, Windows has an additional file-creation capability that creates an empty file for a particular application.

1. Click **Start**, click **Documents**, and open the folder in which you want to create the new file.

2. Right-click a blank area of the subject pane in Windows Explorer, and choose **New**. A menu of all the file types that can be created by the registered applications on your computer will appear.

3. Click the file type you want to create. If you want to work on the file, double-click it to open it in its application.

Encrypt Files and Folders

Windows 7 Professional, Enterprise, and Ultimate editions, but not Windows 7 Starter, Home Basic, or Home Premium editions, have the ability to encrypt files and folders so that they cannot be read without the key to decrypt them. The key is attached to the person who performed the encryption. When she or he logs on to the computer, the files can be used as if they were not encrypted. If someone else logs on, the files cannot be accessed. Even if someone takes the disk to another computer, all that will be displayed is gibberish. To encrypt a file or folder:

1. Click **Start** and click **Computer**. In the navigation pane, open the drive and folders necessary to display the files or folders you want to encrypt in the subject pane.

2. Right-click the file or folder, and choose **Properties**. In the General tab, click **Advanced**. The Advanced Attributes dialog box appears.

3. Click **Encrypt Contents To Secure Data**.

4. Click **OK** twice.

If you are encrypting a file, you will see an Encryption Warning dialog box stating that the file is not in an encrypted folder, which means that when you

NOTE

You can let someone else use an encrypted file by giving him or her your logon user name and password. In addition, in many organizations, an administrator will have the ability to decrypt files so that information cannot be lost through encryption.

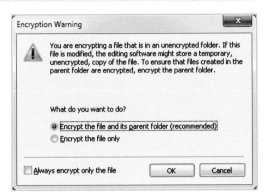

To remove encryption, follow the steps used to encrypt and deselect the relevant option.

Encryption Warning

⚠ You are encrypting a file that is in an unencrypted folder. If this file is modified, the editing software might store a temporary, unencrypted, copy of the file. To ensure that files created in the parent folder are encrypted, encrypt the parent folder.

What do you want to do?

◉ Encrypt the file and its parent folder (recommended)
○ Encrypt the file only

☐ Always encrypt only the file   [OK]   [Cancel]

TIP
It is recommended that folders rather than files be the encrypting container, because many applications save temporary and secondary files during execution.

NOTE
Using the attribute to compress a file or folder is seldom done since the advent of zipping a file (see the "Zipping Files and Folders" QuickSteps later in this chapter), which is more efficient (makes smaller files) and can be more easily "unzipped" or decompressed by most people. Also, a file or folder that has been compressed with attributes cannot also be encrypted and vice versa.

---

edit the file, temporary or backup files might be created that are not encrypted. Options include whether to encrypt the file and its parent folder or just the file.

If you are encrypting a folder, you will see a Confirm Attribute Changes dialog box that asks if the change applies to this folder only or applies to this folder and its subfolders and files.

Choose the option you want, and click **OK**. You may see a message from the Encrypting File System that you should back up your encryption key. Click the icon in the notification area to choose how you want to back up your key. The title under the file or folder icon turns a different color, normally green.

Yellowstone

Change Other File and Folder Attributes

Encryption, described in the previous section, is one of five or six file or folder attributes. The others are shown in Table 3-2.

To set the additional attributes:

1. Click **Start** and click **Computer**. In the navigation pane, open the drive and folders necessary to display in the subject pane the files or folders whose attributes you want to set.

ATTRIBUTE	DESCRIPTION
Read-Only	The file or folder cannot be changed.
Hidden	The file or folder cannot be seen unless Show Hidden Files, Folders, And Drives is selected in the Folder Options View tab.
File Or Folder Is Ready For Archiving	This serves as a flag to backup programs that the file or folder is ready to be backed up.
Allow Files In This Folder Or This File To Have Contents Indexed	This allows the Windows Indexing Service to index the file or folder so that searching for the file can be done quickly. (See Chapter 6 for how to use the Indexing Service.)
Compress Contents To Save Disk Space	The file or folder is rewritten on the disk in compressed format. The file can still be read, but it will take a little longer while it is decompressed.

Table 3-2: Additional File and Folder Attributes

QUICKSTEPS

ZIPPING FILES AND FOLDERS

Windows 7 has a way to compress files and folders called "zipping." *Zipped* files have the extension .zip and are compatible with programs like WinZip. Zipped files take up less room on a disk and are transmitted over the Internet faster.

CREATE A ZIPPED FOLDER

You can create a new zipped folder and drag files to it.

1. Click **Start** and click **Documents**.

2. Navigate to the folder that you want to contain the zipped folder.

3. Right-click in a blank area of the subject pane, click **New**, and click **Compressed (Zipped) Folder**. The zipped folder will appear.

4. Click the folder name, type a new name, and drag files and folders into it to compress them.

New Compressed (zipped) Folder

SEND FILES OR FOLDERS TO A ZIPPED FOLDER

1. In Windows Explorer, select the files and/or folders you want zipped.

2. Right-click the selected objects, click **Send To**, and click **Compressed (Zipped) Folder**. A new zipped folder will appear containing the original files and/or folders, now compressed.

Continued . . .

2. Right-click the file or folder, and choose **Properties**. In the General tab, you can click **Read-Only** and **Hidden**. Do that if you wish, and click **OK**.

3. If you want to set archiving or indexing, click **Advanced**. The Advanced Attributes dialog box appears.

4. Click the attribute you want to set, and click **OK** twice.

Back Up Files and Folders

Backing up copies important files and folders on your disk and writes them on another device, such as a recordable CD or DVD, a USB flash drive, or to another hard disk. To start the backup process:

1. Click **Start**, click **Control Panel**, click **System And Security**, and click **Backup And Restore**. If this is the first time you are doing a backup, you will be asked to set up Windows Backup.

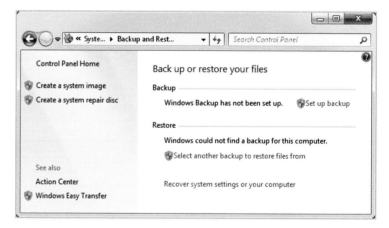

2. Click **Set Up Backup**. The Set Up Backup dialog box will appear, as shown in Figure 3-13.

3. Click a local backup destination drive or click **Save On A Network**.

4. If you chose to save on a network, click **Browse**, select a network drive and folder where you want the backup, click **OK**, and enter your network user name and password. Click **OK**. The network drive will appear on the list of destination drives. Click it.

5. Click **Next**. Accept the recommended Let Windows Choose What To Backup or click **Let Me Choose**, and then click **Next**.

QUICKSTEPS

ZIPPING FILES AND FOLDERS

(Continued)

EXTRACT ZIPPED FILES AND FOLDERS

To unzip a file or folder, simply drag it out of the zipped folder, or you can extract all of a zipped folder's contents.

1. Right-click a zipped folder, and click **Extract All**. The Extract Compressed (Zipped) Folders dialog box will appear.

2. Enter or browse to the location where you want the extracted files and folders, and click **Extract**.

3. Close Windows Explorer when you are done.

TIP

When you zip a group of files, right-click the file whose name you want to give to the zip folder, and then click **Send To**. The file's name will automatically be given to the zip folder.

NOTE

System and program files will not be backed up in an automatic scheduled backup.

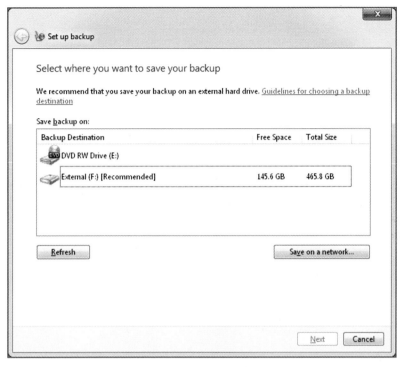

Figure 3-13: **If possible, back up to an external drive.**

6. If you chose the latter option, select the files and drives you want to back up, and click **Next**.

7. Review the Backup Summary that is presented. If it is not correct, click **Back** in the upper-left area, and return to the previous steps.

8. If the proposed schedule is not what you want, click **Change Schedule**. Select how often, what day, and what time you want to do the backup, and click **OK**.

9. Click **Save Settings And Run Backup**. Your next backup will be scheduled and the current backup will begin. You can stop the backup if you wish and change the settings in this window, which replaces the original Backup And Restore window.

10. When the backup is complete, the Backup And Restore window goes into its final form, shown in Figure 3-14. Click the **Close** button to close the Backup And Restore window.

QUICKSTEPS

MANAGING DISKS

Windows 7 provides three tools to help manage the files and folders stored on hard disks.

CLEAN UP A DISK

Disk Cleanup helps you get rid of old files on your hard disk. Windows looks through your hard disk for types of files that can be deleted and lists them, as shown in Figure 3-15. You can then select the types of files you want to delete.

1. Click **Start**, click **Computer**, right-click a disk drive you want to work on, and click **Properties**.

2. Click **Disk Cleanup**. Windows 7 will calculate how much space you could save.

3. Select the types of files to delete, and click **OK**. You are asked if you want to permanently delete these files. Click **Delete Files** to permanently delete them.

4. When you are ready, close the Properties dialog box.

CHECK FOR ERRORS

Error Checking tries to read and write on your disk, without losing information, to determine if bad areas exist. If it finds a bad area, that area is flagged so that the system will not use it. Error Checking automatically fixes file system errors and attempts recovery of bad sectors.

1. Click **Start**, click **Computer**, right-click a disk drive you want to work on, and click **Properties**.

Continued . . .

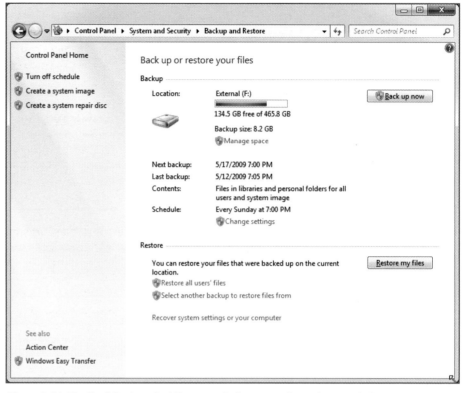

Figure 3-14: *The final Backup And Restore window goes through several changes.*

Write Files and Folders to a CD or DVD

Windows 7 allows you to copy ("burn" or record) files to a writable or rewritable CD or DVD. You must have a CD or DVD writing drive and blank media.

1. Place a blank recordable disc in the drive. You will be asked if you want to burn a CD or DVD using Windows Explorer or Windows Media Player, or possibly other programs on your computer.

QUICKSTEPS

MANAGING DISKS *(Continued)*

2. Click the **Tools** tab, and click **Check Now**. Select whether you want to automatically fix errors and/or attempt recovery of bad sectors, and click **Start**. You may be told you have to restart Windows to use Error Checking. If so, close any open applications, click **Schedule Disk Check** to do a disk check the next time you start your computer, and then restart your computer. Error Checking will automatically begin when Windows restarts.

You will be shown the status of the Error Checking operation and told of any problems that could not be fixed. When Error Checking is complete, your computer will finish restarting.

DEFRAGMENT A DISK

When files are stored on a hard disk, they are broken into pieces (or *fragments*) and individually written to the disk. As the disk fills, the fragments are spread over the disk as space allows. To read a file that has been fragmented requires extra disk activity and can slow down the performance of your computer. To fix this, Windows has a defragmentation process that rewrites the contents of a disk, placing all of the pieces of a file in one contiguous area.

1. Click **Start**, click **Computer**, right-click a disk drive you want to work on, and click **Properties**.

2. Click the **Tools** tab, and click **Defragment Now**. The Disk Defragmenter will open, as shown in Figure 3-16. You can choose to turn off the automatic defragmentation or to modify the schedule.

Continued . . .

2. Click **Burn Files To Disc**. Type a name for the disc. You will be shown two formatting options based on how you want to use the disc:

- **Like A USB flash Drive**, which is the default. This format, called *Live File System,* can only be read on a computer with Windows XP, Windows Server 2003 or 2008, Windows Vista, or Windows 7 operating systems. This option allows you to add one file or folder to the CD or DVD at a time, like you would with a hard disk or a USB flash drive. You can leave the disc in the drive and drag data to it whenever you want and delete previously added objects.

*Figure 3-15: **It is important to get rid of files and folders that you are no longer using.***

- **With A CD/DVD Player**. This format, called Mastered, can be read by most computers, including older Windows and Apple computers and most standalone CD and DVD players. To use this format, you must gather all the files in one place and then burn them all at one time. Use this format for music and video files that you want to play on automobile or standalone devices, such as MP3 and video players.

3. Click the option you want, and click **Next**. The disc will be formatted and, depending on the option you choose, either Media Player will open or a new AutoPlay dialog box will appear.

4. Open another Windows Explorer window, locate the files and folders you want on the CD or DVD, and drag them to the CD/DVD drive subject pane:

- If you are using the Live File System format, as you drag the objects to the drive, they will be immediately written on the disc. When you have written all the files you

UICKSTEPS

MANAGING DISKS *(Continued)*

3. If you wish to go ahead manually, such as with an external drive not otherwise defragmented, shown in Figure 3-16, select the drive and click **Analyze Disk** to see if the disk needs defragmenting. If you wish to continue, click **Defragment Disk**. The process can take up to a couple of hours. Some fragments may remain, which is fine.

4. When you are ready, click **Close** to close the Disk Defragmenter window.

want to the disc, right-click the drive and click **Close Session**. After the "Closing Session" message above the notification area disappears, you can remove the disc from the drive and insert it at a later time to resume adding or removing files and folders.

- If you are using the Mastered format, drag all the objects you want written on the disc to the drive. When all files and folders are in the drive's subject pane, click **Burn To Disc**. You are asked to confirm or change the title, select a recording speed, and click **Next**. When the burn is complete, the disc will be ejected and you can choose to burn the same files to another disc. In any case, click **Finish**. The temporary files will be erased, which might take a few minutes.

5. When you are done, click **Close** to close Windows Explorer.

NOTE

By default, Windows 7 automatically defragments your drives on a periodic basis, so under most circumstances, you won't need to do it.

TIP

The Live File System that lets you use CD-R/DVD-R discs like CD-RW/DVD-RW is a super capability that you can use much as an additional hard disk.

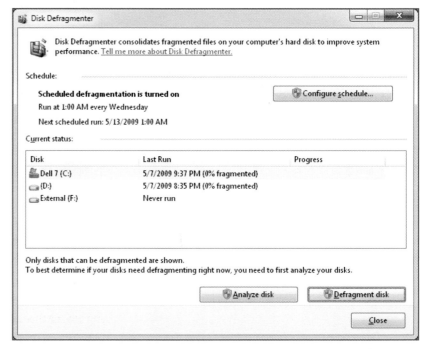

Figure 3-16: Defragmenting brings pieces of a file together into one contiguous area.

Chapter 4
Using the Internet

The Internet provides a major means for worldwide communication between both individuals and organizations, as well as a major means for locating and sharing information. For many, having access to the Internet is the primary reason for having a computer. To use the Internet, you must have a connection to it using one of the many means that are now available. You then can send and receive email; access the World Wide Web; watch movies; and participate in blogs, forums, and newsgroups, among many other things.

Connect to the Internet

You can connect to the Internet using a telephone line, a cable TV connection, a satellite link, or a land-based wireless link. Across these various types of connections there are a myriad of speeds, degrees of reliability, and costs. The most important factor is what is available to you at the location where you want

TYPES OF INTERNET CONNECTIONS

The following Internet connection type descriptions give you a starting place for determining the type you want, if it is available to you. The speeds and costs are representative averages and may not be correct for the Internet service provider (ISP) you are considering or for your location. You must get the correct numbers from your local providers.

TELEPHONE DIAL-UP

A dial-up Internet connection is the oldest and slowest type of connection. It requires a modem in or attached to your computer (many computers come with a modem). To use a dial-up connection, the modem must dial the ISP using a regular phone line each time you want to connect to the Internet. This ties up the phone line while you are connected; thus, it cannot be used for other purposes.

- **Speed—Download**: 48Kbps, **Upload**: 34Kbps
- **Availability**: Almost anywhere
- **Reliability**: Fair
- **Monthly Cost**: From under $10 to over $20
- **One-Time Cost**: Often none

TELEPHONE DSL

Many phone companies offer a DSL (digital subscriber line) service because it is 20 to 40 times faster than dial-up, does not require a dedicated line (phone conversations and faxes can use the same line at the same time without interference), is always connected, and is not all that expensive. Most DSL is actually ADSL, or asymmetric DSL, meaning that the upload and

Continued ...

to use it. In an urban area, you have a number of alternatives from landline phone companies, cell phone companies, and cable TV companies, all with varying degrees of speed, reliability, and cost. As you move away from the urban area, your options will decrease to a telephone dial-up connection and/or a satellite link. With a telephone line, you can connect with a *dial-up* connection, a *DSL* (digital subscriber line) connection, or a high-speed connection of various types. DSL, cable, satellite, and some wireless connections are called *broadband* connections and offer higher speeds and are always on (see "Types of Internet Connections" QuickFacts). You must have access to at least one of these forms of communication in order to connect to the Internet. You must also set up the Internet connection itself.

Choose an Internet Connection

With most forms of Internet connections, you have a choice of speed and ancillary services, such as the number of free email accounts and possibly a personal Web site. Also, depending on the type of connection, you may need dedicated equipment, such as a modem, DSL router, or satellite receiving equipment, which may or may not be included in the price. For any Internet connection service, ask the provider the following questions:

- What is both the best and average experienced download (from the Internet to you) and upload (from you to the Internet) speeds in *Kbps* (kilo or thousands of bits per second) or *Mbps* (millions of bits per second)? (Bits are a series of ones and zeros that represent data.) You will generally do a lot more downloading than you will uploading.

- What is the total cost per month for a given speed, including all applicable taxes and fees?

- What equipment is needed for this service and how much does it cost, either one time or per month? Does the equipment provide hardwired, wireless, or both types of connections? You might want both so you can have both a desktop computer hardwired and a laptop that you can carry around without plugging it in.

- What are the installation, setup, and other one-time charges or fees that are required? If you pay for six months or a year in advance, are these fees waived?

QUICK**FACTS**

TYPES OF INTERNET CONNECTIONS *(Continued)*

download speeds are not the same, which is true with almost all service types.

- **Speed—Download**: 512Kbps to 18Mbps, **Upload**: 256Kbps to 2Mbps

- **Availability**: In urban and many suburban areas. There is a maximum distance limit from equipment facilities.

- **Reliability**: Very good

- **Monthly Cost**: From under $30 to over $60

- **One-Time Cost**: May have setup fees and equipment charges

TELEPHONE FIBER OPTIC

With the advent of phone companies running fiber optic cable to businesses and homes, they have started offering significantly increased Internet connection speeds. Verizon is one example of this with their FiOS service.

- **Speed—Download**: 10Mbps to 50Mbps, **Upload**: 2Mbps to 20Mbps

- **Availability**: Urban and a few suburban areas. There is a maximum distance limit from equipment facilities.

Continued . . .

TIP

Often, setup, installation, and equipment charges for an Internet connection are waived if you sign a one- or two-year contract and/or prepay for a year or two of service.

- How many email accounts are included and how much storage is allowed per account (for example, six accounts and 250MB of storage)? (MB refers to megabytes or millions of bytes, and a byte is eight bits.) How much are additional accounts and storage?

- Are the means for having your own personal or commercial Web site (called web hosting) included? If so, what are the limits in terms of the amount of storage used by the site and the site activity in terms of the number of bits transferred to and/or from your site per month? For a free personal Web site, this commonly is 10 to 100MB of storage and 1 to 5GB (gigabits or billions of bits) of activity.

- How long does it take to get the connection up and running?

Set Up Communications

Communications is the link between your computer and the Internet. To set up communications, you must first choose a type of connection link. With a dial-up connection, you must set up a modem. If you are not using dial-up (and that is recommended, if possible), you do not need to install a modem and can skip the following section.

INSTALL A MODEM

If a modem came with your computer, or if one was already installed when you upgraded to Windows 7, your modem was probably automatically installed and you don't need to do anything more. In that case, or if you are unsure, skip to "Set Up a Dial-Up Connection." Otherwise, if you need to install a modem:

NOTE

As you perform the steps in this and other chapters, you may see a User Account Control (UAC) dialog box appear and tell you that Windows needs your permission to continue. When you see these dialog boxes and if you are an administrator and, in fact, want to continue, click **Continue**. If you are not logged on as an administrator, you will need to enter a password. If you don't want to do whatever is being requested, click **Cancel**. The UAC dialog box and its associated steps are not included in the steps here to simplify the process. When you see the UAC dialog box, process it as you want and continue with the instructions. UAC is discussed in Chapter 8.

- **Reliability**: Very good
- **Monthly Cost**: From under $50 to over $140
- **One-Time Cost**: May have setup fees and equipment charges

TV CABLE SERVICE

Many cable television companies now offer Internet connection service on their lines. This service is advertised as being much faster than DSL, but it often is only slightly faster or not so at all. TV cable Internet service is using a party-line concept where several to many people use the same line (with DSL and FiOS, you have your own private line). In a digital world, this line sharing is not as bad as you might think, but interference can still slow down the actual service, and advertised speeds are seldom attainable for any length of time.

- **Speed—Download**: 3Mbps to 50Mbps, **Upload**: 1Mbps to 10Mbps
- **Availability**: Urban and most suburban areas
- **Reliability**: Very good
- **Monthly Cost**: From under $40 to over $140
- **One-Time Cost**: Normally have installation fees and equipment charges

CELL PHONE WIRELESS

Most cell phone companies offer a mobile broadband Internet service, which can be used both on "smart phones" and with normal computers with a small plug-in device. Like all cell phone service, it is subject to blind areas where the service cannot be received. Also, just

Continued . . .

---

1. Make sure a modem is either physically installed in your computer or, if you have an external modem, that it is connected to your computer, plugged in, and turned on.

2. Click **Start** and click **Control Panel**. On the top-right area, click the **View By** down arrow, and click **Large Icons** if you are not already in that view.

3. In Large Icons view, click **Phone And Modem**.

4. If this is the first time you've set up a modem, you need to enter location information. Select your country, enter your area or city code, and, if necessary, your carrier code and the number to access an outside line. If needed, click **Pulse Dialing** (with old phone systems only), and click **OK**. The Phone And Modem dialog box will appear.

5. Click the **Modems** tab. If it shows a modem, as shown here, your modem is installed and you can skip to "Set Up a Dial-Up Connection."

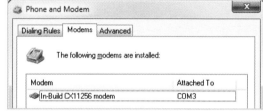

6. If you don't see a modem but you know you have one installed, close the Phone And Modem dialog box, and return to the Large Icons of Control Panel. Click **Device Manager**. You'll see a list of all your hardware in alphabetical order. You should not see a Modems listing yet (because Windows hasn't fully recognized the device at this point), but hopefully, under Other Devices, you'll see a modem with an exclamation point as shown in the illustration.

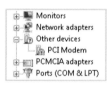

7. If you do not see a modem, it is a good bet that one is not installed and you need to do that. If you do see a modem with an exclamation point, then a device driver needs to be installed. In both of those cases, you need to go outside Windows to locate a solution.

8. If you see the modem listed and have a CD for it, put the CD in the drive. It should automatically start and install the driver. If you need a new modem, talk to the manufacturer of your computer or the store where you bought it.

9. When you are told that your modem has been installed successfully (you should now see your modem listed under a Modems heading), click **Close** twice to close the Device Manager window and Control Panel.

TYPES OF INTERNET CONNECTIONS *(Continued)*

because a company has cell phone service in an area, this does not mean their Internet service extends to that area.

- **Speed—Download**: 600Kbps to 1.4Mbps, **Upload**: 500Kbps to 800Kbps
- **Availability**: Urban and some suburban areas
- **Reliability**: Good
- **Monthly Cost**: From under $40 to over $60
- **One-Time Cost**: Normally have activation fees, a smart phone, and device charge for use with a computer

SATELLITE WIRELESS

Satellite Internet service is available in most areas, including those where other services are not available. Satellite service requires a satellite antenna that can "see" the southern horizon, so you need clear southern exposure. Trees, buildings, and hills or mountains close to you on your south side can block reception. Also, heavy weather can cause interruptions. Generally, satellite service is a last resort. One satellite provider is HughesNet, www.hughesnest.com.

- **Speed—Download**: 1Mbps to 5Mbps, **Upload**: 128Kbps to 300Kbps
- **Availability**: Almost anywhere
- **Reliability**: Fair
- **Monthly Cost**: From under $60 to over $350
- **One-Time Cost**: Purchase or lease of equipment required

SET UP A DIAL-UP CONNECTION

With a modem installed and working, you can set up a *dial-up connection* that uses the modem to dial and connect to another computer at the other end of a phone line.

1. If your Control Panel isn't open, click **Start** and then click **Control Panel**. In Large Icons view, double-click **Network And Sharing Center**.

2. Click **Set Up A New Connection Or Network**. The Set Up A Connection Or Network dialog box will appear.

3. Click **Set Up A Dial-Up Connection**, and click **Next**. The Create A Dial-Up Connection dialog box will appear.

4. Enter the phone number to dial, enter the user name and password given to you by your Internet service provider (ISP), choose whether to show the password and whether to remember the password or require it to be entered each time you connect, and then enter a name for this connection (see Figure 4-1).

Figure 4-1: You will need a user name and a password, as well as other information from your ISP, in order to connect with them. See the second Note on the next page.

NOTE

To connect to the Internet, you need to have an existing account with an ISP and you need to know your ISP's phone number for your modem to dial. You also must have the user name and password for your account. If you want to use Internet mail, you need to know your email address, the type of mail server (POP3, IMAP, or HTTP), the names of the incoming and outgoing mail servers, and the name and password for the mail account. This information is provided by your ISP when you establish your account.

5. Choose whether anyone else can use this user name and password. When you are done, click **Connect**.

6. You will be told when you are connected to the Internet.

7. Click **Browse The Internet Now** to do that. You will be asked if this network is in a home, work, or public location. Click **Public Location**. This will be explained further in Chapter 9. Click **Close**.

8. Internet Explorer (Windows 7's integral Web browser) will open for your use. See "Use the World Wide Web" later in this chapter. When you are done, click the **Close** button on Internet Explorer.

9. To disconnect, right-click the connection icon in the notification area, click **Disconnect From**, and click the name of your connection. Click **Close** to close the Network And Sharing Center window.

SET UP A BROADBAND CONNECTION

A broadband connection—made with a DSL phone line, a TV cable, a satellite connection, or a high-speed wireless connection—is normally made with a device that connects to your local area network (LAN) and allows several computers on the network to use the connection. (See Chapter 9 to set up a network.) With a network set up, your computer connected to the network, and a broadband service connected to the network, your computer is connected to the broadband service. There is nothing else you need to do to set up a broadband connection.

Configure an Internet Connection

In the process of establishing either a dial-up or broadband connection, you may have also configured an Internet connection. The easiest way to check that is to try to connect to the Internet by clicking the **Internet Explorer** icon pinned to the left of the taskbar. If an Internet Web page is displayed, like the MSN page shown in Figure 4-2, then you are connected and you need do no more. If you did not connect to the Internet and you know that your dial-up or broadband and network connections are all working properly, you need to configure your Internet connection.

Call Date: 2nd Call Date:

Initials: Initials:

Disposition: Disposition:

Patron Barcode: 20601000402603

Patron email: stanman2358@gmail.com

Item barcode: 30641003966764

Title: Windows 7 / by Marty Matthews.

Author: Matthews, Martin S.

Call number: 005.4469 WINDOWS 7

Hold note:

Pick-Up Location: Commack Public Library

NOTE

Sometimes, a DSL or TV cable connecting device is called a "modem," but it is not an analog-to-digital converter, which is the major point of a **mo**dulator-**dem**odulator. Therefore, that term is not used for those devices in this book. The correct term is "router," which is a bridge between the Internet and your local network/computer.

NOTE

For the sake of writing convenience and because Windows 7 generally comes with Internet Explorer, this book assumes you are using Internet Explorer to access the Internet.

1. If Internet Explorer did not connect to the Internet, click **Start** and click **Control Panel**.

2. In Category view, click **Network And Internet**, and click **Network And Sharing Center**.

   –Or–

   In Large Icons view, click **Network And Sharing Center**.

3. In either case, click **Set Up A New Connection Or Network**. The Set Up A Connection Or Network dialog box will appear (see Figure 4-3).

Figure 4-2: The easiest way to see if you have an Internet connection is to try to connect to the Internet.

QUICKSTEPS

BROWSING THE INTERNET

Browsing the Internet refers to using a browser, like Internet Explorer, to go from one Web site to another to see the sites' contents. You can browse to a site by directly entering a site address, by navigating to a site from another site, or by using the browser controls. First, of course, you have to start the browser.

START A BROWSER

To start your default browser (assumed to be Internet Explorer), click the **Internet Explorer** icon on the left of the taskbar.

ENTER A SITE DIRECTLY

To go directly to a site:

1. Start your browser and click the existing address, or URL (uniform resource locator), in the address bar to select it.

2. Type the address of the site you want to open, as shown here, and either click **Go To** (the right-pointing arrow) next to the address bar or press **ENTER**.

USE SITE NAVIGATION

Site navigation is using a combination of links and menus on one web page to locate and open another web page, either in the same site or in another site:

- **Links** are words, phrases, sentences, or graphics that always have an open hand displayed when the mouse pointer is moved over them and, when clicked, take you to another location. They are

Continued . . .

Figure 4-3: *Most broadband connections are always on and don't require a user name and password.*

4. Click **Connect To The Internet**, and click **Next**. Click your choice between broadband and dial-up, and click **Next**.

5. Enter a dial-up phone number (if that is your service choice), your user name and password, choose whether to display the password and if it is to be remembered by the system, enter a name for the connection, and choose whether to allow others to use this user name and password. When you are done, click **Connect**.

6. Once more, click the **Internet Explorer** icon on the taskbar. If asked, click **Connect** and then click **Dial**. If you still cannot connect to the Internet, you may need to reinstall your modem, in which case you should go to "Install a Modem" earlier in this chapter. If you are using a broadband connection, you may need to go to Chapter 9 and look at potential network problems.

BROWSING THE INTERNET *(Continued)*

often underlined—if not initially, then when you move the mouse pointer to them.

MSNBC News

Senate OKs credit card reform | Video
- Rules aim to slash carbon output | Video
- Newsweek: Hunt for Africa's last warlord
- Mother of boy resisting chemo faces arrest
- Mega-shrew shot venom through red teeth

- **Menus** contain one or a few words in a horizontal list, vertical list, or both that always have an open hand displayed when the mouse pointer is moved over them and, when clicked, take you to another location.

Home	Local	Nation/World	Business/Tech
Quick links:	Tra	**Home**	
Tuesday, May 19		**Politics**	

USE BROWSER NAVIGATION

Browser navigation is using the controls within your browser to go to another location. Internet Explorer has two controls not discussed elsewhere that are used for navigation:

- **Back** and **Forward** buttons take you to the next or previous page in the stack of pages you have viewed most recently. Moving your mouse over these buttons will display a tooltip showing you the name of the page the button will take you to.

- **Recent Pages** allows you to open a list of the recent pages you have viewed, click one, and quickly return to that page.

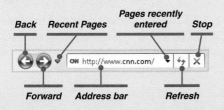

Back   Recent Pages   *Pages recently entered*   Stop

Forward   Address bar   Refresh

Use the World Wide Web

The *World Wide Web* (or just the *Web*) is the sum of all the Web sites in the world—examples of which are CNN, Google, and MSN (which was shown in Figure 4-2). The World Wide Web is what you can access with a *Web browser,* such as Internet Explorer, which comes with Windows 7.

Search the Internet

You can search the Internet in two ways: by using the Microsoft Live Search facility built into Internet Explorer and by using an independent search facility on the Web.

SEARCH FROM INTERNET EXPLORER

To use Internet Explorer's Live Search facility:

1. Click the **Internet Explorer** icon on the taskbar to open it.

2. Click in the Live Search box on the right of the address bar, and type what you want to search for. Click one of the suggestions below the Search box, click **Search** (the magnifying glass) on the right end of the search box, or click **ENTER**. The Windows Live search site will open with the results of the search, as you can see in Figure 4-4.

3. Click the link of your choice to go to that site.

SEARCH FROM AN INTERNET SITE

There are many independent Internet search sites. The most popular is Google.

1. Click the **Internet Explorer** icon on the taskbar to open it.

2. Drag over to highlight the current address in the address bar, type www.google.com, and either click **Go To** (the blue arrow) or press **ENTER**.

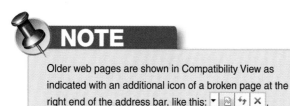

NOTE

Older web pages are shown in Compatibility View as indicated with an additional icon of a broken page at the right end of the address bar, like this: ▼ 🖻 ⁺ ×.

TIP

When you enter search criteria, place quotation marks around certain keywords or phrases to get only results that match those words exactly.

3. In the text box, type what you want to search for, and click **Google Search**. The resulting Web sites are shown in a full web page, as illustrated in Figure 4-5.

4. Click the link of your choice to go to that site.

Keep a Favorite Site

Sometimes, you visit a site that you would like to return to quickly or often. Internet Explorer has a memory bank called Favorites to which you can save sites for easy retrieval.

SAVE A FAVORITE SITE

To add a site to Favorites:

1. Click the **Internet Explorer** icon on the taskbar to open it.

2. Open the web page you want to add to your Favorites list, and make sure its correct address (URL) is in the address bar.

3. Click **Favorites** above the tab row, and click **Add To Favorites**. The Add A Favorite dialog box appears.

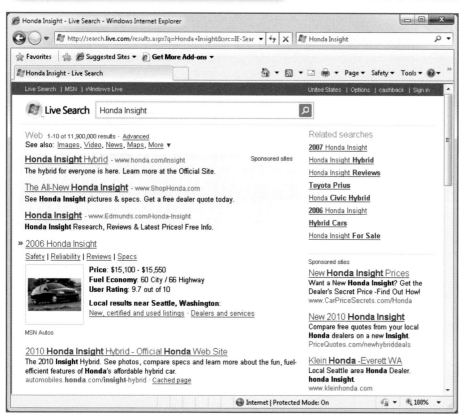

4. Adjust the name as needed in the text box (you may want to type a name you will readily associate with that site), and click **Add**.

Figure 4-4: The results of a search using Internet Explorer's Live Search.

Figure 4-5: *The results of a search using Google.*

OPEN A FAVORITE SITE

To open a favorite site you have saved:

1. Click the **Internet Explorer** icon on the taskbar to open it.

2. Click **Favorites** above the tab row, and click the site you want to open.

Use Tabs

Internet Explorer 8 (IE8), which comes with Windows 7, allows you to have several web pages open at one time and easily switch between them by clicking the tab associated with the page. The tabs reside on the *tab row*, immediately above the displayed web page, as shown in Figure 4-6. Originally, only one page was open at a time, as in versions of Internet Explorer before IE7. If you open a second page, it replaces the first page. IE7 and IE8, however, give you the ability to open multiple pages as separate tabs that you can switch among by clicking their tabs.

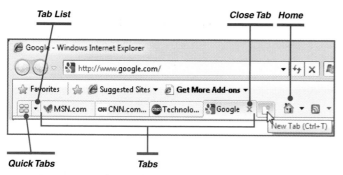

Tab List   Close Tab   Home

Quick Tabs   Tabs

Figure 4-6: Tabs allow you to quickly switch among several Web sites.

OPEN PAGES IN A NEW TAB

To open a page in a new tab:

1. Click the **Internet Explorer** icon on the taskbar to open it.

2. Open your first web page in any of the ways described earlier in this chapter.

3. Click **New Tab** on the right end of the tab row, or press **CTRL+T**, and open a second web page in any of the ways described earlier in this chapter.

–Or–

Type a web address in the address bar, and press **ALT+ENTER**.

–Or–

Type a search request in the search box, and press **ALT+ENTER**.

–Or–

Hold down **CTRL** while clicking a link in an open page.

–Or–

Click the blue arrow on the right of a site in your Favorites list.

4. Repeat any of the alternatives in step 3 as needed to open additional pages.

SWITCH AMONG TABS

To switch among open tabs:

Click the tab of the page you want to open.

–Or–

Click **Quick Tabs** in the tab row, or press **CTRL+Q**, and click the thumbnail of the page you want to open (see Figure 4-7).

–Or–

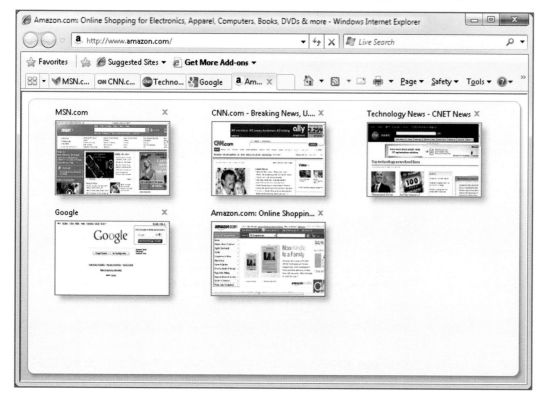

Figure 4-7: Through the Quick Tabs button, you can see thumbnails of all your open pages side-by-side.

Click **Tab List** in the tab row, and click the page you want to open.

–Or–

Press **CTRL+TAB** to switch to the next tab to the right, or press **CTRL+ SHIFT+TAB** to switch to the next tab to the left.

–Or–

Press **CTRL+n**, where *n* is a number from 1 to 8 to switch to one of the first eight tabs numbered from the left in the order they were opened. You can also press **CTRL+9** to switch to the last tab that was opened, shown on the right of the tab row.

CLOSE TABS

To close one or more tabs:

Right-click the tab for the page you want to close, and click **Close Tab** on the context menu, or click **Close Other Tabs** to close all of the pages except the one you clicked, or click **Close This Tab Group** to close all tabs if a group is displayed.

–Or–

Press **CTRL+W** to close the current page.

–Or–

Click the tab of the page you want to close, and click the **X** on the right of the tab.

–Or–

Press **ALT+F4** and click **Close All Tabs** to do that, or click **Close Current Tab**; or click **CTRL+ALT+ F4** to close all tabs except the currently selected one.

Change Your Home Page

When you first start Internet Explorer, a web page is automatically displayed. This page is called your *home page*. When you go to other web pages, you can return to this page by clicking the **Home Page** icon on the tab row. To change your home page:

QUICKSTEPS

ORGANIZING FAVORITE SITES

After a while, you will probably find that you have a number of favorite sites and it is becoming hard to find the one you want. Internet Explorer provides two places to store your favorite sites, a favorites list, which is presented to you in the form of a menu you can open, and a favorites bar, which is displayed at all times. There are several ways to organize your favorite sites.

REARRANGE THE FAVORITES LIST

The items on your Favorites list are displayed in the order you added them, unless you drag them to a new location.

1. Click the **Internet Explorer** icon on the taskbar to open it.

2. Click **Favorites**, locate the site you want to reposition, and drag it to the location in the list where you want it.

CREATE NEW FOLDERS

Internet Explorer comes with several default folders added by Microsoft or by the computer's manufacturer. You can also add your own folders within the Favorites list.

1. Click the **Internet Explorer** icon on the taskbar to open it.

2. Click **Favorites**, click the **Add To Favorites** down arrow, and click **Organize Favorites** to open the Organize Favorites dialog box, shown in Figure 4-8.

3. Click **New Folder**, type the name for the folder, and press **ENTER**.

4. Drag the desired site links to the new folder, drag the folder to where you want it on the list, and then click **Close**.

Continued . . .

Figure 4-8: As with files, organizing your favorite Web sites helps you easily find what you want.

1. Click the **Internet Explorer** icon on the taskbar to open it.

2. Directly enter or browse to the site you want as your home page.

3. Click the **Home Page** down arrow, and click **Add Or Change Home Page**. The Add Or Change Home Page dialog box will appear.

4. Click:

- **Use This Webpage As Your Only Home Page** if you wish to have only a single home page

- **Add This Webpage To Your Home Page Tabs** if you wish to have several home pages on different tabs

QUICKSTEPS

ORGANIZING FAVORITE SITES

(Continued)

PUT FAVORITES IN FOLDERS

You can put a site in either your own folders (see "Create New Folders") or the default ones when you initially add it to your Favorites list.

1. Click the **Internet Explorer** icon on the taskbar to open it.

2. Open the web page you want in your Favorites list, and make sure its correct address or URL is in the address bar.

3. Click **Favorites**, click **Add To Favorites**, adjust the name as needed in the text box, click the **Create In** down arrow, select the folder to use, and click **Add**.

ADD A SITE TO THE FAVORITES BAR

On the same row with and to the right of the Favorites menu is the Favorites bar. By default, it has two sites on it, but you can add others.

Open the site you want to add to the Favorites bar, and click the **Add To Favorites Bar** button on the left of the Favorites bar.

–Or–

Click **Favorites**, click the **Add To Favorites** down arrow, and click **Add To Favorites Bar**.

TIP

To delete a favorite site from either the Favorites list or the Favorites bar, right-click it and click **Delete**.

- **Use The Current Tab Set As Your Home Page** if you want all the current tabs to appear when you start Internet Explorer or click the Home Page icon

5. Click **Yes** to complete your home page selection and close the dialog box.

Access Web History

Internet Explorer keeps a history of the Web sites you visit, and you can use that history to return to a site. You can set the length of time to keep sites in that history, and you can clear your history.

Add a Favorite

Add this webpage as a favorite. To access your favorites, visit the Favorites Center.

Name: US Treasury

Create in: Favorites

- Favorites
  - Favorites Bar
  - Microsoft Websites
  - MSN Websites
  - Websites for United States
  - Windows Live
  - Windows 7 sites

USE WEB HISTORY

To use the Web History feature:

1. Click the **Internet Explorer** icon on the taskbar to open it.

2. Click **Favorites** above the tab row, and click **History** or press **CTRL+H** to open the History pane.

3. Click how you want the history sorted, and then click the day, Web site, and web page you want to open, as shown in Figure 4-9.

Figure 4-9: The Web History feature allows you to find a site that you visited in the recent past.

QUICKSTEPS

CONTROLLING INTERNET SECURITY

Internet Explorer allows you to control three aspects of Internet security. You can categorize sites by the degree to which you trust them, determine how you want to handle *cookies* placed on your computer by Web sites, and set and use ratings to control the content of Web sites that can be viewed. These controls are found in the Internet Options dialog box.

1. Click the **Internet Explorer** icon on the taskbar to open it.

2. Click **Tools** on the tab row, and click **Internet Options**.

CATEGORIZE WEB SITES

Internet Explorer allows you to categorize Web sites into zones: Internet (sites that are not classified in one of the other ways), Local Intranet, Trusted Sites, and Restricted Sites (as shown in Figure 4-10).

From the Internet Options dialog box:

1. Click the **Security** tab. Click the **Internet** zone. Note its definition.

2. Click **Custom Level**. Select the elements in this zone that you want to disable, enable, or prompt you before using. Alternatively, select a level of security you want for this zone, and click **Reset**. Click **OK** when you are finished.

3. Click each of the other zones, where you can identify either groups or individual sites you want in that zone.

HANDLE COOKIES

Cookies are small pieces of data that Web sites store on your computer so that they can remind themselves

Continued . . .

DELETE AND SET HISTORY

You can set the length of time to keep your Internet history, and you can clear this history.

1. Click the **Internet Explorer** icon on the taskbar to open it.

2. Click **Tools** at the right end of the tab row, and click **Internet Options**.

3. In the General tab, under Browsing History, click **Delete** to open the Delete Browsing History dialog box. If needed, select the check box opposite History to delete it. Select any other check box to delete that information, although you should keep the Preserve Favorites Website Data check box selected to *keep* that information (it is a confusing dialog box). Click **Delete**.

–Or–

In the General tab of the Internet Options dialog box, under Browsing History, click **Settings**. Under History, at the bottom of the dialog box, use the **Days** spinner to set the number of days to keep your Web history. Click **OK**.

4. Click **OK** again to close the Internet Options dialog box.

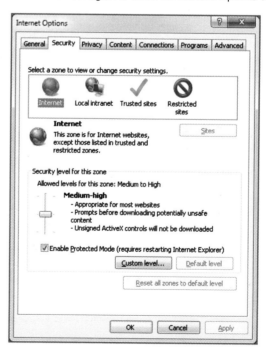

Figure 4-10: Internet Explorer allows you to categorize Web sites into zones and determine what can be done within those zones.

CONTROLLING INTERNET SECURITY *(Continued)*

of who you are. These can save you from having to constantly enter your name and ID. Cookies can also be dangerous, however, letting people into your computer where they can potentially do damage.

Internet Explorer lets you determine the types and sources of cookies you will allow and what those cookies can do on your computer (see Figure 4-11).

From the Internet Options dialog box:

1. Click the **Privacy** tab. Select a privacy setting by dragging the slider up or down.

2. Click **Advanced** to open the Advanced Privacy Settings dialog box. If you wish, click **Override Automatic Cookie Handling**, and select the settings you want to use.

3. Click **OK** to return to the Internet Options dialog box.

4. In the middle of the Privacy tab, you can turn off the pop-up blocker, which is on by default (it is recommended that you leave it on). If you have a site that you frequently use that needs pop-ups, click **Settings**, enter the site address (URL), click **Add**, and click **Close**.

5. At the bottom of the Privacy tab, you can determine how to handle InPrivate Filtering and Browsing. See the Note on InPrivate later in this chapter.

CONTROL CONTENT

You can control the content that Internet Explorer displays.

Continued . . .

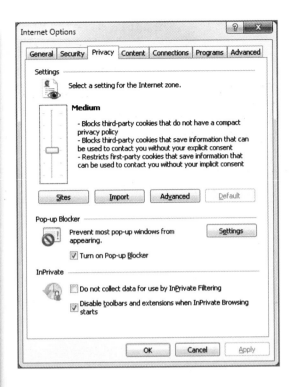

Figure 4-11: Determine how you will handle cookies that Web sites want to leave on your computer.

Copy Internet Information

You may occasionally find something on the Internet that you want to copy—a picture, some text, or a web page.

COPY A PICTURE FROM THE INTERNET

To copy a picture from an Internet web page to a folder on your hard disk:

1. Open Internet Explorer and locate the web page containing the picture you want.

2. Right-click the picture and click **Save Picture As**. Locate the folder in which you want to save the picture, enter the file name you want to use, and click **Save**.

3. Close Internet Explorer if you are done.

QUICKSTEPS

CONTROLLING INTERNET SECURITY *(Continued)*

From the Internet Options dialog box:

1. Click the **Content** tab. Click **Parental Controls**. Click the user you want to control to open the User Controls window, shown in Figure 4-12. Click **On** to turn on parental controls, and configure any other settings you want to use. Click **OK** when you are done, and then close the Parental Controls window.

2. Click **Enable** to open the Content Advisor dialog box. Individually select each of the categories, and drag the slider to the level you want to allow. Detailed descriptions of each area are shown in the lower half of the dialog box.

3. Click **OK** to close the Content Advisor dialog box.

When you are done, click **OK** to close the Internet Options dialog box. (Other parts of this dialog box are discussed elsewhere in this book.)

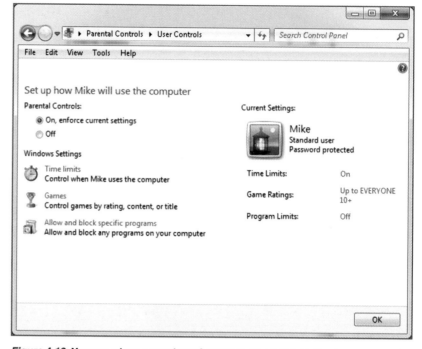

Figure 4-12: **You can place a number of controls on what a particular user can do on a computer using the Parental Controls feature.**

NOTE

Protected Mode—which you can turn on or off at the bottom of the Security tab (the notice for which you'll see at the bottom of Internet Explorer)— is what produces the messages that tells you a program is trying to run in Internet Explorer or that software is trying to install itself on your computer. In most cases, you can click in a bar at the top of the Internet Explorer window if you want to run the program or install the software. You can also double-click the notice at the bottom of Internet Explorer to open the Security tab and turn off Protected Mode (clear the **Enable Protected Mode** check box).

COPY TEXT FROM THE INTERNET

To copy text from a web page to a Microsoft Word document or email message:

1. Open Internet Explorer and locate the web page containing the text you want.

2. Drag across to highlight the text, right-click the selection, and click **Copy**.

3. Open a Microsoft Word document or an email message in which you want to paste the text. Right-click where you want the text, and click **Paste**.

4. Save the Word document and close Internet Explorer, Microsoft Word, or your email program if you are done with them.

COPY A WEB PAGE FROM THE INTERNET

To make a copy of a web page and store it on your hard disk:

1. Open Internet Explorer and locate the web page you want to copy.

2. Click **Page** on the tab row, and click **Save As**. In the Save Webpage dialog box, select the folder in which to save the page, enter the file name you want to use, and click **Save**.

3. Close Internet Explorer if you are done.

Play Internet Audio and Video Files

You can play audio and video files on the Internet with Internet Explorer directly from a link on a web page. Many web pages have links to audio and video files, such as the one shown in Figure 4-13. To play these files, simply click the links.

Figure 4-13: Play an audio or video file on a web page by clicking the link.

If you have several audio players installed (for example, Windows Media Player and Real Player), you will be asked which one you want to use. Make that choice, and the player will open to play the requested piece.

Use Internet Email

Windows 7 does not include a mail program, but you can download Windows Live Mail as part of Windows Live Essentials. Windows Live Mail allows you to send and receive email and to participate in newsgroups. You can also send and receive email through a Web-mail account using Internet Explorer. This section will primarily describe using Windows Live Mail. See the "Using Web Mail" QuickSteps for a discussion of that subject.

Get Windows Mail

For email with Windows 7, this book describes the use of Windows Live Mail because it works well, is freely available from Microsoft, and is designed for Windows 7. There are a number of other alternatives that you can buy or get for free, including Outlook from Microsoft, Eudora, Mozilla Thunderbird, and Opera. Conduct an Internet search on "Windows Mail Clients."

To get Windows Live Mail, you must download Windows Live Essentials from Microsoft. To do that:

1. Click **Start**, click **Getting Started**, and click **Get Windows Live Essentials**. Internet Explorer will open and display Microsoft's download.live.com Web site.

2. Click **Download** and in the File Download – Security Warning box, click **Run**. The download will begin and take from 1 to 10 minutes with a broadband Internet connection. When the download is complete, Windows Live will start.

3. Choose the programs you want to install (see Figure 4-14), and click **Install**. If you are asked to close Internet Explorer, click **Continue**, and it will be closed for you.

4. Choose how much of your Internet experience you want to reveal to Microsoft, and click **Continue**.

Getting Started	▶	Tasks
Windows Media Center		Discover Windows 7
Calculator		Personalize Windows
		Transfer your files
Sticky Notes		Share with a homegroup
		Change UAC settings
Snipping Tool		Get Windows Live Essentials
		Back up your files
Paint		Add new users
		Change text size

Windows Live

Choose the programs you want to install

Click each program name for details.

- ☑ 👥 Messenger
- ☑ 📋 Mail
- ☑ 🖼 Photo Gallery
- ☑ 🔧 Toolbar
- ☑ ✏ Writer
- ☑ 🛡 Family Safety
- ☑ ☑ Microsoft Office Outlook...
- ☑ 🔳 Microsoft Office Live Ad...
- ☑ ◉ Silverlight
- ☐ 🎬 Movie Maker Beta

Messenger

Send instant messages to contacts or groups, play games, share pictures as you chat, and see what's new with people you know.

Installed with this program:

- Microsoft Application Error Reporting
- Microsoft Visual Studio Runtime
- Windows Live Communications Platform
- Windows Live Call

Space needed: 178 MB
Space available: 19.0 GB

[Install]   [Cancel]

Figure 4-14: Windows Live Essentials includes email, instant messaging, blogging, movie making, and more.

5. If you have a Windows Live, Hotmail, Messenger, or Xbox Live account, click **Close**. Otherwise, click **Sign Up** and follow the instructions on the screen to establish an account.

6. For now, click **Close** in the Windows Live Messenger window. It will be opened and discussed at the end of this chapter.

Establish an Email Account

To send and receive email with Windows Live Mail, you must have an Internet connection, an email account established with an ISP, and that account must be set up in Windows Live Mail.

For an email account, you need:

- Your email address, for example: mike@anisp.com
- The type of mail server the ISP uses (POP3, IMAP, or HTTP— POP3 is the most common)
- The names of the incoming and outgoing mail servers, for example: mail.anisp.com
- The name and password for your mail account

With this information, you can set up an account in Windows Live Mail.

1. Click **Start**, click **All Programs**, click **Windows Live**, and click **Windows Live Mail**. If Windows Live Mail has not been previously set up, the Add An Email Account dialog box will appear; if it doesn't, click **Add Email Account** to open it.

2. Enter your email address, press **TAB**, enter your email password, press **TAB**, enter the name you want people to see when they get your email, click the **Manually Configure Server Settings For Email Account** check box, and click **Next**.

3. Select the type of mail server used by your ISP (commonly POP3), enter the name of your ISP's incoming mail server (such as mail.anisp.com), whether this server requires a secure connection (most don't, but your ISP will tell you if it does and how to handle it). Unless your ISP tells you otherwise, leave the default port number and logon authentication.

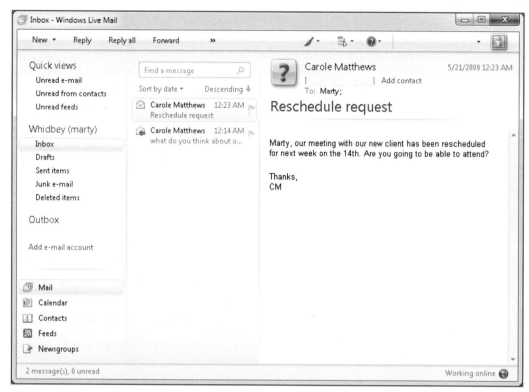

Figure 4-15: Windows Live Mail provides access to email, a calendar, contacts, feeds, and newsgroups.

4. Enter your logon ID or user name, the name of your ISP's outgoing server (often the same as the incoming server), leave the default port number, and select the check box if your ISP tells you the server requires a secure connection or authentication.

5. When you have completed these steps, click **Next** and then click **Finish**. Windows Live Mail will open. Figure 4-15 shows it after receiving two email messages.

Use the next two sections, "Create and Send Email" and "Receive Email," to test your setup.

Create and Send Email

To create and send an email message:

1. Open Windows Live Mail, and click **New** on the toolbar. The New Message window will open, similar to the one in Figure 4-16.

2. Start to enter a name in the To text box. If the name is in your Contacts list (see the "Using the Contacts List" QuickSteps in this chapter), it will be automatically completed and you can press **ENTER** to accept that name. If the name is not automatically completed, finish typing a full email address (such as billg@microsoft.com).

3. If you want more than one addressee, place a semicolon (;) and a space after the first address, and then type a second one as in step 2.

4. If you want to differentiate the addressees to whom the message is principally being sent from those for whom it is just information, click **Show Cc & Bcc**, press **TAB**, and put the second or subsequent addressees in the Cc text box as you did in the To text box.

5. If you want to send the message to a recipient and not have other recipients see to whom it is sent, click **Show Cc & Bcc**, click in the Bcc text box, and type the address to be hidden. (Bcc stands for "blind carbon copy.")

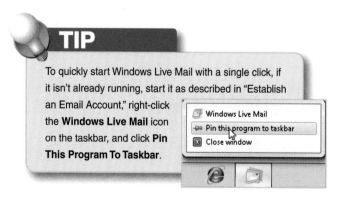

TIP

To quickly start Windows Live Mail with a single click, if it isn't already running, start it as described in "Establish an Email Account," right-click the **Windows Live Mail** icon on the taskbar, and click **Pin This Program To Taskbar**.

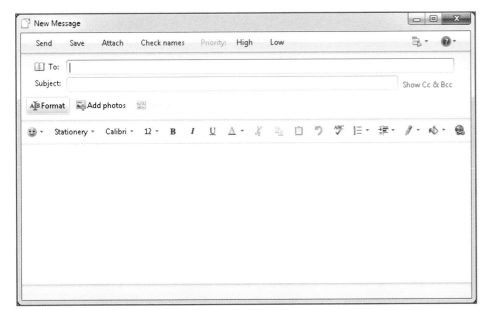

Figure 4-16: Sending email messages is an easy and fast way to communicate.

6. Press **TAB**, type a subject for the message, press **TAB** again, and type your message.

7. When you have completed your message, click **Send** on the toolbar. For a brief moment, you may see a message in your outbox and then, if you look, you will see the message in your Sent Items folder. If you are done, close Windows Live Mail.

Receive Email

Depending on how Windows Live Mail is set up, it may automatically receive any email you have when you are connected to your ISP. If not, or if you need to dial in to your ISP, click **Sync** on the right of the toolbar to synchronize Windows Live Mail with your ISP, in essence sending any mail in your outbox and receiving any mail addressed to you into your inbox. To open and read your mail:

1. Open **Windows Live Mail**, and click **Inbox** in the Folders list to open your inbox, which contains all of the messages you have received and haven't deleted or organized in folders.

2. Click a message in the inbox to read it in the Preview pane on the right of the window, as shown in Figure 4-15, or double-click a message to open the message in its own window, as shown in Figure 4-17.

3. Delete a message in either the inbox or its own window by clicking the relevant button on the toolbar. Close Windows Live Mail if you are finished with it.

Respond to Email

You can respond to messages you receive in three ways. First, click the message in your inbox, and then:

Click **Reply** to return a message to just the person who sent the original message.

–Or–

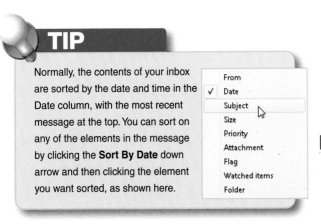

TIP

Normally, the contents of your inbox are sorted by the date and time in the Date column, with the most recent message at the top. You can sort on any of the elements in the message by clicking the **Sort By Date** down arrow and then clicking the element you want sorted, as shown here.

USING THE CONTACTS LIST

The Contacts list, shown in Figure 4-18, allows you to collect email addresses and other information about the people with whom you correspond or otherwise interact.

OPEN THE CONTACTS LIST

To open the Contacts list:

Click **Contacts** in the lower-left corner of Windows Live Mail. [Contacts]

ADD A NEW CONTACT

To add a new contact to the Contacts list:

1. With Windows Live Contacts open, click **New** on the toolbar. The Add A Contact window opens.

2. Enter as much of the information as you have or want. For email, you need a name and an email address, as shown in the Quick Add category. If you have additional information, such as a nickname, several email addresses, several phone numbers, or a home address for the contact, click the other categories on the left and fill in the desired information.

3. When you are done, click **Add Contact** to close the Add A Contact window.

Continued . . .

TIP

When you have several email addresses in a single contact's record, they are all displayed when you go to enter the contact in an email message so you can select the address you want.

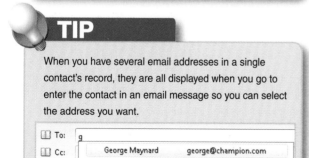

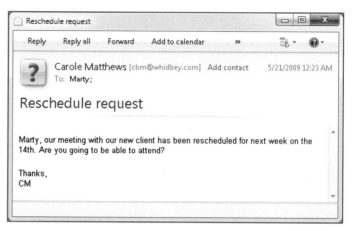

Figure 4-17: Work with a message you have received in the inbox or in its own window.

Figure 4-18: The Contacts list provides a place to store information about the people with whom you correspond.

USING THE CONTACTS LIST *(Continued)*

ADD CONTACT CATEGORIES

You can group contacts by category and then send messages to everyone in the category. To categorize a group of contacts:

1. In Windows Live Contacts, click the **New** down arrow, and click **Category**. The Create A New Category dialog box appears.

2. Enter the category name, and click the names in your Contacts list that you want in the category. When you have selected all the names, click **Save**.

3. When you are done, click **Close** to close the Contacts list.

When you want to address a message to a category of people, start typing the category—it will be displayed with the contacts that are included in it. Click the category name to send the message to everyone in the category, or select an individual in the category to send the message to only that individual.

Click **Reply All** to return a message to all the people who were addressees (both To and Cc) in the original message.

–Or–

Click **Forward** to relay a message to people not shown as addressees on the original message. | Reply   Reply all   Forward |

In all three cases, a window similar to the New Message window opens and allows you to add or change addressees and the subject, and add a message.

Use Stationery

If you would like to add some character to your email messages, you can include a background image with them. You can do this individually for each message or for all your messages.

APPLY STATIONERY TO INDIVIDUAL MESSAGES

1. Open Windows Live Mail and click **New** on the toolbar.

2. In the New Message window, click **Stationery**, click **More Stationery** for stationery options, select one (as shown in Figure 4-19), and then click **OK**. The New Message window will open with your stationery displayed.

3. Address, enter, and send the message as you otherwise would, and then close Windows Live Mail.

APPLY STATIONERY TO ALL MESSAGES

1. Open Windows Live Mail, click the **Menus** icon 🔲 ▾ on the toolbar, and click **Options**.

2. Click the **Compose** tab, and, under Stationery, click **Mail**.

3. Click **Select**, select the stationery that you want to apply to all your email, click **OK** twice, and then close Windows Live Mail.

Apply Formatting

The simplest messages are sent in plain text without any formatting. These messages take the least bandwidth and are the easiest to receive. If you wish, you can send messages with formatting using Hypertext Markup Language (HTML), the language with which many Web sites have been created. You can do this for an individual message and for all messages.

TIP

If you see an email address in an email message that you want to add to your Contacts list, open the message in its own window and click **Add Contact**. This creates a new contact and opens its Add A Contact window so that you can make changes and add other information.

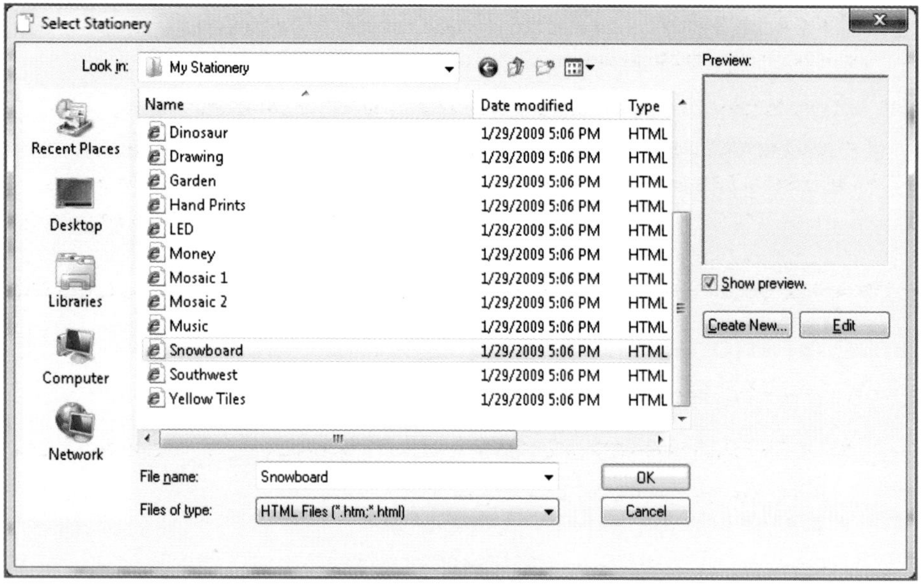

Figure 4-19: *In addition to the stationery that comes with Windows Live Mail, you can create your own by saving either a web page or a photograph in the My Documents\My Stationery folder.*

APPLY FORMATTING TO ALL MESSAGES

1. Open Windows Live Mail, click the **Menus** icon, and click **Options**.

2. Click the **Send** tab. Under Mail Sending Format, click **HTML**.

3. Click **OK**, and then close Windows Live Mail.

SELECT A FONT AND A COLOR FOR ALL MESSAGES

To use a particular font and font color on all of your email messages (you must send your mail using HTML in place of plain text—see "Apply Formatting to All Messages"):

1. Open Windows Live Mail, click the **Menus** icon, and click **Options**.

2. Click the **Compose** tab. Under Compose Font, click **Font Settings** opposite Mail.

3. Select the font, style, size, effects, and color that you want to use (see Figure 4-20) with all your email, click **OK** twice, and then close Windows Live Mail.

CAUTION

Not all email programs can properly receive HTML messages, which results in messages that are not very readable. However, most programs released in the last 10 years can handle HTML.

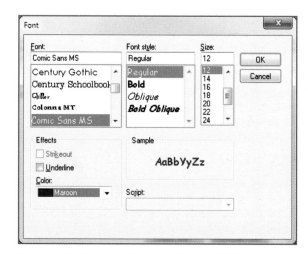

Figure 4-20: *If you send your mail using HTML instead of plain text, you can apply fonts and color and do many other things not available with plain text.*

NOTE

If you have several email accounts, you can click **Advanced** in the Signatures tab of the Options dialog box and select the account(s) with which to use a selected signature.

QUICKSTEPS

USING WEB MAIL

Web mail is the sending and receiving of email over the Internet using a browser, such as Internet Explorer, instead of an email program, such as Windows Live Mail. There are a number of Web mail programs, such as Windows Live Hotmail (www.hotmail.com), Yahoo! Mail (http://mail .yahoo.com), and Google's Gmail (http://mail.google.com). So long as you have access to the Internet, you can sign up for one or more of these services. The basic features (simple sending and receiving of email) are often free. For example, to sign up for Windows Live Hotmail:

1. Open Internet Explorer. In the address bar, type www.hotmail.com, and press **ENTER**.

2. If you already have a Windows Live account, enter your ID and password, and click **Sign In**. Otherwise, under Windows Live Hotmail, click **Sign Up**, fill in the requested information, and click **I Accept The Terms Of Use**.

3. When you are done, the Windows Live Hotmail page will open and display your mail, as shown in Figure 4-22.

4. Click the envelope icon to open and read a message.

5. Click **New** on the toolbar to write an email message. Enter the address, a subject, and the message. When you are done, click **Send**.

6. When you are finished with Hotmail, close Internet Explorer.

ATTACH A SIGNATURE

To attach a signature (a closing) on all of your email messages:

1. Open Windows Live Mail, click the **Menus** icon, and click **Options**.

2. Click the **Signatures** tab, and click **New**. Under Edit Signature, enter the closing text you want to use, or click **File** and enter or browse to the path and filename you want for the closing. The file could be a graphic image, such as a scan of your written signature, if you wished.

3. Click **Add Signatures To All Outgoing Messages**, as shown in Figure 4-21, and click **OK**. Then close Windows Live Mail.

Attach Files to Email

You can attach and send files, such as documents or images, with email messages.

1. Open Windows Live Mail, and click **New** on the toolbar.

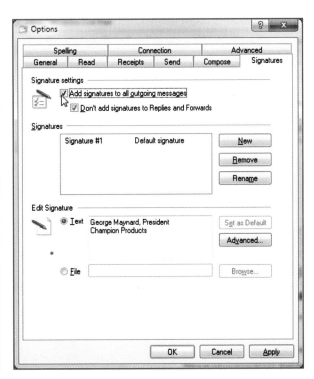

Figure 4-21: A "signature" in Windows Live Mail is really a closing.

TIP

A way to quickly open Windows Live Hotmail, if you still have the Windows Live toolbar in Internet Explorer, is to click **Mail** in this toolbar. Otherwise, with Hotmail already open in Internet Explorer, click the **Add To Favorites Bar** icon above the tab row. Windows Live Hotmail will appear in the Favorites bar. In the future, click it once to open Windows Live Hotmail.

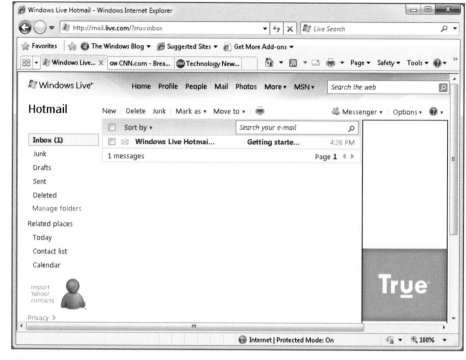

Figure 4-22: Web mail accounts are a quick and free way to get one or more email accounts.

TIP

With a New Message window open, you can drag a file from Windows Explorer or the desktop to the message, and it will automatically be attached and sent with the message.

2. Click **Attach** on the toolbar. Select the folder and file you want to send, and click **Open**. The attachment will be shown below the subject.

3. Address, enter, and send the message as you normally would, and then close Windows Live Mail.

Use Calendar

Windows Live Mail includes a calendar capability to keep track of scheduled events. To open the Calendar:

Click **Calendar** in the lower-left corner of Windows Live Mail. Calendar will open, as shown in Figure 4-23. 📅 Calendar

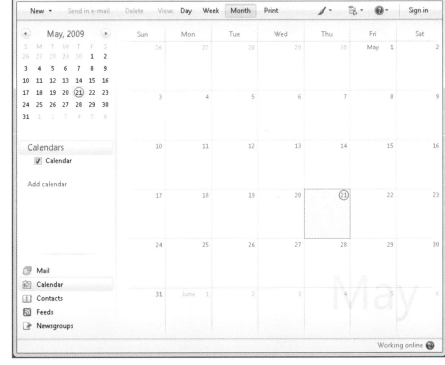

Figure 4-23: *The Windows Live Mail calendar looks similar to the Microsoft Office Outlook calendar.*

DIRECTLY ADD EVENTS TO A CALENDAR

To add an event to a calendar date:

1. With the calendar open, right-click a date on the calendar, and click **New Event**. The New Event window will open.

2. Enter the subject, location, dates and times, and a message, as shown in Figure 4-24.

3. If you have multiple calendars, click the **Calendar** down arrow, and select the calendar you want to use. Also, select how you want the calendar to reflect your time during the event.

4. If the event will happen on a repeated basis, click the **No Recurrence** down arrow, and click the period for this event.

5. When you have completed the event, click either **Save & Close** to store the event on your calendar or **Send In Email** to send this to others for their schedules.

6. If you selected Send In Email, an email message will open. Make any desired changes, and click **Send**.

ADD AN EMAIL MESSAGE TO A CALENDAR

When you receive an email message with scheduling ramifications, you can directly add its information to your calendar.

1. In Windows Live Mail, click the message that has calendar information. You can click **Add To Calendar** from the mail window, or double-click the message to open it and click **Add To Calendar** from the message window. In both cases, an event window will open.

2. Unfortunately, the subject and the body are the only fields that are filled in for you. You must fill in the location, dates and times, and whether it is recurring.

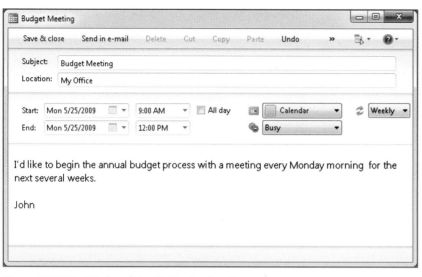

Figure 4-24: *The Windows Live Mail calendar allows you to send scheduled events to others to put on their calendars.*

3. After filling in the pertinent information, click **Save & Close**. The event will appear on your calendar.

4. Click **Close** to close the Windows Live Mail Calendar window when you are ready.

Participate in Newsgroups

Newsgroups are organized chains of messages on a particular subject. Newsgroups allow people to enter new messages and respond to previous ones. To participate in one or more newsgroups, you need to set up a newsgroup account, then locate and open a particular newsgroup, and finally send and receive messages within the newsgroup.

SET UP A NEWSGROUP ACCOUNT

Setting up a new account for a newsgroup is similar to setting up the account for your email. To set up a newsgroup account, you need the name of the news server and, possibly, an account name and password.

1. Open Windows Live Mail, and click **Newsgroups**. Click **Yes** when asked if you want to set Windows Live Mail as your news client.

2. Click **View Newsgroups**. A list of Microsoft public newsgroups will appear. If you wish to just view a newsgroup, select that newsgroup and click **Go To**. If you wish to view a newsgroup over a period of time, click **Subscribe**. Click **OK**.

3. To participate in newsgroups outside of Microsoft, click **Add Newsgroup Account**. Enter the name you want displayed, and click **Next**. Enter your email address if not already displayed, and click **Next**.

NOTE

To unsubscribe to a newsgroup, right-click the newsgroup name in the list of groups on the left of the newsgroup window, and click **Unsubscribe**. Click **OK** to confirm.

4. Enter the name of your news server. Your ISP or sponsoring organization will give you this. If you do not need to enter an account name and password, your ISP or sponsoring organization also will tell you this, and you can skip to step 6.

5. To enter an account name and password, click **My News Server Requires Me To Log On**, and click **Next**. Enter your account name and password, and click **Remember Password** (if desired).

6. Click **Next**, click **Finish**, and click **OK** to show available newsgroups and turn on communities. Newsgroups will be downloaded from your news server. This could take several minutes. A new account will appear in the Newsgroup Subscriptions window and a list of newsgroups will be displayed, as shown in Figure 4-25.

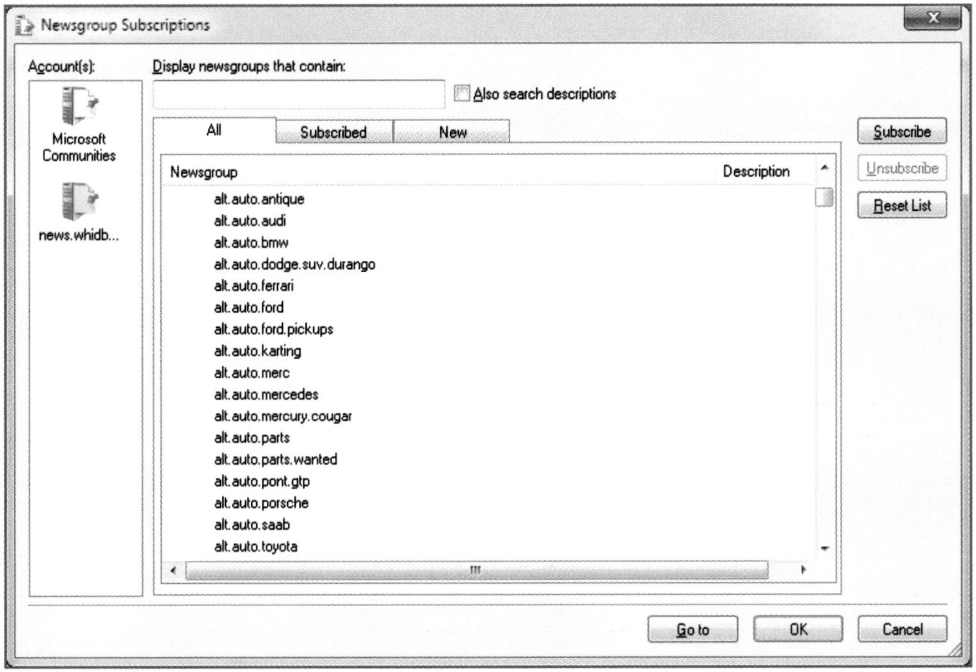

SUBSCRIBE TO A NEWSGROUP

Most general-purpose news servers, such as those maintained by ISPs, have a great many newsgroups, probably only some of which might interest you. To subscribe to a newsgroup (meaning to read and reply to messages they contain on a recurring basis):

1. If you have just come from setting up a newsgroup account, skip to step 2. Otherwise, open Windows Live Mail and click **Newsgroups**.

2. Click the news server you want to use in the left column, and click **View Newsgroups**.

3. To search for a particular newsgroup, type a keyword (such as Computers) in the Display Newsgroups That Contain text box, and press **ENTER** (newsgroups start popping up as you type your search keywords and you may not need to press **ENTER**).

4. Double-click the newsgroups to which you want to subscribe. An icon appears to the left of each newsgroup you double-click. After you have selected the newsgroups, click **OK**. You are returned to Windows Live Mail Newsgroups.

Figure 4-25: A list of newsgroups to which you can subscribe.

READ AND POST MESSAGES IN A NEWSGROUP

For newsgroups to which you have subscribed, you can read and send messages like email messages, but with two differences. You can choose to reply to the newsgroup or to the individual, and a new message is called a write message. If someone replies to this message, it gets added to the end of the original message, thereby creating a chain, or *thread*, of messages on a given subject.

1. Open Windows Live Mail, open your news server, and click a newsgroup you want to open. A list of messages will be displayed.

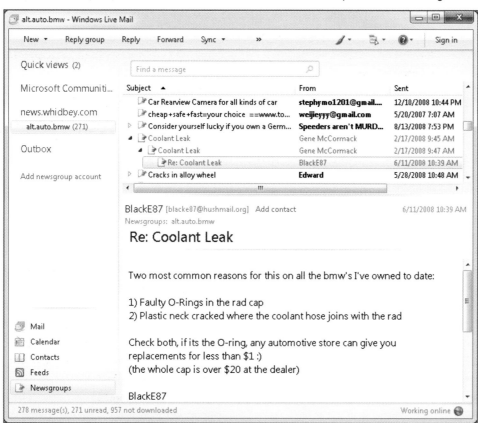

2. Click the triangular icon on the left of a message (this identifies that there are replies) to open the related messages.

3. Click a message to display it in the bottom pane, as shown in Figure 4-26. Or, double-click the message to have it displayed in its own window.

4. To initiate a newsgroup thread or respond to a newsgroup thread:

   Click **New** on the toolbar to create a public message that will begin a new thread.

   –Or–

   Click **Reply Group** on the toolbar to create a public message in the thread you have selected.

   –Or–

   Click **Reply** on the toolbar to create a private message to the person who wrote the message you have selected.

   –Or–

   Click **Forward** on the toolbar to send a copy of the message you have selected to one or more individuals.

Figure 4-26: A newsgroup provides a thread on a given topic to which you can add your comments.

5. Create and send the message as you would any email message. When you are done, close Windows Live Mail.

Use Windows Live Messenger

Windows Live Messenger allows you to instantly send and receive messages (or *chat*) with others who are online at the same time as you. (It is frequently called "instant messaging" or IM.)

Set Up Windows Live Messenger

When you installed Windows Live Essentials to get Windows Live Mail, you probably also installed Windows Live Messenger; it is selected by default. If so, its icon 👤 may be on the taskbar or at least it is in the Start menu. If you didn't install it and want to now, return to the "Get Windows Mail" section and follow the instructions there.

The use of Windows Live Messenger requires that you first have a Microsoft Live account or an MSN or Hotmail account, which you may have done earlier in this chapter in the "Using Web Mail" QuickSteps. Once you have an account, you are able to set up your contacts and personalize Messenger to your tastes.

ESTABLISH A WINDOWS LIVE ACCOUNT

With Windows Live Messenger installed, open it and establish a Windows Live account.

1. Click **Start**, click **All Programs**, click **Windows Live**, and click **Windows Live Messenger**. The Windows Live Messenger window will open, as you can see here.

2. If you already have a Windows Live account, enter your email address and password, and click **Sign In**. Go to the next section, "Add Contacts to Messenger."

3. If you don't have a Windows Live account, click **Sign Up**. Internet Explorer will open and the Windows Live registration will appear. Enter the information requested, click **I Accept**, and when you are told you have successfully registered your email address, close your browser. You will be returned to Windows Live Messenger.

4. Enter your email address and your password, and then click **Sign In**.

ADD CONTACTS TO MESSENGER

To use Windows Live Messenger, you must enter contacts for people you want to "talk" to.

1. If Windows Live Messenger is not already open, click its icon in the taskbar. If the icon isn't there, click **Start**, click **All Programs**, click **Windows Live**, and click **Windows Live Messenger**.

2. Click the **Add A Contact Or Group** icon 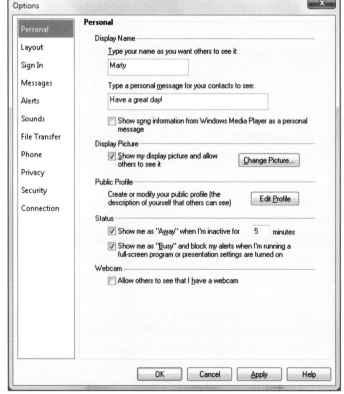 in the Windows Live Messenger window, and then click **Add A Contact**. If you know your contact's IM address, click in the **Instant Messaging Address** text box, and enter the address; if text messaging, enter a country and the cell phone number, select a category, and click **Next**. Enter a brief message, and click **Send Invitation**. Depending on the person's status—whether they are online and whether they accept your invitation—you will get a response accordingly.

3. If you want, click **Search Contacts**, enter the person's name as best you can, and press **ENTER**. If more than one person fits your criteria, click **Add** for the one you want, or click the name for more information; if you then want to add them, click **Add** and their name. You can also send the person an email message by clicking **Send Message**, entering a subject and your message, and clicking **Send**.

4. When you are done adding contacts, close Internet Explorer. If want to exit Windows Live Messenger, click **Close**.

PERSONALIZE MESSENGER

There are a number of ways to personalize Windows Live Messenger.

1. Open **Windows Live Messenger**, click the **Show Menu** icon, click **Tools**, and click **Options**.

2. Click the **Personal** tab (see Figure 4-27), enter the name you want to use, click **Change Picture**, select or browse for the picture you want, and click **OK**.

3. Click the **Privacy** tab, and place your contacts on either the Allow or Block list. To move a contact from one column to the other, select that contact and click **Allow** or **Block**.

4. Click the other tabs, and set the options that are best for you.

5. When you have personalized Windows Live Messenger the way you want, click **OK**. If you want to exit Windows Live Messenger, click **Close**.

Figure 4-27: Setting Windows Live Messenger options.

QUICKSTEPS

USING WINDOWS LIVE MESSENGER

Using Windows Live Messenger is simple: double-click a contact. If they are online, the Conversation window will open, as shown in Figure 4-28. If they are not online, you will be told the contact will be given the message the next time they are online.

SEND A MESSAGE

With the Conversation window open (done by double-clicking a contact), send a message by typing it in the bottom pane and pressing **ENTER**. You can add emoticons (smiley faces), change the font, and/or change the message background with the icons below the text box.

RECEIVE A MESSAGE

With a conversation in process, a received message appears in the Conversation window, as you can see in Figure 4-28. If someone sends you an instant message without a Conversation window open, you will get a little pop-up message from your notification area. Double-click this message to open a Conversation window with the sender.

TIP

If you want to stop receiving comments permanently from another person (for example, if that person's remarks are getting offensive) click **Block**, which only appears in the menu bar during an active conversation.

Figure 4-28: When a conversation is in process, you can see who said what in the Conversation window.

Chapter 5
Managing Windows 7

Running programs is one of Windows 7's major functions. The managing of Windows 7, the subject of this chapter, entails setting up the starting and stopping of programs in a number of different ways. Management also includes the maintenance and enhancement of Windows 7 and the setting up of Remote Assistance so that you can have someone help you without that person actually being in front of your computer.

Start and Stop Programs

Previous chapters discussed starting programs from the Start menu, through All Programs, through a shortcut on the desktop, and by locating the program with Windows Explorer. All of these methods require a direct action by you. Windows also provides several ways to automatically start programs and to monitor and manage them while they are running.

Automatically Start Programs

Sometimes, you will want to start a program automatically and have it run in the background every time you start the computer. For example, you might automatically run an antivirus program or a screen-capture program (such as SnagIt, which was used to capture the figures and illustrations you see here). To automatically start a program, open a folder, or open a file in a program:

1. Click **Start**, click **All Programs**, right-click **Startup**, and click **Open All Users**. The Startup folder will open.

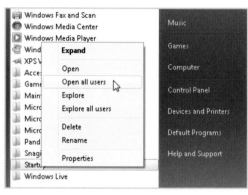

2. Click **Start** and click **Computer** to open Windows Explorer. Position the Explorer window so that you can see both it and the Startup window on the desktop at the same time (right-click the taskbar and click **Show Windows Side By Side** to arrange both windows).

3. In Explorer, open the drive and folders needed to display the program file you want to automatically start, or the folder or disk drive you want to automatically open, or the file you want to automatically start in its program.

4. Hold the right mouse button while dragging (right-drag) the program file, the folder, or the file to the open Startup folder, as you can see in Figure 5-1. When you reach the Startup folder, click **Create Link In Startup**.

5. Close the Startup folder and Windows Explorer. The next time you start your computer, the action you want will take place.

Figure 5-1: Programs in the Startup folder are automatically started when you start Windows 7.

NOTE

Some programs automatically start when Windows 7 is started without being in the Startup folder. You can see these programs and manage them using MSConfig, discussed later in this chapter.

Start Programs Minimized

Sometimes, when you start programs automatically, you want them to run in the background—in other words, minimized. To do that:

1. Click **Start**, click **All Programs**, right-click **Startup**, and click **Open All Users** to open the Startup folder.

2. Right-click the program you want minimized, and click **Properties**. Click the **Shortcut** tab.

3. Click the **Run** down arrow, and click **Minimized**, as shown in Figure 5-2.

4. Click **OK** to close the Properties dialog box, and then close the Startup folder.

Schedule Programs

You can schedule a program to run automatically using Windows 7's Task Scheduler, although you may need to specify how the program is to run using command-line parameters or arguments. See how to use Help in step 2 of "Start Older Programs" later in this chapter to learn what parameters are available for the program you want to run.

1. Click **Start**, click **All Programs**, click **Accessories**, click **System Tools**, and click **Task Scheduler**. The Task Scheduler window will open, as you can see in Figure 5-3.

2. Click **Create Basic Task** in the Actions pane or in the Action menu. The Create A Basic Task Wizard opens. Type a name and description, and click **Next**. Select what you want to use as a trigger, and again click **Next**.

3. Depending on what you choose for the trigger, you may have to select the start date and time and enter additional information, such as the day of the week for a weekly trigger. Click **Next**.

4. Choose whether you want to start a program, send an email, or display a message, and click **Next**.

5. If you want to start a program, select it either from the list of programs or by browsing to it, add any arguments that are to be passed to the program when it starts, and indicate if you would like the program to be looking at a particular folder when it starts (Start In).

–Or–

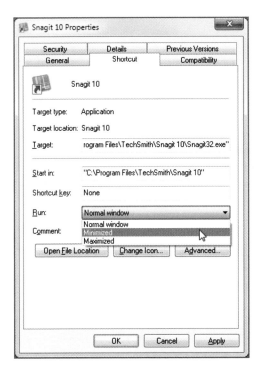

*Figure 5-2: **Minimizing a program, when it has automatically started, lets it run in the background.***

NOTE

Many programs, such as backup and antivirus programs, use their own scheduler to run automatically on a scheduled basis.

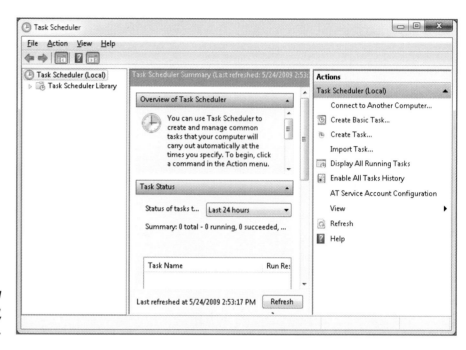

Figure 5-3: The Task Scheduler is used by Windows 7 for many of its tasks, but you can also use it to repeatedly perform a task you want.

NOTE

The Create Task dialog box, basically identical to the Task Scheduler Properties dialog box, can be used to set up a scheduled task instead of using the Task Scheduler Wizard. Click **Create Task** instead of clicking **Create Basic Task**.

If you want to send an email, type the From and To email addresses, the subject, and text; browse to and select an attachment; and type your SMTP email server (this your outgoing mail server that you entered when you set up Windows Mail—see Chapter 4).

–Or–

If you want to display a message, type a title and the message you want it to contain.

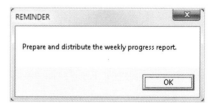

6. Click **Next**. The Summary dialog box will appear, as shown in Figure 5-4. Click **Open The Properties Dialog For This Task When I Click Finish**, and click **Finish**. The Task Properties dialog box will appear.

TIP

Right-click a task in the center pane of the Task Scheduler to work with it. Click **Properties** to edit the task's settings.

Run
End
Disable
Export...
Properties
Delete

QUICKSTEPS

SWITCHING PROGRAMS

You can switch programs that are running on the desktop, on the taskbar, and on the task list. You can also switch them using the Task Manager (see "Control Programs with the Task Manager" later in this chapter).

SWITCH PROGRAMS ON THE DESKTOP

If you have several programs running and arranged so that you can see all of them, switch from one to another by clicking the program you want to be active. However, if you have more than two or three programs running, it may be hard to see them on the desktop and, therefore, to select the one you want.

SWITCH PROGRAMS ON THE TASKBAR

If you have up to five or six programs running, you should be able to see their tasks on the taskbar. Clicking the task will switch to that program.

If you have multiple instances of a single program open, they will, by default, be grouped in a single icon. For example, in the illustration shown here, the taskbar icon indicates that there are multiple instances open for Internet Explorer, Microsoft Word, and Microsoft Excel.

Continued . . .

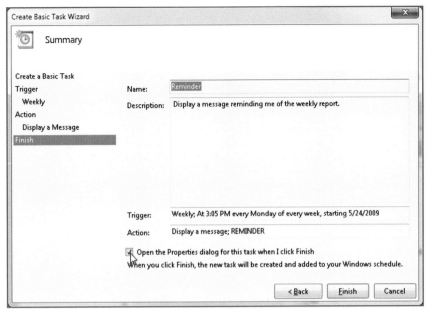

Figure 5-4: *The Task Scheduler can be used to send email messages and display a message on your screen, as well as to start a program.*

7. Look at each of the tabs, review the information you have entered, and determine if you need to change anything.

8. When you are done reviewing the scheduled task, click **OK**. Click **Task Scheduler Library** in the left pane (called the console tree). You should see your scheduled task in the middle pane. Close the Task Scheduler window.

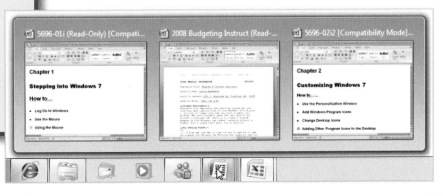

QUICKSTEPS

SWITCHING PROGRAMS (Continued)

To select a particular instance of a program when there are multiple instances running, mouse over the icon on the taskbar to open thumbnails of the several instances, then mouse over the one you want to see enlarged. Finally, when you are ready to fully open one particular instance, click the thumbnail for that instance, as you can see in Figure 5-5.

SWITCH PROGRAMS ON THE TASK LIST

The oldest method of switching programs, which predates Windows 95 and the taskbar, is using the task list.

1. Press **ALT+TAB** and hold down **ALT**. The task list will appear.

2. While continuing to hold down **ALT**, press **TAB** repeatedly until the highlight moves to the program and instance you want or the desktop on the right. Then release **ALT** or click an icon to select the program you want.

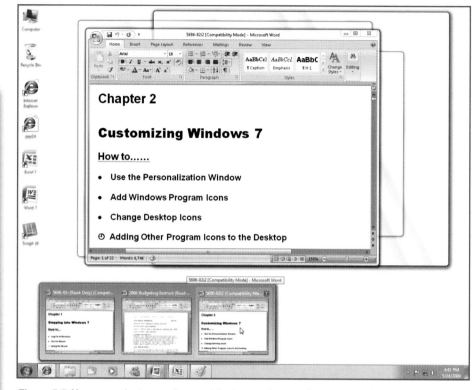

Figure 5-5: *You can select one of several instance of a running program by mousing over the taskbar icon and the thumbnails, and then clicking the thumbnail you want.*

Control Programs with the Task Manager

The Windows Task Manager, shown in Figure 5-6, performs a number of functions, but most importantly, it allows you to see what programs and processes (individual threads of a program) are running and to unequivocally stop both. A display of real-time

QUICKSTEPS

STOPPING PROGRAMS

You may choose to stop a program simply because you are done using it or in an attempt to keep a program from harming your data or other programs.

USE THE CLOSE BUTTON

One of the most common ways to close a program is to click the **Close** button on the upper-right corner of all windows.

USE THE EXIT COMMAND

Almost all programs have an Exit command in a menu on the far left of the menu bar; often, this is the File menu (in Microsoft Office 2007, the Office Button is the "menu" and the exit command is located in the lower-right corner). Open this menu and click **Exit**.

CLOSE FROM THE TASKBAR

There are two ways to close a program from the taskbar.

Mouse over the icon, move the mouse to the red X in the upper-right corner of the thumbnail, and click.

–Or–

Right-click a task on the taskbar, and click **Close Window**.

Recent
- Expenses
- 2010 Budget Summary
- 2010 Manufacturing Plan
- 2010 Manufacturing Plan
- 2010 Budget Projection
- 2010 Budget Summary
- Yellowstone Expenses

- Excel 7
- Pin this program to taskbar
- Close window

CLOSE FROM THE KEYBOARD

With the program you want to close open and selected, press **ALT+F4**.

If none of these options work, see "Control Programs with the Task Manager."

Figure 5-6: *The Task Manager shows you what programs are running and allows you to stop them.*

graphs and tables also shows you what is happening at any second on your computer, as you can see in Figure 5-7. To work with the Task Manager:

1. Press **CTRL+ALT+DELETE** and click **Start Task Manager**. Alternately, you can right-click a blank area of the taskbar, and click **Start Task Manager**.

2. Click the **Applications** tab. You'll see a list of the programs you are running, as shown in Figure 5-6.

3. Click a program in the list. Click **End Task** to stop the program, or click **Switch To** to activate that program.

4. Click **New Task** to open the Run command, where you can enter a program you want to start. See "Start a Program in Run," next.

5. Click the **Processes** tab. Here you see a list of all the processes that are currently running and their CPU (percentage) and memory (KB) usage. Most of these processes are components of Windows 7.

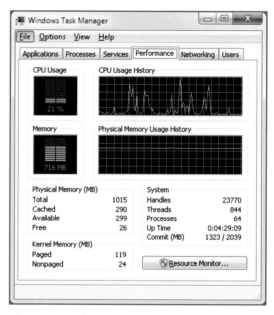

Figure 5-7: *Under most circumstances, on a personal computer, only a small fraction of the computer's resources are being used.*

6. Click the **Services** tab. This is a list of the Windows 7 services that are active and their status. There is nothing that you can do here except observe it.

7. Click the **Performance** tab. This tab graphically shows the CPU and memory usage (see Figure 5-7), while the Networking tab shows the computer's use of the network. The Users tab shows the users that are logged on to the computer. You can disconnect them if they are coming in over the network or log them off if they are directly logged on.

8. When you are done, close the Windows Task Manager.

Start a Program in Run

The Start menu has an option called "Run" that opens the Run dialog box. This is the same dialog box that is opened by clicking New Task in the Task Manager (see "Control Programs with the Task Manager" earlier in

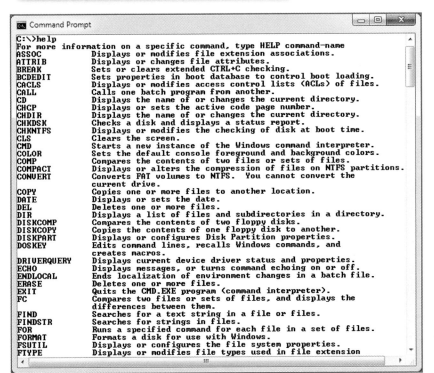

this chapter). From this dialog box, you can start most programs if you know the path to the program, its name, and don't mind typing all that information.

1. Click **Start**, click **All Programs**, click **Accessories**, and click **Run**.

   –Or–

   Click **Start**, type <u>run</u> in the Search Programs And Files box, and press **ENTER**.

2. In either case, the Run dialog box will appear. Type the path and filename of the program you want to run, and press **ENTER**.

Start Older Programs

While you can start most programs from the desktop or Start menu, older, less sophisticated programs require that they be run in their own isolated window named Command Prompt (also called a DOS, or Disk Operating System, window). Here, you can type DOS commands at the flashing underscore, which is called the *command prompt*.

1. Click **Start**, click **All Programs**, click **Accessories**, and click **Command Prompt**. The Command Prompt window will open.

2. Type <u>help</u> and press **ENTER**. A list of commands that can be used at the command prompt will be displayed, as shown in Figure 5-8 (the colors of the background and text have been switched for printing purposes).

3. To run a program in the Games folder on the C: drive (if you have one—it is not there by default), type <u>cd c:\games</u> (change directory to c:\games), press **ENTER**, type <u>dir /p</u> (to display the contents of the directory), press **ENTER** to see the name of the program, type the name of the program, and press **ENTER**. The program should run, although not all programs will run in Windows 7.

4. When you are done with the Command Prompt window, type <u>exit</u> and press **ENTER**.

Figure 5-8: At the command prompt, you can type DOS commands, which Windows 7 will carry out.

If you open the Command Prompt window, you will
see white text on a black background. For Figure 5-8,
the text and background colors have been reversed by
clicking the control menu in the upper-left corner, clicking
Properties, clicking the **Colors** tab, and selecting black in
the Screen Text field and white in the Screen Background
field. Click **OK** to close the Properties dialog box.

Unless you are trying to diagnose a problem and have
some experience doing this, you normally do not want to
change the settings in the System Configuration Utility
dialog box. However, you can safely stop obvious known
Windows-related programs without harm.

(handwritten note)

① copy chart B-6 answer questions.

② chart B-8 and study it

③ copy chart B-9 to own event

④ study chart B-2

⑤ Practice chart B-6 ✳
    answer all questions.

⑥ after master B-6 Practice chart B-8

Primary Basic Strategy

Control Automatic Programs

Sometimes, when you install a program, it sets up itself or other programs
to run in perpetuity, even if that is not what you had in mind. Many of these
programs are not started from the Startup folder. To control these programs and
prevent them from running, Windows 7 has a program named MSConfig, and
the easiest way to start it is from the Run dialog box.

1. Click **Start**, click **All Programs**, click **Accessories**, and click **Run**.

   –Or–

   Click **Start**, type <u>run</u> in the Search Programs And Files box, and press **ENTER**.

2. Type <u>msconfig</u> and press **ENTER**. The System Configuration Utility dialog box appears.

3. Click the **Startup** tab. You will see a list of all the programs that start when Windows 7
   starts, as shown in Figure 5-9.

4. Clear the check box to deselect a program so that it is not started the next time
   Windows 7 starts. When you are done, click **OK** to close the System Configuration
   Utility dialog box. A System Configuration message box will appear. Click **Restart** to
   restart your computer and reflect the changes you have made.

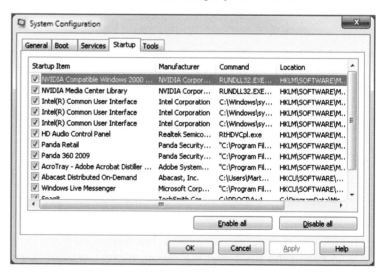

*Figure 5-9: In the System Configuration Utility (MSConfig) dialog box, you
can see and stop from running all of the programs that Windows 7 starts
automatically.*

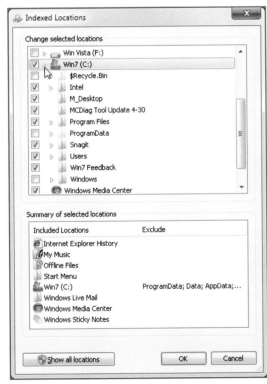

NOTE

Unlike earlier versions of Windows, in Windows 7, you cannot turn off indexing—it is an integral part of the search facility. Windows Indexing has become quite efficient and seldom affects the performance of the computer. Also, you shouldn't index your full C: drive, as it this includes program files that will slow down the search for your own data, music, and other personal files.

Control Windows Indexing

Windows 7 automatically indexes the files that are stored on a computer to substantially speed up your searches of files and folders.

1. Click **Start**, click **Control Panel**, select **Large Icons** view if it is not already selected, and click **Indexing Options** to open the Indexing Options dialog box.

2. If you want to change what is being indexed, click **Modify**, click the triangle icon to open the drives on your computer, and click the folders, as shown in Figure 5-10. Then click **OK**.

3. If you want to change the types of files being indexed, click **Advanced**. Choose if you want encrypted files indexed, or if you want similar words that have different marks (diacritics such as the accent, grave, and umlaut) that change the sound and meaning of the word indexed differently. Click the **File Types** tab, and select the types of files you want included. When you are done, click **OK**.

4. Close the Indexing Options dialog box.

Figure 5-10: Windows Indexing uses idle time to index your files and folders.

RUNNING ACCESSORY PROGRAMS

Windows 7 comes with a number of accessory programs. You can open these by clicking **Start**, clicking **All Programs**, and choosing **Accessories**. Many of these programs are discussed elsewhere in this book, but Calculator, Character Map, Notepad, and Paint will be briefly looked at here. You should also explore these on your own.

CALCULATOR

The Calculator, started from Accessories, has four alternative calculators, each with its own view:

- Standard desktop calculator
- Scientific calculator, shown in Figure 5-11
- Programmer calculator
- Statistics calculator

A unit converter, a date calculator, and four worksheets for calculating a mortgage, a vehicle lease, and fuel economy in both mpg and L/100 km are included that are extensions to the current view. To switch from one view to the other, click **View** and click the other view. To use a calculator, click the numbers on the screen or type them on the keyboard.

CHARACTER MAP

The Character Map, which is in System Tools, allows you to select special characters that are not available on a standard keyboard.

1. Click the **Font** down arrow, and click the font you want for the special character.

Continued . . .

Maintain Windows 7

Windows 7 maintenance consists of periodically updating fixes and new features, restoring Windows 7 when hardware or other software damages it, getting information about it, and installing new hardware and software.

Update Windows 7

Microsoft tries hard to encourage you to allow Windows 7 to update itself, from the point of installation, where you are asked to establish automatic updates, to periodically reminding you to do that. If you turn on Automatic Updates, on a regular basis, Windows will automatically determine if any updates are available, download the updates (which come from Microsoft) over the Internet, and install them. If Automatic Updates was not turned on during installation, you can do that at any time and control the updating process once it is turned on.

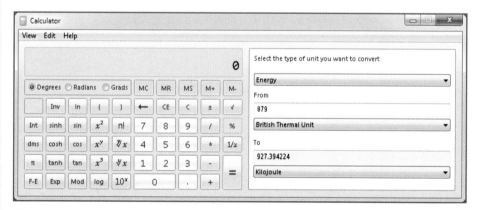

Figure 5-11: The Scientific view of the Calculator provides a number of advanced functions, including several extensions such as the unit converter shown here.

RUNNING ACCESSORY PROGRAMS

(Continued)

2. Scroll until you find it, and then double-click the character, or click the character and click **Select**, to copy it to the Clipboard.

3. In the program where you want the character, right-click an open area, and click **Paste** or press **CTRL+V**.

NOTEPAD

Notepad is a simple text editor you can use to view and create unformatted text (.txt) files. If you double-click a text file in Windows Explorer, Notepad will likely open and display the file. If a line of text is too long to display without scrolling, click **Format** and click **Word Wrap**. To create a file, simply start typing in the Notepad window, click the **File** menu, and click **Save**. Before printing a file, click **File**; click **Page Setup**; and select the paper orientation, margins, header, and footer.

PAINT

Paint lets you view, create, and edit bitmap image files in .bmp, .dib, .gif, .ico, .jpg, .png, and .tif formats. Several drawing tools and many colors are available to create simple drawings and illustrations (see Figure 5-12).

Figure 5-12: Paint allows you to make simple line drawings or touch up images.

TURN ON AUTOMATIC UPDATES

To turn on, off, and control Windows Update:

1. Click **Start** and click **Control Panel**. In Category view, click **System And Security**, and click **Windows Update**. In Large Icons view, click **Windows Update**.

2. Click **Change Settings**, determine the amount of automation you want, and click one of the following four choices after clicking the **Important Updates** down arrow (see Figure 5-13):

   • The first and recommended choice, which is the default, automatically determines if there are updates that are needed, downloads them, and then installs them on a frequency and at a time you specify.

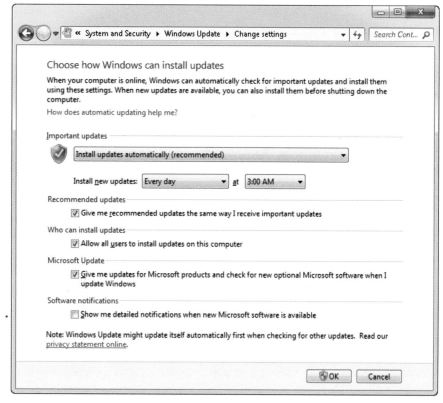

Choose how Windows can install updates

When your computer is online, Windows can automatically check for important updates and install them using these settings. When new updates are available, you can also install them before shutting down the computer.

How does automatic updating help me?

Important updates

✅ [Install updates automatically (recommended)]

Install new updates: [Every day ▼] at [3:00 AM ▼]

Recommended updates

☑ Give me recommended updates the same way I receive important updates

Who can install updates

☑ Allow all users to install updates on this computer

Microsoft Update

☑ Give me updates for Microsoft products and check for new optional Microsoft software when I update Windows

Software notifications

☐ Show me detailed notifications when new Microsoft software is available

Note: Windows Update might update itself automatically first when checking for other updates. Read our privacy statement online.

[OK] [Cancel]

Figure 5-13: *Automatic Updates determines which updates you need and can automatically download and install them.*

- The second choice automatically determines if there are updates that are needed and downloads them; it then asks you whether you want to install them.

- The third choice automatically determines if there are updates that are needed, asks you before downloading them, and asks you again before installing them.

- The fourth choice, which is not recommended, never checks for updates.

3. Choose whether to include recommended updates when you are otherwise online with Microsoft, whether all users can install the updates, and whether to use Microsoft Update Service to receive updates for other Microsoft products you have installed, like Microsoft Office.

4. Click **OK** when you are finished, and close Windows Update.

APPLY UPDATES

If you choose either the second or third option for handling updates, you will periodically see a notice that updates are ready to download and/or install.

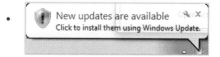

When you see the notice:

1. Click the notice. The Windows Updates dialog box will appear and show you the updates that are available.

2. Click the individual updates to see detailed information for the updates being proposed.

3. Select the check box for the updates you want to download and/or install, and then click **OK**.

4. After you have selected all the updates you want, click **Install Updates**. You will see a notice that the updates are being installed.

5. When the updates have been downloaded and installed, Windows Update will reopen, tell of this fact, and often ask to restart your computer.

6. Close any open programs, and click **Restart Now**.

Use the Action Center

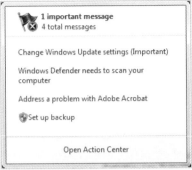

The Windows Action Center contains messages that have been sent to you from Windows and other programs that, at least from the viewpoint of the program, you need to respond to. When a message is sent to you by a program, a flag with a red X appears in the notification area.

Click the notification area Action Center flag to open the Action Center jump list. Click any option on the jump list to go directly to the window or dialog box, where you can view the message and possibly take corrective actions.

–Or–

1. Click **Open Action Center** to review recent messages and resolve problems, as you can see in Figure 5-14.

2. Click the relevant item to address the issue, and when you are ready, close the Action Center.

CHANGE ACTION CENTER SETTINGS

You can change how the Action Center informs you of an alert message.

1. From the Action Center, click **Change Action Center Settings**.

2. Select the security and maintenance messages you want to see. Open any of the related settings that seem pertinent, returning to the Action Center when you are ready.

3. When your Action Center settings are the way you want them, click **OK** and close the Action Center.

Restore Windows 7

System Restore keeps track of the changes you make to your system, including the software you install and the settings you make. If a hardware change, a software

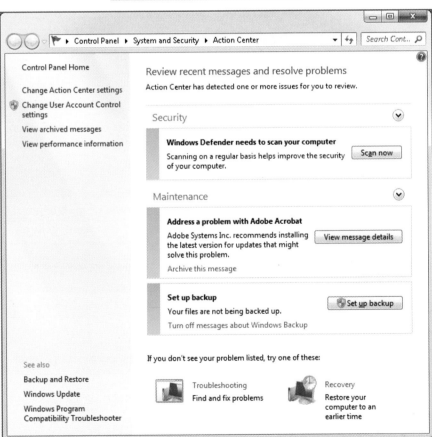

Figure 5-14: The Action Center consolidates and maintains alert messages that are sent to you by the programs you run.

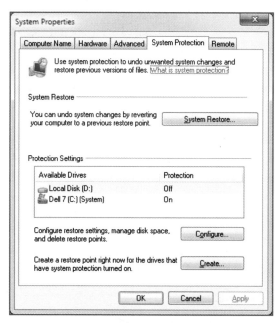

*Figure 5-15: **System Restore returns the system to a previous time when it was functioning normally.***

installation, or something else causes the system not to load or not to run properly, you can use System Restore to return the system to the way it was at the last restore point.

SET UP SYSTEM RESTORE

In a default installation of Windows 7, System Restore is automatically installed. If you have at least 300MB of free disk space after installing Windows 7, System Restore will be turned on and the first restore point will be set. If System Restore is not enabled, you can turn it on and set a restore point:

1. Click **Start** and click **Control Panel**. In Category view, click **System And Security**, click **System**, and click **System Protection** in the left pane. The System Properties dialog box will appear with the System Protection tab displayed, as you can see in Figure 5-15.

2. By default, the disk on which Windows 7 is installed should have system protection turned on, indicating that System Restore is automatically operating for that disk. Again by default, your other hard drives are not selected.

3. If any drive does not have protection on and you want it on, select the disk, click **Configure**, click **Restore System Settings And Previous Versions Of Files**, adjust the disk space usage as desired, and click **OK**.

4. When you have made the adjustments you want, click **OK**.

CREATE RESTORE POINTS

A *restore point* is an identifiable point in time when you know your system was working correctly. If your computer's settings are saved at that point, you can use those settings to restore your computer to that time. Normally, Windows 7 automatically creates restore points for the system drive on a periodic basis. But if you know at a given point in time that your computer is operating exactly the way you want it to, you can create a restore point.

1. Click **Start** and click **Control Panel**. In Category view, click **System And Security**, click **System**, and click **System Protection** in the left pane. The System Properties dialog box will appear with the System Protection tab displayed.

2. Click **Create** and type a name for the restore point. The date and time are automatically added, and you cannot change the name once you create it.

3. Click **Create** again. You will be told when the restore point is created. Click **OK** and click **Close** to close the System Properties dialog box.

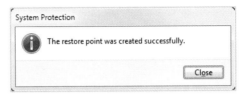

System Protection

The restore point was created successfully.

Close

RUN SYSTEM RESTORE FROM WINDOWS

If you can start and operate Windows 7 normally, try to execute the following steps. If you can't make it through these steps without Windows 7 crashing, go to the next section.

1. Click **Start** and click **Control Panel**. In Category view, click **System And Security**, click **System**, and click **System Protection** in the left pane. The System Properties dialog box will appear with the System Protection tab displayed.

TIP

You can restore from a system restore. Immediately before doing a system restore, a restore point is created and can be used to return to the point the system was at prior to performing this action. Simply re-run System Restore as described in either of the System Restore sections in this chapter, choose **Undo System Restore**, and follow the remaining instructions.

2. Click **System Restore**; a message explains the restore. Click **Next** to open the System Restore dialog box shown in Figure 5-16.

3. Select the restore point you want to use, and click **Scan For Affected Programs**. This will tell you if any programs have been updated or had a driver installed after the restore point. If you go ahead with the restore, these programs will be restored to their state before the update.

4. Click **Close** and click **Next**. You are asked to confirm the restore point the system will be returned to and given information about that point. If you do not want to restore to that point, click **Back** and return to step 3.

5. System Restore will need to restart your computer, so make sure all other programs are closed. When you are ready to restore to the described point, click **Finish**.

6. A confirmation dialog box appears, telling you that the restore process cannot be interrupted or undone until it has completed. Click **Yes** to continue. Some time will be spent saving files and settings for a new restore point, and then the computer will be restarted.

7. When the restore is completed, you will be told that it was successful. Click **Close**.

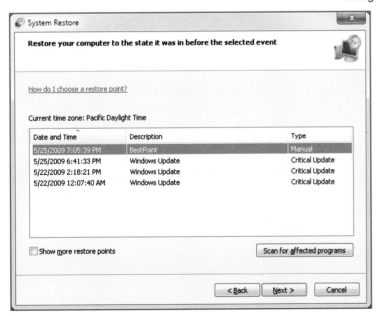

Figure 5-16: You can do a system restore at any of the restore points on the computer and return all of the Windows 7 settings and registry to that point in time.

You must log on as the administrator, with the appropriate password, in order to run System Repair.

You can also run System Restore by clicking **Start**, clicking **All Programs**, clicking **Accessories**, clicking **System Tools**, and clicking **System Restore**.

RUN SYSTEM RESTORE FROM SYSTEM RECOVERY

Windows 7 has a System Recovery mode that allows you to start Windows in a minimal way and fix many problems. You can start System Restore in this mode.

1. If your computer is turned on, turn it off (use Shut Down and make sure the power is off) and let it sit for at least two full minutes. This allows all of the components to fully discharge and will give you a clean restart.

2. After your computer has sat for at least two minutes without power, remove any disks in the floppy, CD, or DVD drives, or any flash or USB drives, and turn the computer on. As soon as the memory check is complete, hold down the **F8** key. After a moment, the Advanced Boot Options menu will appear.

3. If necessary, use the **UP ARROW** key to go to the top choice, **Repair Your Computer**, and then press **ENTER**. Windows 7 will begin loading.

4. Select the type of keyboard you want to use, and click **Next**. Select and/or type your user name and password, and click **Next**.

5. Click **System Restore**. The System Restore window will open, as you saw earlier. Click **Next**.

6. Follow the instructions in "Run System Restore from Windows" earlier in this chapter, from step 3 on.

7. The restoration process will begin and Windows 7 will restart. The System Restore dialog box will appear, telling you that the restoration was successful. Click **OK**.

Get System Information

When you are working on a computer problem, you, or possibly a technical support person working with you, will want some information about your computer. The two primary sources are basic computer information and advanced system information.

BASIC COMPUTER INFORMATION

Basic computer information provides general system information, such as the Windows edition, the processor and memory, and the computer name and workgroup (see Figure 5-17). To see the basic computer information:

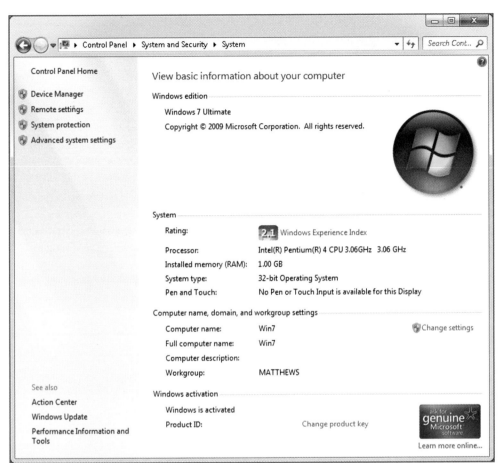

Click **Start** and click **Control Panel**. In Category view, click **System And Security**, and click **System**. The System window will open. After you have reviewed the information, click **Close**.

ADVANCED SYSTEM INFORMATION

Advanced system information provides detailed system information and lets you look at services that are running, Group Policy settings, and the error log. To see the advanced system information:

Click **Start** and click **All Programs**. Click **Accessories**, click **System Tools**, and click **System Information**. The System Information window will open. Click any of the topics in the left pane to display that information in the right pane. Figure 5-18 shows the summary-level information that is available. Click **Close** when you are done.

Figure 5-17: Basic computer information provides an overview of the computer and its operating system.

Set Power Options

Setting power options is important on laptop and notebook computers that run at least some of the time on batteries. It can also be useful on desktop computers to conserve power. The Windows 7 Power Options feature provides a number of settings that allow you to manage your computer's use of power.

1. Click **Start** and click **Control Panel**. In Category view, click **System And Security**, and click **Power Options**.

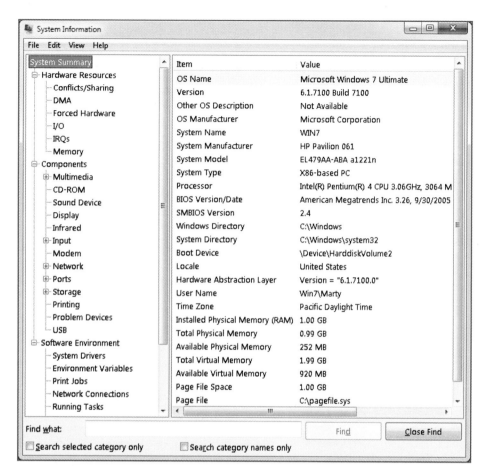

Figure 5-18: *Advanced system information provides a great depth of information useful in troubleshooting.*

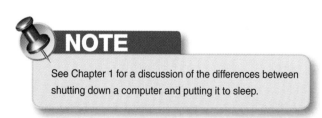

See Chapter 1 for a discussion of the differences between shutting down a computer and putting it to sleep.

2. Choose one of the power plans, depending on whether you want to emphasize battery life (energy savings on desktops) or performance (see Figure 5-19). You can also reduce the screen brightness on a laptop or notebook computer to reduce the power drain.

3. To see a more detailed setting, click **Choose When To Turn Off The Display**. If you are using a laptop or notebook computer, your power options will look like those in Figure 5-20. (A desktop computer won't have the battery settings.)

4. Click each of the drop-down lists, select the setting that is correct for you, and adjust the screen brightness. If you would like to control individual pieces of hardware (disk drives, USB ports, and so on), click **Change Advanced Power Settings**, click the plus signs to open the lists, click the action you want to change, and click the spinners to adjust the values. Click **OK** when you are finished.

5. When you are ready, click **Save Changes** to accept the changes you have made to your power options settings.

Add and Remove Software

Today, almost all application and utility software come in one of two ways: on a CD or DVD, or downloaded over the Internet.

INSTALL SOFTWARE FROM A CD

If you get software on a CD and your computer is less than 10 years old, all you need to do is put the CD in the drive, wait for the install program to automatically load, and follow the displayed instructions, of which there are usually only a few. When the installation is complete, you may need to acknowledge that by clicking **OK** or **Finish**. Then remove the CD from its drive. That is all there is to it.

Figure 5-19: *Windows 7 has two preferred power plans that let you emphasize either performance or energy consumption.*

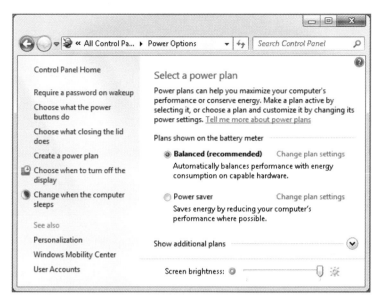

NOTE

In medium to larger organizations, application software might be available over the LAN (local area network) on a server. Generally, it is better to download the software and then do the installation from your computer than to do the installation over the network in case the network connection is lost during installation (the same can be said for online software; better to download and then install rather than installing directly through an Internet home network connection).

TIP

If you are having trouble installing a program for no discernable reason, make sure you are logged on with administrative permissions. Some programs or installation situations require these permissions; without them, the program refuses to install. See Chapter 8 to see how to establish and work with administrative permissions.

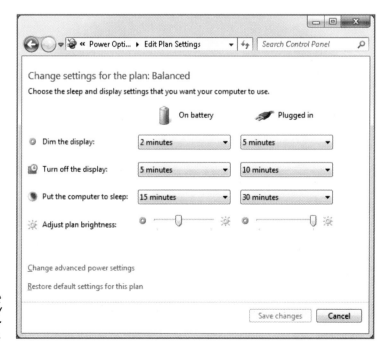

Figure 5-20: *You can set the amount of idle time before the display and/ or the computer are turned off or put to sleep, respectively.*

INSTALL SOFTWARE FROM THE INTERNET

To download and install a program from the Internet:

1. Click the **Internet Explorer** icon on the taskbar. In the address bar, type the URL (uniform resource locator, also called the address) for the source of the download, and press **ENTER**. (For this example, I'm downloading the Firefox web browser whose URL is http://www.mozilla.com, but you don't need to type the http://.)

2. Locate the link for the download, and click it, as shown in Figure 5-21. You may need to approve the downloading in Internet Explorer by clicking the bar at the top of the window and clicking **Download File**.

3. A dialog box will appear, asking if you want to run or save the program. Click **Save**. The Save As dialog box will appear and let you choose where you want to save the file. The desktop is a good place, at least initially, because you can easily double-click the program to start it. With the desktop or a folder you choose opened in the Save As dialog box, click **Save**.

4. When you are told the download is complete, if you are offered this choice, click **Run**. If you are not offered the choice to run the program, open Windows Explorer, navigate to the drive and folder where you stored the program (possibly your desktop), and double-click the program you downloaded. At this point, click **Run**.

Figure 5-21: Mozilla's Firefox is a good alternative browser to Internet Explorer.

5. If the program does not have a valid digital signature (many do not) a message will appear telling you this and asking if want to continue. Decide that and, if so, click **Run** again; otherwise, click **Don't Run**. User Account Control will also ask you if you are sure you want to go ahead. Click **Yes** if you do, or click **No** if you don't.

6. Follow the program's installation instructions, making the choices that are offered to you.

7. When the installation is complete, you may be notified, the program may be started, Windows Explorer may be opened to show where the program is installed, and/or one or more shortcuts may be left on the desktop.

8. Close the Windows Explorer window and any other windows and dialog boxes that were opened by this process.

REMOVE SOFTWARE

There are at least two ways to get rid of a program you have installed and one way not to do it. You do not want to just delete the program files in Windows Explorer. That leaves files in other locations and all the settings in the registry. To correctly remove a program, you need to use either the uninstall program that comes with many programs or Windows 7's Uninstall Or Change A Program feature. To do the latter:

1. Click **Start** and click **Control Panel**. In Category view, click **Programs** and click **Programs And Features**. The Uninstall Or Change A Program window will open, as you can see in Figure 5-22.

2. Click the program you want to uninstall, and click **Uninstall** on the toolbar. Follow the instructions as they are presented, which vary from program to program.

3. When the uninstall has successfully completed, close the Uninstall Or Change A Program window.

Add Hardware

Most hardware today is *Plug and Play*. That means that when you plug it in, Windows recognizes it and installs the necessary driver software automatically and you can immediately begin using it. Often, when you first turn on the computer after installing the hardware, you see a message telling you that you

TIP

Unless you are specifically told otherwise, always save a downloaded file to your hard disk and then, if a program-specific dialog box doesn't automatically appear, allowing you to start the program, start it by double-clicking the file on your hard disk. That way, if there is a problem, you can restart it without having to download it a second time.

NOTE

The "change" part of the Uninstall Or Change A Program window is used to install updates and patches to programs. It requires that you have either a CD with the changes or have downloaded them. With some programs you will get a third option: Repair.

Uninstall or change a program

To uninstall a program, select it from the list and then click Uninstall, Change, or Repair.

Organize ▼

Name	Publisher	Installed On	Size	Version
Abacast Distributed Live	Abacast, Inc.	5/5/2009	1.95 MB	2.2b1
Abacast Distributed On-Demand		5/5/2009		
Adobe Acrobat 8.1.3 Professional	Adobe Systems	5/21/2009		8.1.3
Adobe Flash Player 10 ActiveX	Adobe Systems Incorpor...	5/1/2009		10.0.22.
Intel(R) Graphics Media Accelerator Driver		4/30/2009		6.14.10.
Microsoft Feedback Data Collector	Microsoft	5/4/2009	391 KB	1.0.0
Microsoft Office Live Add-in 1.3	Microsoft Corporation	5/7/2009	494 KB	2.0.231
Microsoft Office Professional 2007	Microsoft Corporation	4/30/2009		12.0.64.
Microsoft Silverlight	Microsoft Corporation	5/8/2009	23.8 MB	2.0.401
Microsoft SQL Server 2005 Compact Editi...	Microsoft Corporation	5/7/2009	1.72 MB	3.1.000
Microsoft Sync Framework Runtime Nativ...	Microsoft Corporation	5/7/2009	625 KB	1.0.121!
Microsoft Sync Framework Services Nativ...	Microsoft Corporation	5/7/2009	1.44 MB	1.0.121!
Mozilla Firefox (3.0.10)	Mozilla	5/26/2009		3.0.10 (
Panda Antivirus Pro 2009	Panda Security	4/30/2009		8.00.82
PlayReady PC Runtime x86	Microsoft Corporation	4/30/2009	1.64 MB	1.3.0

Currently installed programs   Total size: 96.1 MB
22 programs installed

Figure 5-22: Programs are removed through the Uninstall Or Change A Program feature.

have new hardware or that Windows is installing the device driver. Frequently, you need do nothing more; the installation will complete by itself. With other equipment, you must click the message for the installation to proceed. In either case, you are told when it has successfully completed.

Problems may occur when you have older hardware and the programs that run it, called *drivers,* are not included with Windows 7. In that case, you will see a dialog box saying you must locate the drivers. Here are some options for locating drivers:

- Let **Windows 7** see what it can do by itself by clicking **Locate And Install Driver Software** in the Found New Hardware dialog box. Windows 7 will scan your computer and see what it can find. The original dialog box appears only because a driver wasn't in the standard Windows 7 driver folder. It may well be in other locations.

- **Microsoft** has drivers for the most popular and recent devices and, as a part of Windows Update (discussed earlier in this chapter), the ability to scan your system and see if it has any drivers to help you. The first step is to look at Windows Update by clicking **Start**, clicking **All Programs**, and clicking **Windows Update**. Click **Check For Updates** in the upper-left area, and see if a driver for your device is found.

- The **manufacturer of the device** is generally a good source, but as hardware gets older, manufacturers stop writing new drivers for more recent operating systems. The easiest way to look for manufacturer support is on the Internet. If you know the manufacturer's Web site, you can enter it; or you may have to search for it. If you must search, start out by typing the manufacturer's name in the Internet Explorer address bar. This uses Windows Live search and gives you a list of sites.

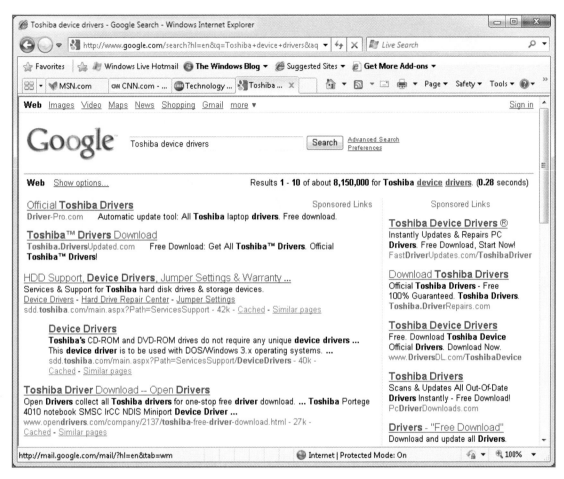

*Figure 5-23: **Many device drivers can be found by searching the Internet, although you may have to pay for them.***

- **Third-party sources** can be found using search engines like Google (www.google.com) and searching for "device drivers." You should find a number of sources, as you can see in Figure 5-23. Some of these sources charge you for the driver; others are free. Make sure the driver will work with Windows 7.

Use Remote Assistance

Remote Assistance allows you to invite someone to remotely look at your computer and control it for purposes of assisting you. The other person must be using Windows 7, Windows Vista, Windows XP, or Windows Server 2003 or 2008, and it will be helpful if both of you have an email account. To use Remote Assistance, you must set it up, and then you can be either the requester or the helper.

SET UP REMOTE ASSISTANCE

Although Remote Assistance is installed with Windows 7, you must turn it on and set your firewall so that Windows 7 will allow it through. Both of these tasks are done in Control Panel.

1. Click **Start** and click **Control Panel**. In Category view, click **System And Security**, click **System**, and click **Remote Settings** in the left pane. The System Properties dialog box will appear with the Remote tab displayed (see Figure 5-24).

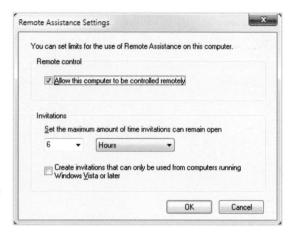

2. Select **Allow Remote Assistance Connections To This Computer**, if it isn't already, and click **Advanced**.

3. Determine if you want a person to control your computer, and select the check box under **Remote Control** accordingly. Set the time an invitation for Remote Assistance is to remain open.

4. Click **OK** twice to close the two open dialog boxes. In Control Panel, click **Control Panel** in the address bar, click **System And Security**, and click **Windows Firewall**.

5. Click **Allow A Program Or Feature Through Windows Firewall**. The Allow Programs To Communicate Through Windows Firewall window will open and show the programs and features that are allowed through the firewall.

6. Click **Change Settings** toward the top of the window, then scroll through the list until you see **Remote Assistance**, and click it, if it isn't already selected (see Figure 5-25).

7. Click **OK** to close the dialog box, close the Windows Firewall window, and then close Control Panel.

Figure 5-24: *Before using Remote Assistance, it must be turned on.*

NOTE

If you are using Windows 7 and want to use Remote Assistance with someone using Windows XP or Windows Server 2003, you must be on the receiving end of the assistance and you cannot use Windows 7's Pause feature. Also, the person using Windows XP/Server 2003 cannot use Start Talk for voice capability.

REQUEST REMOTE ASSISTANCE

To use Remote Assistance, first find someone willing to provide it and request the assistance. Besides the obvious invitation text, the request for assistance message will include a password to access your computer and the code to allow the encryption of information to be sent back and forth. All this is provided for you with Windows Remote Assistance. To begin a Remote Assistance session:

1. Click **Start**, click **All Programs**, click **Maintenance**, and click **Windows Remote Assistance** to open the Windows Remote Assistance dialog box.

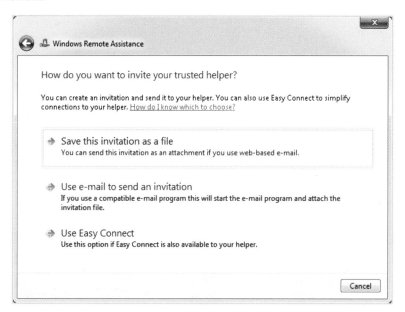

Allow programs to communicate through Windows Firewall

To add, change, or remove allowed programs and ports, click Change settings.

What are the risks of allowing a program to communicate? **Change settings**

Allowed programs and features:

Name	Home/Work (Private)	Public
☑ Microsoft Office Outlook	☑	☐
☐ Netlogon Service	☐	☐
☑ Network Discovery	☑	☐
☐ Performance Logs and Alerts	☐	☐
☑ Remote Assistance	☑	☑
☐ Remote Desktop	☐	☐
☐ Remote Event Log Management	☐	☐
☐ Remote Scheduled Tasks Management	☐	☐
☐ Remote Service Management	☐	☐
☐ Remote Volume Management	☐	☐
☐ Routing and Remote Access	☐	☐
☐ Secure Socket Tunneling Protocol	☐	☐

Details... Remove

Allow another program...

OK Cancel

*Figure 5-25: **Before you can use Remote Assistance, you must make sure that your firewall will let it through.***

NOTE

Remote Desktop, which is discussed in Chapter 10, is different from Remote Assistance, even though it is on the same Remote tab of the System Properties dialog box. Remote Desktop lets you sit at home and log on and use your computer at work as though you were sitting in front of it.

2. Click **Invite Someone You Trust To Help You**, and then click one of the following methods:

Windows Remote Assistance

How do you want to invite your trusted helper?

You can create an invitation and send it to your helper. You can also use Easy Connect to simplify connections to your helper. How do I know which to choose?

→ Save this invitation as a file
You can send this invitation as an attachment if you use web-based e-mail.

→ Use e-mail to send an invitation
If you use a compatible e-mail program this will start the e-mail program and attach the invitation file.

→ Use Easy Connect
Use this option if Easy Connect is also available to your helper.

Cancel

- **Save This Invitation As A File** that you can transfer as an attachment to an email message using any email program or Web-based email such as Google's gmail, or via a CD or USB flash drive.

- **Use Email To Send An Invitation** if you are using Windows Live Mail or Microsoft Office Outlook or another compatible email package.

- **Use Easy Connect** if the other computer is using Windows 7.

3. If you choose **Use Email To Send An Invitation**, your email program will open and display a message to your helper and contain the invitation as an attachment, as shown in Figure 5-26. Address the email and click **Send**. Skip to step 6.

4. If you choose **Save This Invitation As A File**, select the drive and folder where you want to store the invitation—it may be across a network on your helper's computer. Click **Save**.

5. Attach the saved file to an email message or store it on a CD or flash drive, and send or deliver it to your helper.

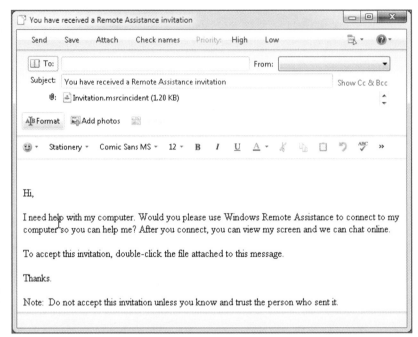

Figure 5-26: *You need to send an invitation that asks a person for assistance and gives him or her the means to communicate in an encrypted manner.*

6. If you choose **Easy Connect**, in either of the other two cases, a Windows Remote Assistance window will open, providing you with the password you must also communicate to your helper, say via phone. This window will wait for your helper to answer.

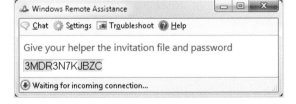

7. When your helper answers, you will be asked if you want to allow the person to see your computer. Click **Yes** if you do. Your computer screen will appear on your helper's computer.

8. Click **Chat**, click in the text box at the bottom, and type a message to the other person, who can see everything on your computer (see "Provide Remote Assistance," next). Click **Send**.

9. If the other person requests control of your computer, you'll see a message asking if that is what you want to do. If you do, select the check box, and then click **Yes**. If you become uncomfortable, you can click **Stop Sharing** or press **ALT+T** at any time.

10. To end the session, send a message to that effect, and close the Remote Assistance window.

PROVIDE REMOTE ASSISTANCE

If you want to provide remote assistance:

1. Upon receiving an invitation as a file, drag it to the desktop and double-click it.

2. If you are using Easy Connect, click **Start**, click **All Programs**, click **Maintenance**, and click **Windows Remote Assistance**. Click **Help Someone Who Has Invited You**. It may take a couple of minutes to connect.

3. Enter the password you have been given, click **OK**, and, if the other person approves, you are shown his or her screen and can request control of the other person's computer. You can view the screen in its actual size or scale it to fit your screen, as shown in Figure 5-27.

4. To request control of the other computer, click **Request Control**. Click **Stop Sharing** to give up control.

5. Click **Close** to end the session and close the Remote Assistance window.

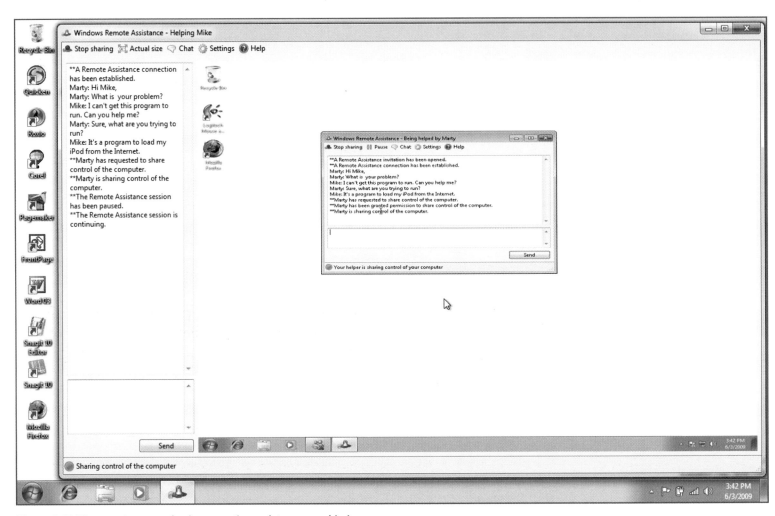

Figure 5-27: *The remote screen is shown on the assistance provider's screen.*

Chapter 6
Working with Documents and Pictures

In this chapter you will discover many aspects of creating documents and pictures, installing and using digital cameras and scanners, and installing and using printers and their fonts with documents and pictures.

Create Documents and Pictures

Creating documents and pictures is primarily done with programs outside of Windows 7, although Windows has simple programs to do this. Windows 7 also has facilities to bring documents and pictures in from other computers, from the Internet, and from scanners and cameras.

Create a Picture

Pictures are really just documents that contain an image. They can be created or brought into your computer in the same way as any other document (see the

QUICKSTEPS

ACQUIRING A DOCUMENT

The documents in your computer got there because they were created with a program on your computer, or they were brought to the computer on a disk, transferred over a local area network (LAN), or downloaded from the Internet.

CREATE A DOCUMENT WITH A PROGRAM

To create a document with a program:

1. Start the program. For example, start Microsoft Word by clicking **Start**, clicking **All Programs**, clicking **Microsoft Office**, and clicking **Microsoft Office Word**.

2. Create the document using the facilities in the program. In Word, for example, type the document and format it using Word's formatting tools.

3. Save the document by (in Word), clicking the **Office Button**. Then click **Save As**, if needed, click **Browse Folders**, and select the disk drive and folder in which to store the document. Enter a filename, and click **Save**, as shown in Figure 6-1.

4. Close the program used to create the file.

Continued . . .

"Acquiring a Document" QuickSteps). For example, to create and save a picture in Microsoft Paint:

1. Click **Start**, click **All Programs**, click **Accessories**, and click **Paint**.

2. Create a picture using the tools in Paint. For example, click the **Pencil** tool, choose a color, and create the drawing.

3. Save the document by clicking the **Paint** menu (next to the Home tab). Then click **Save As**, select the disk drive and folder in which to store the document, enter a filename, select a Save As Type, and click **Save**. Close Paint.

Install Cameras and Scanners

Installing cameras and scanners depends a lot on the device—whether it is Plug and Play (you plug it in and it starts to function), what type of connection it has,

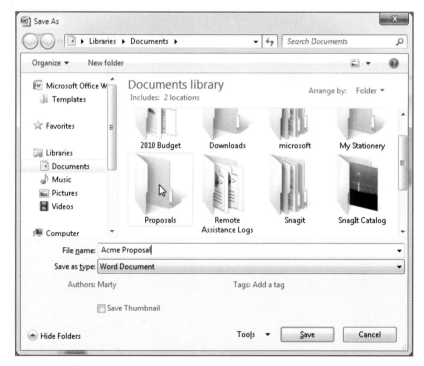

Figure 6-1: *Most document-creation programs let you choose where you want to save the files you create.*

ACQUIRING A DOCUMENT *(Continued)*

BRING IN A DOCUMENT FROM A DISK

Use Windows Explorer to bring in a document from a disk or other removable storage device.

1. Click **Start** and click **Computer**.

2. Double-click the drive from which you want to retrieve a document (this could be another hard drive, floppy disk, CD, DVD, flash drive, or other device), and double-click to open any necessary folders to locate the document file and display it in the subject (middle) pane (assuming your Windows Explorer window displays a three-pane view: navigation, subject, and preview).

3. In the navigation pane, display (but do not select or open) the drive and folder(s) in which you want to store the file by clicking their respective triangles on the left.

4. Drag the document file to the displayed folder, as illustrated in Figure 6-2. When you are done, close Windows Explorer.

DOWNLOAD A DOCUMENT ACROSS A NETWORK

Use Windows Explorer to bring in a document from another computer on your network (the folder on the other computer will need to be shared; see Chapter 8 for more information on sharing files and folders).

1. Click **Start**, click **Computer**, and click **Network** in the left column.

2. Double-click the other computer from which you want the document, and double-click to open any necessary drives, folders, and subfolders to locate the document file.

Continued . . .

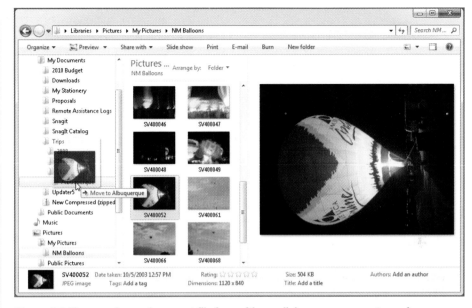

Figure 6-2: *You can drag a document file from either a disk on your computer or from another computer on your network.*

and so on. Most recent cameras and scanners are Plug and Play devices. To use them:

1. Plug the device into the computer, and turn it on. If it is Plug and Play, the first time you plug it in, you will see a message that a device driver is being installed and then that it is ready to use. Finally an AutoPlay dialog box may appear and allow you to choose what you want to do. If this happens for you and you plugged in a scanner, skip to "Scan Pictures" later in this chapter. If you plugged in a camera, skip to "Import Camera Images," also later in this chapter. Otherwise, continue to step 2.

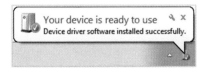

2. Click **Start** and click **Devices And Printers**. If you see your device, installation is complete, as shown in Figure 6-3 (DigiMax V4 is my camera, which Windows thinks is a disk), and you can skip the remainder of these steps.

ACQUIRING A DOCUMENT *(Continued)*

3. In the navigation pane, display (but do not select or open) the drive and folder(s) in which you want to store the file by clicking their respective triangles on the left.

4. Drag the document file to the displayed folder. When you are done, close Windows Explorer.

DOWNLOAD A DOCUMENT FROM THE INTERNET

Use Internet Explorer to bring in a document from a site on the Internet.

1. Click the **Internet Explorer** icon on the taskbar.

2. Type an address, search, or browse to a site and page from which you can download the document file.

3. Use the links and tools on the Web site to select and begin the file download. For example, right-click a picture and click **Save Picture As**.

4. In the Save Picture dialog box, select the disk and open the folder(s) in which you want to store the file on your computer.

5. Type or edit the filename and press **ENTER** to complete the download. When you are done, close your browser.

*Figure 6-3: **Most recent Plug and Play cameras and scanners are automatically detected and installed.***

3. Click **Add A Device**. The Add A Device Wizard Starts. Click the device you want to install and click **Next**. Scroll through the manufacturer and model lists, and see if your device is there. If so, select it and click **Next**. Confirm the name you want to use, click **Next**, and then click **Finish** to complete the installation.

4. If you don't see your device on the lists and you have a disk that came with it, place the disk in the drive, and click **Have Disk**. If a driver appears, complete the installation and close the Add A Device Wizard. If you cannot find the driver, close the Add A Device Wizard and the Devices And Printers window, and use the manufacturer's installation program on the disk.

Scan Pictures

Scanners allow you to take printed images and convert them to digital images on your computer. The scanner must first be installed, as described in "Install Cameras and Scanners" earlier in this chapter. If you ended up using the manufacturer's software to install the scanner, you might need to use it to scan images too. If you used Windows to install the scanner, use the following steps to scan an image.

TIP

The scanning software in Windows may or may not be superior to the software that comes with your scanner.

1. Turn on your scanner, and place what you want to scan onto the scanning surface.

2. Click **Start**, click **All Programs**, and click **Windows Fax And Scan**. The Windows Fax And Scan window opens.

3. Click **New Scan** on the toolbar. The New Scan dialog box appears. The scanner you installed should be displayed in the upper-left area. Change the scanner if you wish.

4. Choose the color, file type, and resolution you want to use, and click **Preview**. The image in the scanner will appear in the dialog box.

5. Adjust the margins around the page by dragging the dashed lines on the four sides, as shown in Figure 6-4. When you are ready, click **Scan**.

6. The scanned image will appear in the Windows Fax And Scan window (see Figure 6-5). Select the image in the list at the top of the window and, using the toolbar, choose to:

- **Forward As Fax** using the Windows fax capability described later in this chapter
- **Forward As E-mail** using your default email application

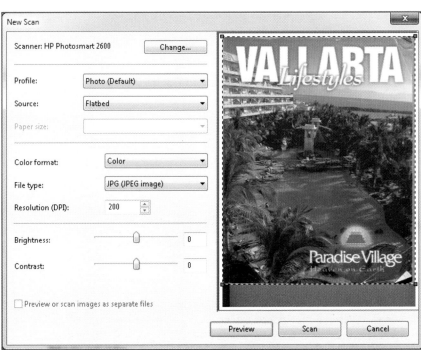

Figure 6-4: In the Windows 7 scanning software you can change a several of the parameters including the margins of what to include, and see the results in the preview pane.

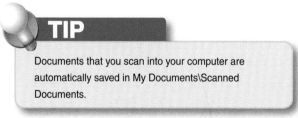

Figure 6-5: *Images that you scan can be faxed, emailed, saved, and printed.*

- **Save As** using Windows Explorer to save the image as a file on one of the storages devices available to you
- **Print** using a printer available to you
- **Delete** the image

7. Work through the related dialog box(es) that appear to complete the scanning process. When you are ready, close the Windows Fax And Scan window.

Import Camera Images

When most digital cameras are plugged into the computer, turned on, and installed (see "Install Cameras and Scanners" earlier in this chapter), the AutoPlay dialog box should automatically appear, calling the camera a removable disk and asking if you want to:

- **Import Pictures And Videos**, in essence, copying them to your hard disk
- **View Pictures** in your camera using Windows Photo Viewer
- **Import Pictures And Videos** in your camera using Windows Live Photo Gallery
- **View Pictures** in your camera using Windows Live Photo Gallery
- **Open Folder To View Files** to look at your camera as if it were a disk and the pictures as files using Windows Explorer

1. Click **Import Pictures And Videos Using Windows Live Photo Gallery**. The Import Photos And Videos dialog box should appear.

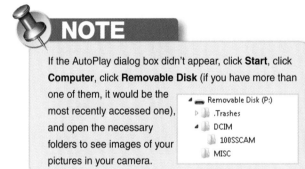

2. Choose if you want to review and organize your photos first or import them all immediately.

3. If you choose to review and organize, click **Next**. A window opens that allows you to select the photos you want imported. You can group photos by date, add names to groups, and add tags to groups that will form the basis of photo names (the date is already a part of the name). When you are ready, click **Import**.

4. If you choose to import all items at once, select that option, enter a name, if desired click **Add Tags** and type a tag to add to the filename of all the pictures, and click **Import**. The first time you do this, you will see a message box asking if you want to use Windows Live Photo Gallery to open picture file types instead of the default Windows viewer. Click **Yes**.

5. In either case, you will see each of the pictures as they are imported. When the process is completed, the Windows Live Photo Gallery will open and show thumbnails of the pictures, as you can see in Figure 6-6.

Work with Photo Gallery Pictures

Once you have brought pictures into your computer from a camera, a scanner, an Internet download, or a removable disk, you can look at them on your computer screen. Assuming that you brought your pictures into Photo Gallery as discussed in "Import Camera Images" or "Scan Pictures" earlier in this chapter:

1. Click **Start**, click **All Programs**, click **Windows Live**, and click **Windows Live Photo Gallery** (you may be asked to sign in to Windows Live, but you don't have to do that—click **Cancel**). The Windows Live Photo Gallery should open.

2. Select the tag you assigned or date your pictures were taken to open the category that contains them, as was shown in Figure 6-6.

3. Hover your mouse over a picture to see an enlarged image.

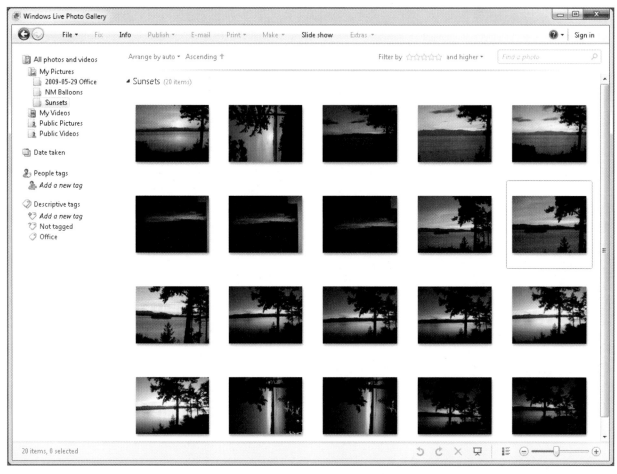

Figure 6-6: **The Windows Live Photo Gallery gives you a quick way to organize and work with your pictures.**

4. To see an even larger image, double-click its thumbnail. The image will expand to fit the Photo Gallery window, similar to what is shown in Figure 6-7. The controls at the bottom of the window allow you to cycle through a number of pictures and work with them.

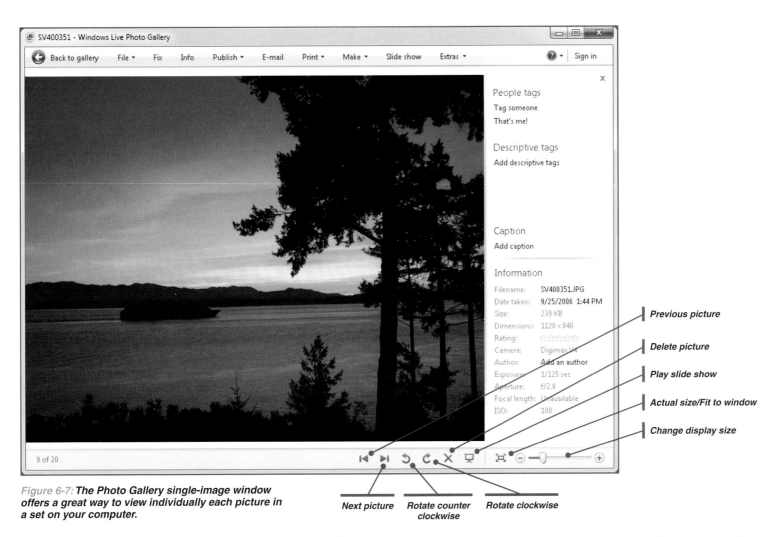

SV400351 - Windows Live Photo Gallery

Back to gallery   File ▾   Fix   Info   Publish ▾   E-mail   Print ▾   Make ▾   Slide show   Extras ▾   ❓ ▾   Sign in

People tags

Tag someone
That's me!

Descriptive tags

Add descriptive tags

Caption

Add caption

Information

Filename: SV400351.JPG
Date taken: 9/25/2006 1:44 PM
Size: 239 KB
Dimensions: 1120 x 840
Rating: ☆☆☆☆☆
Camera: Digimax V4
Author: Add an author
Exposure: 1/125 sec
Aperture: f/2.8
Focal length: Unavailable
ISO: 100

9 of 20

Previous picture

Delete picture

Play slide show

Actual size/Fit to window

Change display size

Figure 6-7: The Photo Gallery single-image window offers a great way to view individually each picture in a set on your computer.

Next picture   **Rotate counter clockwise**   **Rotate clockwise**

5. If you have several pictures you want to view, click the right and left arrows on the bottom of the window to go through them sequentially. You can also use the other controls at the bottom of the window or in the menus at the top to perform their stated functions.

6. When you are done, click **Back To Gallery** to view the photo thumbnails or close the Windows Live Photo Gallery.

If you have two computers, such as a laptop and a desktop, both running Windows 7, Windows Live Photo Gallery can synchronize your photos and videos on both computers using Windows Live Sync. On one computer open Windows Live Photo Gallery, click the **File** menu, and click **Setup Gallery Sync**. On the second computer, given that both computers have activated Windows Live with the same ID and password, simply open Windows Live Photo Gallery. With Windows Live Sync activated, you or someone with your Windows Live ID and password can sign on and view your Photo Gallery by clicking **Start**, clicking **All Programs**, clicking **Windows Live**, and clicking **Windows Live Sync**.

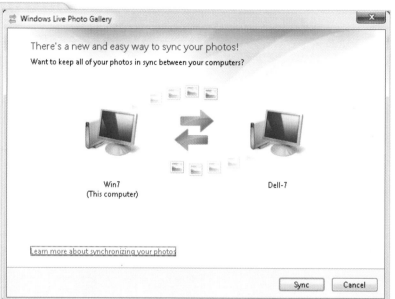

QUICKSTEPS

VIEWING OTHER PICTURES

If your pictures are not in the Photo Gallery, to locate and view them:

1. Click **Start**, click **Computer**, and open the drive and folders necessary to locate your pictures.

2. Click the **Change Your View** menu down arrow, , and click **Extra Large Icons**; or adjust the slider so that you can adequately see the thumbnail images.

3. Double-click the picture you want to view in a larger size. The Windows Photo Viewer will open and display the picture. From here, you can work with the picture.

Capture Snips

Windows 7 includes the Snipping Tool to capture images of the screen, called "screen shots" or "snips." This can capture four areas of the screen:

- **Full screen** captures the entire screen

- **Window** captures a complete window

- **Rectangular area** captures a rectangle you draw around objects

- **Free-form area** captures any area you draw around objects

Once you have captured an area it is temporarily stored on the Clipboard and displayed in the mark-up window where you can write and draw on the snip to annotate it, and, when you are ready, save the snip where you want it. To do all of that:

1. Display the windows or other objects on the screen whose images you want to capture (see the Note on capturing a menu).

2. Click **Start**, click **All Programs**, click **Accessories**, and click **Snipping Tool**. The screen will be dimmed, the Snipping Tool dialog box will appear, along with a cross-hair to use to outline the area to be captured—by default you will see a rectangle (see Figure 6-8).

3. If you want to capture a rectangular area, drag the cross-hair from one corner of the rectangle to its opposite. To capture a different type of area, click the **New** down arrow, and click one of the other three types of areas. Then, with:

- **Free-Form Snip**, drag the cross-hair around the area to be captured

- **Window Snip**, click on the window to be captured

- **Full Screen Snip**, the screen is automatically captured

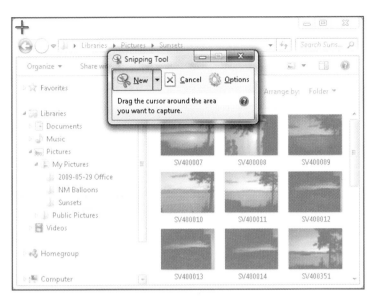

Figure 6-8: *The Snipping Tool allows you to capture an image of an area of the screen for future reference or use.*

Figure 6-9: *The Snipping Tool mark-up window allows you to annotate, email, and save a snip.*

TIP

To capture a snip of a menu, open the Snipping Tool, press **ESC**, display the menu to be captured, press **CTRL+PRINT SCREEN**, click **New**, select the type of area to be captured (Free-Form, Rectangle, and so forth), and delineate that area as you would otherwise.

4. In all cases, the mark-up window opens showing you the area that was captured, as you can see in Figure 6-9, and allowing you to use the pen, highlighter, and eraser to annotate the snip.

5. From the mark-up window you can also directly email the snip to someone by clicking **Send Snip**, which opens an email message with the snip in it; save the snip by clicking **Save Snip**, select a folder, enter a name, select a file type, and click **Save**.

Print Documents and Pictures

It is important to be able to install and fully use printers so that you can transfer your digital documents to paper.

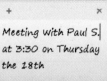

UICK**STEPS**

USING STICKY NOTES

Sticky Notes are exactly what the name implies: little notes to yourself that you can place anywhere on your screen. You can type messages on these notes; change their color; cut, copy, and paste the text on them with the Clipboard to and from other programs; create additional notes; and delete the note. Here's how:

> ＋ ✕
>
> Meeting with Paul S.
> at 3:30 on Thursday
> the 18th

1. Click **Start**, click **All Programs**, click **Accessories**, and click **Sticky Notes**. If you don't already have a note on your desktop, one will appear.

2. If you already have one or more notes on the desktop, the most recent one will be selected. If you want a new note, click **New Note** (the plus sign in the upper-left corner).

3. On the new note, type the message you want it to contain, or, having copied some text from another source, right-click the note and click **Paste**.

4. Right-click the note, and click the color you want it the note to be, and then drag the note to where you want it.

5. When you no longer want the note on the desktop, click **Delete Note** (the **X** in the upper-right), and click **Yes**.

Install a Printer

All printers are either automatically installed or done so using the Devices And Printers window. Because there are differences in how the installation is done, look at the sections in this chapter on installing local Plug and Play printers, installing other local printers, installing network printers, and selecting a default printer. Also, if you are installing a local printer, first consider the following checklist.

PRINTER INSTALLATION CHECKLIST

A local printer is one that is attached to your computer with a cable or wireless connection. Make sure that your printer meets the following conditions *before* you begin the install:

- It is plugged into the correct port on your computer (see manufacturer's instructions).
- It is plugged into an electrical outlet.
- It has fresh ink, toner, or ribbon, which, along with the print heads, is properly installed.
- It has adequate paper.
- It is turned on.

INSTALL A LOCAL PLUG AND PLAY PRINTER

Installing Plug and Play printers is supposed to be fairly automatic, and, for the most part, it is.

1. With your computer and printer turned off, connect the devices to each other. Then make sure the other points in the previous checklist are satisfied.

2. Turn on your computer, let it fully boot, and then turn on your printer. Your computer should find and automatically install the new printer and briefly give you messages to that effect.

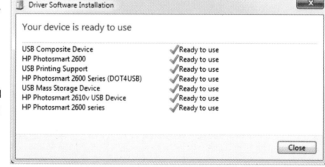

NOTE

Some laptop computer-and-printer combinations are connected through an infrared beam or other wireless connection. In this case, "plugging the printer into the computer" means to establish that wireless connection.

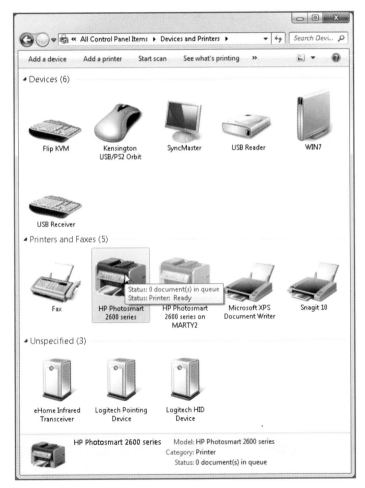

Figure 6-10: **When you connect a Plug and Play printer, it should be recognized by the computer and automatically installed.**

3. Click **Start** and click **Devices And Printers**. The Devices And Printers window will open, and you should see your new printer. Hover the mouse pointer over that printer and you should see "Status: Ready," as shown in Figure 6-10. (If you don't see your printer, it was not installed. Go to the next section.)

4. Right-click the new printer, click **Printer Properties**, and click **Print Test Page**. If the test page prints satisfactorily, click **Close**. Otherwise, click **Get Help With Printing**, follow the suggestions, and close the Help and printer windows when you are done. When you are ready, click **OK** to close the printer's Properties dialog box.

5. If you want the new printer to be the default printer used by all applications on the computer, right-click the printer and click Set As Default Printer.

6. Close the Devices And Printers window.

INSTALL LOCAL PRINTER MANUALLY

If a printer isn't automatically installed in the process of using steps 1 through 3 in the previous section, you must install it manually.

1. If a CD came with your printer, providing it says that it is for Windows 7, place that CD in the drive, and follow the on-screen instructions to install the printer. When this is complete, go to step 3 in "Install a Local Plug and Play Printer," and determine if the printer will print a test page. If so, skip to step 7.

2. If you don't have a manufacturer's CD, click **Start** and click **Devices And Printers**. The Devices And Printers window should open.

3. Click **Add A Printer** on the toolbar, and click **Add A Local Printer**.

4. Click **Use An Existing Port:**, open the drop-down list, and select the correct port (on newer printers, it is probably USB001; on the majority of other printers, it is LPT1), and click **Next**.

Choose a printer port

A printer port is a type of connection that allows your computer to exchange information with a printer.

◉ Use an existing port: LPT1: (Printer Port)

○ Create a new port:
      Type of port: Local Port

5. Select the manufacturer and model of the printer you want to install (see Figure 6-11). If you can't find your printer, click **Windows Update** to download the latest printer drivers. Then, once more, search for the manufacturer and model. When you find the correct printer. Click **Next**.

6. Confirm or change the printer name and click **Next**. Determine if you want to share this printer; if so, enter its share name, location, and comments. Click **Next.**

7. Choose whether you want this printer to be your default printer. Click **Print A Test Page**. If the test page prints satisfactorily, click **Close**. Otherwise, click **Get Help With Printing**, follow the suggestions, and close the Help and Printer windows when you are done. When you are ready, click **Finish** to close the Add Printer dialog box and close the Devices And Printers window.

INSTALL A NETWORK PRINTER

Network printers are not directly connected to your computer, but are available to you as a result of your computer's connection to a network and the fact that the printers have been shared. There are three types of network printers:

- Printers connected to someone else's computer, which are shared
- Printers connected to a dedicated printer server, which are shared
- Printers directly connected to a network (which, in effect, have a built-in computer)

The first two types of network printers are installed with the Network Printer option in the Add Printer dialog box and will be described here. The third option is installed with the Local Printer option, often automatically.

1. Click **Start** and click **Devices And Printers**. The Devices And Printers window will open.

2. Click **Add A Printer** on the toolbar, and click **Add A Network, Wireless Or Bluetooth Printer**. Windows will search for network printers (as shown in Figure 6-12).

3. Scroll through the printers to locate the one you want. Click that printer and click **Next**. Skip to step 5.

4. If the search did not find the network printer you were looking for, click **The Printer That I Want Isn't Listed**. Click **Browse For A Printer**, and click **Next**. Double-click the computer to which the printer is attached, double-click the printer, and click **OK**.

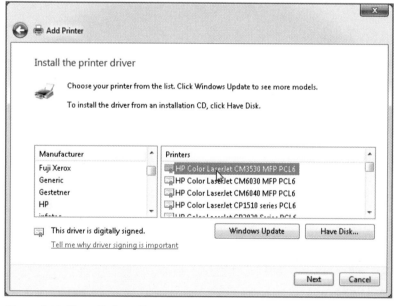

Figure 6-11: **Manually installing a printer requires that you know some facts about the printer.**

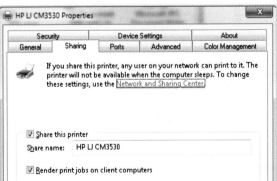

5. Adjust the name of the printer if you want and click **Next**. Click **Set As The Default Printer**, if you want to do that. Click **Print A Test Page**. If the test page prints satisfactorily, click **Close**. Otherwise, click **Get Help With Printing**, follow the suggestions, and close the Help window when you are done. When you are ready, click **Finish** to close the Add Printer dialog box and close the Devices And Printers window.

IDENTIFY A DEFAULT PRINTER

If you have several printers available to you, one must be identified as your default printer—the one that will be used for printing whenever you don't select another one. To change your default printer:

1. Click **Start** and click **Devices And Printers**. The Devices And Printers window will open.

2. Right-click the printer you want to be the default, and click **Set As The Default Printer**.

3. Close the Devices And Printers window when finished.

Figure 6-12: *A printers on another computer must be shared by that computer before you can use it.*

SHARE A PRINTER

If you have a printer attached to your computer and you want to let others use it printer, you can share the printer.

1. In the Devices And Printers window, right-click the printer you want to share, and click **Printer Properties**. The printer's Properties dialog box will appear.

2. Click the **Sharing** tab, click **Share This Printer**, enter a share name, and click **OK.**

3. Close the printers Properties dialogue box.

NOTE

The search for network printers will find those printers that: (1) have been published to Active Directory—normally in larger organizations; (2) are attached to computers on the network; (3) use a Bluetooth wireless system and a Bluetooth transceiver is connected to the computer doing the search; and (4) are directly connected to the network (not through another computer) and have their own IP address (probably automatically assigned).

UICKSTEPS

PRINTING

Most printing is done from a program. Using Microsoft Office Word 2007, whose Print dialog box is shown in Figure 6-13, as an example:

PRINT DOCUMENTS

To print the document currently open in Word:

Click **Quick Print** on Word's Quick Access toolbar to immediately print using the default settings.

CHOOSE A PRINTER

To choose which printer you want to use:

Click the **Office Button**, and click **Print** to open Word's Print dialog box shown in Figure 6-13. Open the printer **Name** drop-down list, and choose the printer you want.

DETERMINE SPECIFIC PAGES TO PRINT

In the Page Range section of the Print dialog box, you can select:

- **All** to print all pages
- **Current Page** to print only the currently selected page
- **Selection** to print the text that has been selected
- **Pages** to print a series of individual pages and/or a range of pages by specifying the individual pages separated by commas and specifying the range with a hyphen. For example: typing 4,6,8-10,12 will cause pages 4, 6, 8, 9, 10, and 12 to be printed.

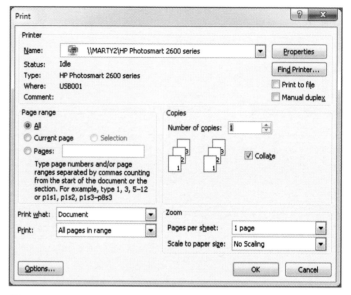

Figure 6-13: **The Microsoft Office Word 2007 Print dialog box is similar to those in other programs.**

Print Pictures

Printing pictures from a program is exactly the same as described in the "Printing" QuickSteps. In addition, Windows has a Print Pictures dialog box used to print pictures from either Windows Explorer or the Photo Gallery.

1. Click **Start** and click **Pictures** to use Windows Explorer; or click **Start**, click **All Programs**, click **Windows Live**, and click **Windows Live Photo Gallery** to use that program.

2. In either program, select the picture(s) you want to print. To select one, click it. To select a contiguous set of pictures, click the first one, hold down **SHIFT**, and click the last picture. To select noncontiguous pictures, hold down **CTRL** while clicking the pictures you want.

3. Click **Print** on the toolbar. To print on a local or network printer, click **Print** again; alternately you can order prints online. Using the selected printer, the Print Pictures dialog box will appear, as shown in Figure 6-14.

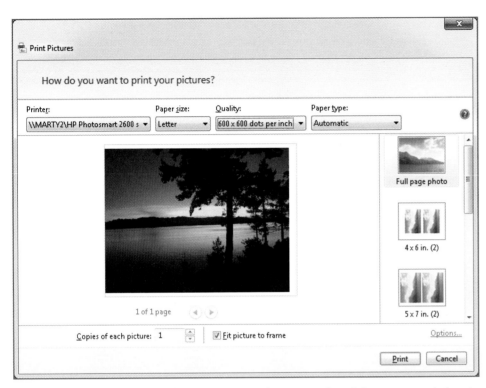

Figure 6-14: *If you use high-quality photo paper and a newer color printer, you can get almost professional-grade pictures.*

4. Select the printer, paper size, quality, paper type, number to print on a page, number of copies, and whether to fit the picture to a frame. You can also click **Options** above the Cancel button to look at and possibly change several print settings. Click **OK** after looking at (and possibly selecting) the options.

5. When you are ready, click **Print**. The pictures will be printed. When you are done, close Windows Explorer or Windows Live Photo Gallery, whichever you have open.

Print to a File

There are two primary reasons to print to a file: to have a file you can take to a remote printer, and to get information out of one program and into another. The first requires formatting the information for a printer and then sending it to a file. The actual printer must be installed on your computer even though it is not physically connected to your computer. In the second case, you must create a "printer" to produce unformatted generic text. The following sections explain first how to create a text file printer and then how to print to a file.

CREATE A TEXT FILE PRINTER

1. Click **Start**, click **Control Panel**, and, in Category view, click **View Devices And Printers** under Hardware And Sound; in Large Icons view, click **Devices And Printers**. The Devices And Printers window will open.

2. Click **Add A Printer** on the toolbar, and click **Add A Local Printer**. Click the **Use An Existing Port** down arrow, and click **File (Print To File)**.

3. Click **Next**. In the Install The Printer Driver dialog box, scroll down and click **Generic** as the manufacturer and **Generic/Text Only** as the printer.

4. Click **Next**. Enter a name for the printer and click **Next**. Determine if you want to share this printer and, if so, enter a share name. Click **Next.**

TIP

If Quick Print isn't on your Quick Access toolbar, click the **Customize** down arrow to the right of the Quick Access toolbar and click **Quick Print**.

NOTE

You can print just the even or odd pages in a document by opening the **Print** drop-down list in the bottom-left corner of the Print dialog box and making the relevant selection.

5. Click **Set As The Default Printer**, (if you want to do that), skip printing a test page, and click **Finish**. A new icon will appear in your Devices And Printers window. Close the Devices And Printers window when you are done.

Print to a File

SELECT PRINT TO FILE

Whether you want to print to a file so that you can print on a remote printer or so that you can create a text file, the steps are same once you have created a text file printer.

1. In the program in which you are printing, click the **File** menu (or the *program* **Button** in Microsoft Office 2007 and other programs, where *program* is the name of the program you are using), and click **Print**.

2. Select the ultimate printer or the generic text file printer, and click **Print To File**. Select the print range, number of copies, and other settings; and click **OK**. Select the folder, type the file name to use, and click **OK**.

Configure a Printer

Configuring a printer is usually done for special purposes and often isn't required. Nevertheless, all configuring is done from the printer's Properties dialog box.

1. Click **Start** and click **Devices And Printers**. The Devices And Printers window will open.

2. Right-click the printer you want to configure, and click **Printer Properties**. The printer's Properties dialog box will appear (you cannot change most settings for networked printers).

In the General tab (shown in Figure 6-15), you can change the printer name, its location, and enter a comment. In the Ports tab, you can specify the port used by the printer, configure ports, and set up printer pooling. In the Device Settings tab, you can set what is loaded in each paper tray, how to handle font substitution, and what printer options are available (your printer may be different). Though most printer configurations are self-explanatory, several items are worthy of further discussion and are explained in the following sections.

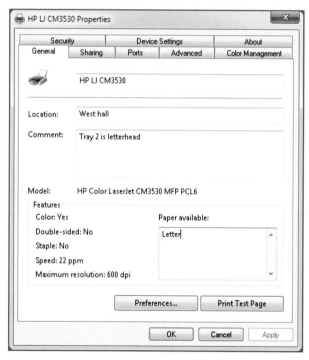

Figure 6-15: **Printers, while having many settings, are often run without ever changing the default settings.**

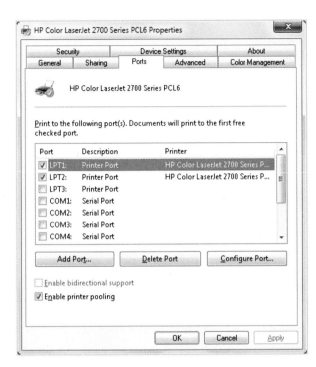

ENABLE PRINTER POOLING

Printer pooling allows you to have two or more physical printing devices with the same print driver assigned to one printer. When print jobs are sent to the printer, Windows determines which of the physical devices is available and routes the job to that device.

1. In the Properties dialog box for the printer to which all work will be directed, click the **Ports** tab, and click **Enable Printer Pooling**.

2. Click each of the ports with a printing device that is to be in the pool. When all the ports are selected, click **OK** to close the Properties dialog box.

3. If the printer that contains the pool isn't already selected as the default printer, right-click the printer and click **Set As Default Printer**.

SET PRINTER PRIORITY

Assigning several printers to one printing device allows you to have two or more settings used with one device. If you want to have two or more priorities automatically assigned to jobs going to a printer, create two or more printers that all point to the same printer port but that have different priorities. Then have high-priority print jobs printed to a printer with a priority of 99 and low-priority jobs printed to a printer with a priority of 1.

1. Install all printers as previously described in "Install a Printer," all with the same port. Name each printer to indicate its priority, such as "High-Priority Printer" and "Low-Priority Printer."

2. In the Devices And Printers window, right-click the high-priority printer, and click **Printer Properties**.

3. Click the **Advanced** tab, type a priority of <u>99</u>, and click **OK**.

4. Similarly, right-click the other printers, open their Properties dialog boxes, click the **Advanced** tab, and set the priority, from 1 for the lowest priority to 98 for the second highest priority.

Jobs with the highest priority will print before jobs with a lower priority if they are in the *queue* (waiting to be printed) at the same time.

TIP

If you have a program that automatically prints certain tasks, such as incoming orders, you might want to assign it a lower priority than a word-processing task, such as a new proposal.

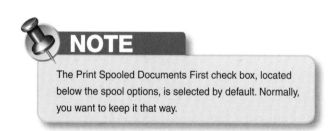

Figure 6-16: *You can set the paper type and size in each paper tray.*

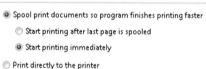

ASSIGN PAPER TRAYS

Some printers have more than one paper tray, and each tray can have different types or sizes of paper. If you assign types and sizes of paper to trays in the printer's Properties dialog box and a user requests a specific type and size of paper when printing, Windows 7 automatically designates the correct paper tray for the print job.

1. In the Printer Properties dialog box for the printer whose trays you want to assign, click the **Device Settings** tab.

2. Click the type of paper in a tray, open the drop-down list, and select the type and size of paper in that tray, similar to what you see in Figure 6-16.

3. When you have set the paper type and size in each tray, click **OK**.

CONFIGURE SPOOL SETTINGS

The time it takes to print a document is normally longer than the time it takes to transfer the information to the printer. *Printer spooling* temporarily stores information on disk, allowing Windows to feed it to the printer as it can be handled. Under most circumstances, you want to use printer spooling and not tie up the program waiting for the printer. The printer's Properties Advanced tab lets you choose to spool or not and gives you two options if you spool.

- **Start Printing After Last Page Is Spooled** waits to print until the last page is spooled, allowing the program to finish faster and the user to get back to the program faster, but it takes longer to finish printing.

- **Start Printing Immediately** allows printing to be done sooner, but the program will be tied up a little longer.

The default, Start Printing Immediately, provides a middle ground between getting the printing done and getting back to the program.

USE SEPARATOR PAGES

If you have several jobs on a printer, it might be helpful to have a separator page between them. A separator page can also be used to switch a printer between

PostScript (a printer language) and PCL (Printer Control Language) on Hewlett-Packard (HP) and compatible printers. Four sample SEP separation files come with Windows 7 and are installed in the \Windows\System32\ folder:

- **Pcl.sep** prints a separation page before the start of each print job on PCL-compatible printers. If the printer handles both PostScript and PCL, it will be switched to PCL.

- **Pscript.sep** does *not* print a separation page, but printers with both PostScript and PCL will be switched to PostScript.

- **Sysprint.sep** prints a separation page before the start of each print job on PostScript-compatible printers.

- **Sysprtj.sep** is the same as Sysprint.sep, but in the Japanese language.

You can choose to have a separator page added at the beginning of each print job by clicking **Separator Page** on the Advanced tab of the Printer Properties dialog box, browsing for and selecting the page you want, clicking **Open**, and clicking **OK** twice.

Control Printing

To control printing means to control the process as it is taking place, whether with one print job or with several in line. If several print jobs are spooled at close to the same time, they form a *print queue*, waiting for earlier jobs to finish. You may control printing in several ways, as described next. These tasks are handled in the printer's window, which is similar to that shown in Figure 6-17, and is opened by clicking **See What's Printing** in the Devices And Printers window or by double-clicking the printer icon in the notification area of the taskbar 🖨 and then clicking **See What's Printing**.

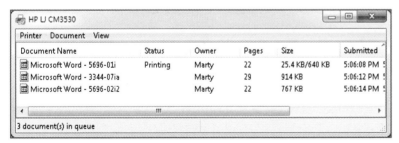

Figure 6-17: *Controlling printing takes place in the printer's window and allows you to pause, resume, restart, and cancel printing.*

PAUSE, RESUME, AND RESTART PRINTING

While printing, a situation may occur (such as needing to add toner) where you want to pause and then resume printing, either for one or all documents.

- **Pause all documents**: In the printer's window, click the **Printer** menu and click **Pause Printing**. "Paused" will appear in the title bar, and, if you look in the Printer menu, you will see a check mark in front of Pause Printing.

- **Resume printing all documents**: In the printer's window, click **Printer** and click **Pause Printing**. "Paused" disappears from the title bar and the check mark disappears from the Pause Printing option in the Printer menu.

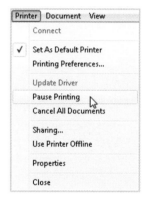

- **Pause a document**: In the printer's window, select the document or documents to pause, click **Document**, and click **Pause**. "Paused" will appear in the Status column of the document(s) you selected.

- **Resume printing a paused document where it left off**: In the printer's window, select the document, click **Document**, and click **Resume**. "Printing" will appear in the Status column of the document selected.

- **Restart printing at the beginning of a document**: In the printer's window, select the document, click **Document**, and click **Restart**. "Restarting" and then "Printing" will appear in the Status column.

CANCEL PRINTING

Canceling printing can be done either at the printer level for all the jobs in the printer queue or at the document level for selected documents. A canceled job is deleted from the print queue and must be restarted by the original program.

- **Cancel a job**: In the printer's window, select the job or jobs that you want canceled. Click **Document** and click **Cancel**. Click **Cancel** a second time to confirm the cancellation. The job or jobs will disappear from the window and the queue.

<div class="note">

NOTE

You cannot change the order in which documents are being printed by pausing the current document that is printing. You must either complete printing the current document or cancel it. You can, however, use Pause to get around intermediate documents that are not currently printing. For example, suppose you want to immediately print the third document in the queue, but the first document is currently printing. You must either let the first document finish printing or cancel it. You can then pause the second document before it starts printing, and the third document will begin printing when the first document is out of the way.

</div>

- **Cancel all the jobs in the queue**: In the printer's window, click **Printer** and click **Cancel All Documents**. You are asked whether you are sure you want to cancel all documents. Click **Yes**. All jobs will disappear from the queue and the printer window.

REDIRECT DOCUMENTS

If you have two printers with the same print driver, you can redirect all the print jobs that are in the queue for one printer to the other, where they will be printed without having to be resubmitted. You do this by changing the port to which the queue is directed.

1. In the printer's window, click **Printer**, click **Properties**, and click the **Ports** tab.

2. If the second printer is in the list of ports, select it. Otherwise, click **Add Port** to open the Printer Ports dialog box. Click **Local Port** and click **New Port**, which opens the Port Name dialog box.

3. Enter the UNC (Uniform Naming Convention) name for the printer (for example, \\Server3\HPLJ9050 for an HP printer to the Server3 computer), and click **OK**.

4. Click **Close** and then click **OK**. The print queue will be redirected to the other printer.

CHANGE A DOCUMENT'S PROPERTIES

A document in a print queue has a Properties dialog box, shown in Figure 6-18, which is opened by right-clicking the document and selecting **Properties**. The General tab allows you to change a number of things:

- **Priority:** To change a document's default priority of 1, the lowest priority, so that the document can be printed before another that hasn't started printing yet, set the document's priority in the document's Properties dialog box to anything higher than the other document by dragging the **Priority** slider to the right.

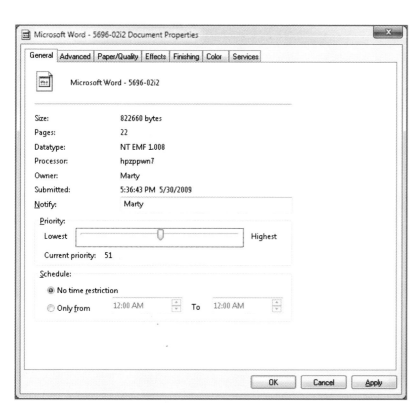

*Figure 6-18: **Setting the properties of a document in the print queue can change its priority and when it prints.***

HANDLING FONTS

A *font* is a set of characters with the same design, size, weight, and style. A font is a member of a *typeface* family, all with the same design. The font 12-point Arial bold italic is a member of the Arial typeface with a 12-point size, bold weight, and italic style. Windows 7 comes with a large number of fonts, a few of which are shown in Figure 6-19.

ADD FONTS

To add fonts to those that are installed by Windows 7:

1. Click **Start**, click **Control Panel**, click **Appearance And Personalization** in Category view, and click **Fonts**. The Fonts window opens as shown in Figure 6-19.

2. Either use Windows Explorer to locate a font (or fonts) on your computer (this can be a flash drive, a CD/DVD, or a hard disk) or on your network, or use Internet Explorer to download a font to your computer and then, with Windows Explorer, locate it so you can see and then select the actual font(s) you want to install, as shown in Figure 6-20.

3. Right-click the selected fonts and then click **Install**. A message will tell you the fonts are being installed. When you are done the new fonts will appear in the Fonts window.

DELETE FONTS

Remove fonts simply by selecting them in the Fonts window and pressing **DELETE** or by right-clicking the font(s) and clicking **Delete**. In either case, you are told you are deleting a font collection and asked whether you are sure you want to do that. Click **Yes** if you are. The fonts will be deleted *permanently* and can*not* be retrieved from the Recycle Bin.

Continued . . .

- **Who to notify:** To change who is optionally notified of any special situations occurring during printing, as well as when a document has finished printing, put the name of another person (the individual's user name on a shared computer or network) in the **Notify** text box of the document's Properties dialog box.

- **Set print time:** To change when a job is printed, open a document's Properties dialog box, click **Only From** at the bottom under Schedule, and then enter the time range within which you want the job printed. This allows you to print large jobs, which might otherwise clog the print queue, at a time when there is little or no load.

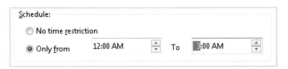

*Figure 6-19: **Windows 7 comes with a large number of fonts, but you can add others.***

QUICKSTEPS

HANDLING FONTS *(Continued)*

USE FONTS

Fonts are used or specified from within a program. In Microsoft Word, for example, you can select a line of text and then open the Font drop-down list on the Formatting toolbar (in versions prior to Office 2007) or in the Font group (in Office 2007). Every program is a little different. One nice feature in recent versions of Word is that the list shows what the fonts look like.

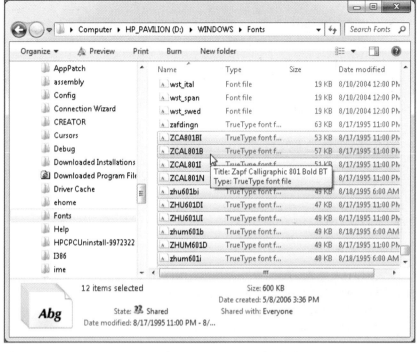

Figure 6-20: **Fonts can be added from many sources, including another computer on the network.**

TIP

To select several fonts, hold down **SHIFT** and click the first and last font (to select several contiguous fonts), or hold down **CTRL** and click each font (to select several noncontiguous fonts).

Chapter 7
Working with Multimedia

Multimedia is the combination of audio and video, with the term *media* referring to either audio or video. As an operating system, Windows 7 has to be able to handle audio and video files and accept their input from a number of different devices. It has four major programs—Windows Media Player, Windows DVD Maker, Windows Media Center, and Windows Live Movie Maker—that enable you to work with these files and read and write them onto CDs, DVDs, flash drives, and music players, as well as *stream* them to other computers (streaming sends audio or video files to another computer in such a way that the other computer can display the files as they are being sent). We'll look first at sound by itself, then at video with sound.

Work with Audio

Audio is sound. Windows 7 works with and uses sound in several ways, the simplest being to alert you of various events, like an incoming email message or closing down the system. Chapter 2 shows you how to customize the use of sounds for these purposes.

The other use of sound is to entertain or inform you—be it listening to music or lectures from CDs, Internet radio, or another Internet site. It is this use of sound that is the subject of this section.

Play CDs

Playing a CD is as easy as inserting a disc in the drive. When you do that, by default, Windows Media Player opens and starts playing the CD. The other alternative is that you will be asked if you want Windows Media Player to play the disc. In that case, if you click **Play Audio CD Using Windows Media Player**, Media Player will open and begin playing the disc. Initially, the on-screen view, called "Now Playing," is a small window, as shown in Figure 7-1. If you click **Switch To Library** in the upper-right corner under the Close button, a larger, more comprehensive window will open, as you can see in Figure 7-2. The Media Player library window has a variety of controls that enable you to determine how it functions and looks.

Figure 7-1: Windows Media Player Now Playing view shows you its controls when you move the mouse over it.

These controls are located either in the functional controls and option menus at the top of the window or in the playback controls at the bottom.

- **Menu options** includes facilities to:
  - **Organize** the Media Player window
  - **Stream** media from your computer
  - **Create a playlist** of selected tracks

Menu options   Functional controls

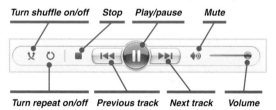

Turn shuffle on/off   Stop   Play/pause   Mute

Turn repeat on/off Previous track   Next track   Volume

Media Guide   Playback controls

*Figure 7-2: **Windows Media Player Library view gives you access to a wide range of audio and video entertainment.***

- **Functional controls** allow selection of the primary Media Player functions:
  - **Rip CD** copies audio CDs to the Media Library.
  - **Rip settings** for audio being copied from a CD.
  - **Play** plays selected tracks and creates a playlist.
  - **Burn** copies playlists from the library to writable CDs and DVDs.
  - **Sync** synchronizes content between portable music devices and your PC.
  - **Media Guide** opens the Windows Media Guide, an online media source for music, movies, TV, and radio.
- **Playback controls** provides CD player–like controls to play/pause, stop, go to a previous track, go to the next track, and adjust volume.

When you click any of the three tabs for the functional controls in the upper-right area, the list pane opens. The Play tab initially lists what is currently being played, but can be cleared and used to build your own playlist. The parts of the Media Player in Play mode are shown in Figure 7-3, and include:

- **List options** hides (closes) the list pane and manipulates the list.
- **Play to** starts an audio or video stream to a media device.
- **Clear list** stops what is being played and prepares the pane for creating a playlist.
- **Save list** saves the current playlist to your media library.
- **Shop for CD/DVD** enables you to buy the item you are listening to or watching.
- **Previous and Next** let you cycle through the playlists in your library.
- **Switch to Now Playing** collapses the window to just the small window shown in Figure 7-1.

Navigation pane   Detail pane   Shop for CD/DVD   List pane   Play to   List options

Windows Media Player

Time Out (J:)

Organize ▾ »

Search

Play   Burn   Sync

Save list   Clear list

01 Fanfare fc
50 Miler
My John Dei
Untitled Play
Music
  Artist
  Album
  Genre
Videos
Pictures
Recorded TV
Other media
Time Out (J:)

Album

Audio CD (J:)

Time Out
The Dave Brubeck ...

Title

1   Blue Rondo à la Turk
2   Strange Meadow Lark
3   Take Five
4   Three to Get Ready
5   Kathy's Waltz
6   Everybody's Jumpin'
7   Pick Up Sticks

Three to Get Ready

Time Out
The Dave Brubeck Quartet

Shop

Time Out

Blue Rondo à la Turk   6:47
Strange Meadow Lark   7:27
Take Five   5:29
Three to Get Ready   5:26
Kathy's Waltz   4:54
Everybody's Jumpin'   4:27
Pick Up Sticks   4:17

7 items, 38 minutes

Dave Brubeck ...   03:55

Previous/
next playlist

Switch to
Now Playing

Figure 7-3: *The list pane shows what is currently playing and is where playlists are created.*

Control the Volume

You can control your computer's audio volume from several places, including the physical volume control on your speakers or on your laptop computer, the volume control on the bottom-right of the playback controls of the Media Player, and the volume icon in the notification area on the right of the taskbar.

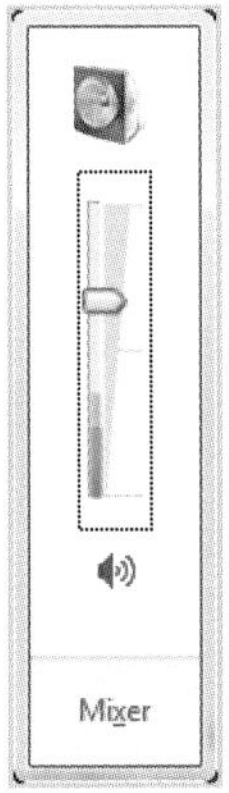

Clicking the **Volume** icon in the notification area opens a small Volume slider that you can drag for louder or softer sound, or you can click **Mute** (the blue speaker at the bottom of the slider) to do just that. Click anywhere on the desktop to close the Volume slider.

Mixer

Access Online Media

If you have a broadband Internet connection (as described in Chapter 4) of at least 512Kbps (more will improve your experience) and sound capability, you can find a large amount of media, including music, movies, and TV. Windows Media Player gives you access to this media through the Media Guide, whose icon is in the lower-left corner of the Media Player and opens into the window shown in Figure 7-4.

Figure 7-4: *The Media Guide facilitates locating music, movies, and TV media.*

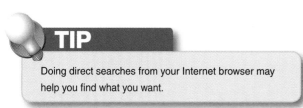
To use the Media Guide to locate media from a closed Media Player.

1. Click the **Windows Media Player** icon  on the taskbar (it is pinned there by default). If you don't have a Media Player icon on the taskbar, click **Start**, click **All Programs**, and click **Windows Media Player**.

2. Click the **Media Guide** icon in the lower-left corner of the Media Player. It may be that the Media Guide icon has been replaced by the Online Stores icon because that is what was last used. In that case, click the **Online Stores** down arrow, and click **Media Guide**.

3. Click in the **Search** text box; type the name of the piece, the performer, or the genre; and either press **ENTER** or click the **Search** magnifying glass. The search results list will appear.

4. Select your choice within the results list, or if you don't find what you want, try a different search. From the results, you often are able to listen to or view a segment and find out where you can buy the entire piece.

5. Close the Media Player when you are ready.

Buy Media Online

There are many sources of media on the Internet. The Online Stores in the Media Player provides links to many of these sites—links that you can follow to featured sites and categories of sites. You can also search for a site—the site of a particular artist, for example.

1. Click the **Windows Media Player** icon on the taskbar. If you don't have a Media Player icon on the taskbar, click **Start**, click **All Programs**, and click **Windows Media Player**.

2. Click the **Online Stores** icon if it is displayed; otherwise, click the **Media Guide** down arrow, and click **Browse All Online Stores**. The Online Stores home page will open.

3. Follow any links that look promising; or type in the **Search** text box (the cursor should be there by default) the name of an artist, song, or movie about whom or which you would like to locate sites. Click **Search**. The search results will appear.

4. Click the link that interests you, and buy what you want. Then follow the instructions to download it to your computer and into your music or video library.

5. Close the Media Player when you are ready.

NOTE

Where it makes sense, consider that when I say "CD" I mean "CD or DVD."

Figure 7-5: Media Player can be used to build a music library from your CDs.

Copy (Rip) CDs to Your Computer

Media Player gives you the ability to copy (or "rip") CD tracks that you like to your hard disk so that you can build and manage a library of your favorite music and copy this material to a recordable CD or DVD. To copy from a CD (see Figure 7-5):

1. Insert the CD from which you want to copy tracks. If it doesn't automatically start playing, click **Play Audio CD Using Windows Media Player** to open Windows Media Player.

NOTE

The material on most CDs and DVDs is owned and copyrighted by some combination of the composer, the artist, the producer, and/or the publisher. Copyright law prohibits using the copyrighted material in ways that are not beneficial to the owners, including giving or selling the content without giving or selling the original CD or DVD itself. To enforce this, most CDs and DVDs are protected to make copying difficult. Media Player provides the ability to copy copyrighted material to your hard disk and then to a recordable CD or a USB Flash drive with the understanding that the copy is solely for your own personal use and you will not sell or give away copies. This is both a great gift and a responsibility. As one who makes his living on copyrighted material, I urge you not to abuse it.

2. In the details pane, select the tracks you want to copy to your hard disk by clicking the check boxes to the left of each track. Click **Play** in the playback controls to listen to the tracks and to make sure your choices are correct.

3. If you wish, click **Rip Settings** and review the settings that are available to you. For the most part, the default settings provide the best middle ground between high quality and file size.

4. When you are satisfied that you have selected the correct tracks and settings, click **Rip CD**. The selected tracks will be copied to your hard disk. When you are done, remove the CD and close Media Player.

Organize Music

Once you have copied several CDs and have downloaded other music to your hard disk, you will likely want them organized. When music and videos are copied to the library, the contents are automatically indexed alphabetically by album, artist, and genre. You may want to combine selected tracks into a *playlist* that allows you to play pieces from several albums. To build a new playlist:

1. Open Media Player and click **Create Playlist** in the menu options area. Enter the name you want for the new playlist, and press **ENTER**. A new playlist will appear in the list of playlists in the navigation pane.

2. Open an album, artist, or genre, and select a piece or the pieces (by holding down **CTRL** as you click multiple pieces) that you want in the new playlist. Drag the piece(s) to the playlist title in the navigation pane.

3. Select additional pieces you want to add, and drag them to the playlist title in the navigation pane. Click the playlist to display the contents of the playlist in the details pane, or double-click the playlist to display it in the Play tab in the list pane and begin to play it.

TIP

When listening to a playlist, you can randomize the order in which the pieces will play by clicking **Turn Shuffle On**  in the playback controls, which is the first button on the left. Click it a second time to return to normal play.

–Or–

1. Open Media Player and click the **Play** tab to open it in the list pane. Select and display in the details pane the music you want in the playlist. Drag the piece(s) you want to the list pane, as you can see in Figure 7-6.

2. When you have added all the pieces that you initially want (you can always add more later), click **Save List**, type a name, and press ENTER.

3. Listen to the playlist by clicking the play button in the playback controls. When you are done, click **Clear List**, click the **Play** tab to close the list pane, and close Media Player.

*Figure 7-6: **Media Player provides a way to manage the media you store on your computer, including building playlists.***

Make (Burn) a Music CD

Once you have created a playlist (see "Organize Music" earlier in this chapter), you can write (or "burn") it to a writable or rewritable CD or DVD using Media Player's Burn feature.

1. Put a blank recordable disc in the CD or DVD recording drive. The AutoPlay dialog box will appear and ask what you want to do. Click **Burn An Audio CD** to open Windows Media Player with the Burn functional area displayed.

2. Open your playlists in the navigation pane, and drag a playlist (or individual songs from an open playlist) that you want on the CD or DVD to the Burn List on the right. You can see how much of the CD is being used and the amount of time remaining just above the Burn List, as shown in Figure 7-7.

Figure 7-7: *Burning a playlist to a writable CD or DVD allows you to create a disc that has just your favorite songs.*

UICKSTEPS

DISPLAYING VISUALIZATIONS IN WINDOWS MEDIA PLAYER

The Media Player's Now Playing window, shown in Figure 7-1, can, as an alternative to the cover art, display a graphic visualization of the music that is playing. Several visualizations come with Media Player, and you can download more. To display a visualization:

1. Right-click the **Now Playing** window, click **Visualizations**, select one of the three types of visualizations (Album Art and Info Center View are static displays), and then click the visualization you want to use, as shown in Figure 7-8.

2. If you want to download additional visualizations, right-click the **Now Playing** window, click **Visualizations**, and click **Download Visualizations**. Then follow the instructions on the Web sites you will visit.

3. You can make corrections to the Burn List by dragging additional songs there until you use up the remaining time, or by right-clicking a song on the Burn List and clicking **Remove From List** in the context menu that opens. You can also clear the Burn List and start over.

4. When you are sure you have the list of pieces you want to burn, click **Start Burn**. The digital files will first be converted to analog music files and then written to a CD or DVD. You can see the progress in the thermometer bar near the top of the list pane (it is not very fast!). When the burn is complete and if no one has changed the default settings, the disc will be ejected from the drive. Write the title on the disc with a soft felt-tip marker, or use a LightScribe drive to burn a label on the special discs you use for this purpose.

The resulting CD should be playable in most CD players.

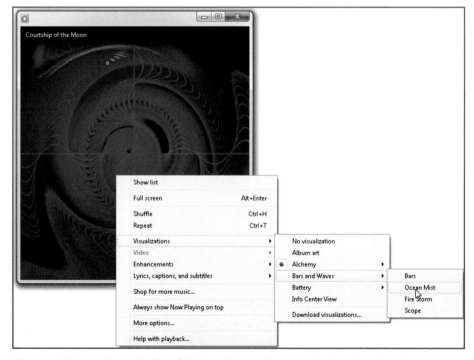

Figure 7-8: **You can have the Now Playing window display a visualization of music that is being played.**

Copy to (Sync with) Music Players

Windows Media Player allows you to plug in a digital music device, such as an MP3 player, and transfer music to and from (sync with) the device.

1. Start Windows Media Player, and click **Sync** in the Windows Media Player functional controls. You will be told to connect your device.

2. Start your device and then plug it into your computer. The first time you do that, Windows will install a driver for it, and then the AutoPlay dialog box will appear.

   You can manually select playlists and songs that you want copied to the device, as shown in Figure 7-9.

Figure 7-9: A digital music device can mirror your Media Player library if it has enough room and that is what you want.

3. In the Devices Setup dialog box, click **Finish** or **Cancel**, depending on your situation. If you click **Cancel**, drag the playlists and/or songs you want on the device to the Sync List on the right. If you wish, you can play the Sync List by double-clicking the first playlist or song.

4. When you are certain that you have all the music in the Sync List that you want on your device, click **Start Sync**. The music will be copied to the device.

Work with Video

Windows 7 lets you watch videos from a DVD, from live or recorded TV, or downloaded from the Internet using Windows Media Player or Windows Media Center. It also allows you to capture videos and still images from a digital camcorder or digital camera using Windows Live Photo Gallery and then edit those into your own movie using Windows Live Movie Maker.

Play DVDs

Playing DVDs is as easy as playing CDs: Simply insert a DVD into its drive. When you do that, the AutoPlay dialog box will appear, and you will be asked if you want to play the DVD using Windows Live Media Player. We'll discuss Media Center later in this chapter, but if you click **Play DVD Movie** using Windows Media Player, the player will open and play the disc. The Media Player controls are virtually the same for DVDs as they are for CDs, except the View Full Screen option enlarges the movie or video you are watching to fit the full screen, and the DVD menu has options for viewing menus and special features on the DVD.

UICKSTEPS

PREPARING TO MAKE A MOVIE

Making a movie with a computer takes more hardware than any other task. The faster your CPU, the more memory it has, the better your video display adapter, and the larger your disk, the more smoothly the task will go. The beauty is that most recent computers have what you need by default.

REQUIREMENTS CHECKLIST

The recommended hardware requirements for making movies are as follows:

COMPONENT	RECOMMENDED HARDWARE
CPU	2.4 GHz dual core
RAM memory	2GB
Hard drive free space	60GB
Optical drive	DVD±R
Video display card	Supports DirectX 9.0c, WDDM driver, Windows Aero, Pixel Shader 2.0, 32 bits/pixel, 128MB dedicated video memory or more
Video recording from DV camcorders	IEEE 1394 FireWire card, OHCI-compliant
Video capture from analog VCR/camera/TV	Windows 7–compatible video capture card
Audio capture from microphone, tape	Windows 7–compatible audio card and microphone

NOTES ON REQUIREMENTS

- Memory is most important. The more, the better.
- CPU capability is a close second in importance. To work with full-motion video, you need a lot of it. 2.4 MHz dual core is really the minimum.

Continued . . .

Import Video from a Camcorder

Importing video directly from your camcorder to your hard disk is done using the Windows Live Photo Gallery.

1. Click **Start**, click **All Programs**, click **Windows Live**, and click **Windows Live Photo Gallery**. Click the **File** menu, and click **Import From A Camera Or Scanner**.

2. Plug your camcorder into an OHCI-compliant FireWire port on your computer, and turn it on. Windows 7 will detect it, install the necessary driver software, and display it in the list of devices.

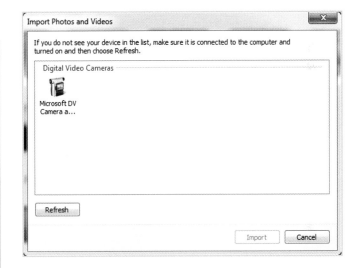

3. Select your digital video camera, and click **Import**. The Import Video dialog box will appear. Type the name you want for the video, click either **Import The Entire Video** or **Choose Parts Of The Video**, and click **Next** (you can also burn the entire video to a DVD, but here we want to make a movie from the video).

If you chose to import the entire video and your camcorder uses tape, it will be rewound, and then the capture will begin playing and importing the video without controls to pause, rewind, or fast-forward it. When the end of the video is reached,

QUICKSTEPS

PREPARING TO MAKE A MOVIE

(Continued)

- The initial capture of video from a camcorder to your computer can use approximately 12GB per hour captured in disk space.

- The video display card has become quite important to Windows Live Movie Maker. It will not work without the minimum shown in the table. See the Note on how to check this.

- With a digital video (DV) camcorder and an IEEE 1394 FireWire interface, get an Open Host Controller Interface (OHCI)–compliant FireWire card for your computer, if one isn't built in.

- A video capture card can bring in a video signal from a TV, a VCR, an analog camcorder, and (in most cases) a DV camcorder; however, the result is not as good as a digital recording.

the importation will stop, the Import Video dialog box will close, and you will see a message telling you it is finished. Click **OK**.

–Or–

If you chose to import portions of the video, the camcorder will not be rewound and you can use its controls to position the video. Also, you are given controls in the Import Video dialog box. Position the video in your camcorder to a little before where you want to start recording using either its controls or those in the Import Video dialog box, and press the **Stop** icon. Then, in the dialog box, click the **Play** icon. When you are at the spot you want to start importing, click **Import**. You can import some, stop it, reposition the video, and again click **Play** and **Import**. When you are done with the importation, click **Finish** to close the Import Video dialog box.

Windows Live Photo Gallery will show you where your video is stored. From either Photo Gallery or Windows Media Player, you can play the captured video by locating and double-clicking it.

Make a Movie

Making a movie out of the imported camcorder video and other material involves selecting and editing the available material; assembling it into the order in which you want it; adding narration, titles, and special effects; and finally publishing the finished product. Windows Live Movie Maker provides the means to do that. While working in Movie Maker, you are working on what Movie Maker calls a "project," which is a fluid collection of video clips, still pictures, titles, audio clips, narration, and special effects that you have added and laid out along a timeline. So long as you are in the project and have not published the movie, you can change almost anything. Projects can be saved and reopened for as long as you like.

To begin making a movie using the imported camcorder video and other material:

1. Click **Start**, click **All Programs**, click **Windows Live**, and click **Windows Live Movie Maker**. Movie Maker opens with a new project tentatively named "My Movie." Start the project by adding content.

2. Click **Add** in the Home tab Videos And Photos group. In the Add Videos And Photos dialog box that appears, locate and select the video footage you want to work with, and click **Open**.

3. Repeat step 2, as shown in Figure 7-10, adding video footage, still pictures, and music (clicking Add in the Soundtrack group) that you want to use. Most audio, video, and picture file types are supported. When you have all the material you want, drag it around the content (right) pane until it is in the order that you want.

You can continue to add, remove (right-click and click **Remove**), and rearrange elements in your project throughout its creation. You can also:

- **Trim** video clips
- **Add transitions** between pictures
- **Adjust the duration** for which a still image is shown
- **Add titles** to the video
- **Adjust the mix** between the sound on a video and the added music

In Chapter 4, when I suggested you install Windows Live, Movie Maker was not selected by default so you may not have installed it at that time. Therefore, it may not be in your Windows Live list and you will need to go back to the Windows Live site and install it. See Chapter 4 for more information.

Figure 7-10: *The process of making a movie entails selecting and editing video, audio, and still images.*

While you are still working with a project and have not published the movie, you can think of trimming as simply "hiding" the ends of the clips. You can recover what you have trimmed until you publish the movie. Do this by selecting **Trim** and dragging the trim handles out to include more material.

TRIM VIDEO CLIPS

You can remove unwanted frames by *trimming,* or deleting, frames from the beginning or end of a video clip.

1. Select the video clip you want to trim.

2. Click the **Edit** tab, and click **Trim** in the Video group. Trim handles will appear at either end of the progress slider.

3. If you want to trim the beginning of the clip, play the clip to the point at which you want to trim, and then drag the trim handle to that point, dragging it back and forth until it is correctly placed.

4. To trim the right end of the clip, drag the right trim handle to the left until you get to the point where you want to trim off the rest of the clip.

5. When the trim handles are positioned at both ends where you want them, click **Save And Close** in the Trim tab to save the trim positions and close the Trim operation.

ADD TRANSITIONS

When you bring in or drag a clip or a still image to the workspace, it simply abuts the preceding clip. The last frame of the preceding clip plays or a still image is displayed, and then the first frame of the new clip plays or the next still image is displayed. Movie Maker provides several transitions that you can add to smooth out the progression from one element to the next.

1. Click the rightmost clip or image of a pair where you want a transition.

2. Click the **Visual Effects** tab, and click the transition you want to use. The focus will shift back to the left member of the pair so you can click the **Play** icon to see the transition.

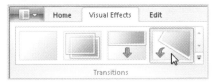

ADJUST DURATION OF STILL IMAGES

By default, still images that are used in a movie are displayed for three seconds. You can adjust this to anything from 1 to 30 seconds.

1. Select the still image whose duration you want to change.

2. Click the **Edit** tab, click the **Duration** down arrow, and click the duration (in seconds) you want to use.

ADD TITLES

Windows Live Movie Maker provides the means to add titles and text to movies you create. This text will overlay the video and still images you have.

1. Select the video or still image where you want the text, click the **Edit** tab, and click **Text Box**. A text box with eight sizing handles will appear on the selected image.

2. Select the font, its size, whether it is bold and/ or italic, and its color. Then type the text you want in the title.

**Mike's Eagle
Project &
Court of Honor
Spring 2004**

00:00 / 28:31

3. When you have entered all the text you want, use the sizing handles to size the box to position the text. Use **SHIFT+ENTER** to create a line break.

4. Point on an edge of the text box to get a four-headed arrow, and then drag the text box to where you want it in the image.

5. Drag over all the text to select it, and then use:

   ● **CTRL+L** to left-align it

   ● **CTRL+R** to right-align it

   ● **CTRL+E** to center it

6. When you are ready, click on another image to close the text box and leave the text.

7. At any time you can return to the image with the text and click **Text Box** to edit the text.

MIX SOUND

After adding a sound clip you have two sound tracks—one that was on the original video and one that you have added. By default, the volume level of both tracks is the same. You can adjust the relative level between the two soundtracks in the Home tab by clicking **Mix**. The Mix slider will appear. Dragging the slider to the left increases the relative level of the video soundtrack, dragging it to the right increases the relative level of the audio you have added. In both cases, the change is for the entire project. The slider closes when you complete a change, or you can close it when you are done by clicking anywhere below the slider.

Complete a Movie

The final step in making a movie is to create a movie file that you can upload to the Internet or output, either for a DVD or a portable device.

OUTPUT TO A DVD

If you want to save your movie to replay on your computer or put it on a DVD:

1. In the Home tab, click **Output** and click how you want to replay this movie, as shown in Figure 7-11.

2. In the Output Movie dialog box that appears, select the drive and folder in which you want to save your movie, enter a name for it, and click **Save**.

3. With the DVD choice, Movie Maker will save the project, which may take a considerable amount of time if your video is of any length, and you will be told when it is complete.

4. Click **View Folder** to open the folder in Windows Explorer that contains your new video. Leave this window open; you will be using it again in a minute.

*Figure 7-11: **Saving a movie for replay on either your computer or a DVD player is the most versatile option.***

SAVE A MOVIE TO DVD

With your new movie file, you can burn it onto a DVD.

1. Click **Start**, click **All Programs**, and click **Windows DVD Maker**. If this is the first time you have used Windows DVD Maker, click **Choose Photos And Videos**.

2. Position the Windows DVD Maker window and the Windows Explorer window with your video so you can see them both.

3. Drag your video from Windows Explorer to DVD Maker. Type a name for the DVD title, and click **Next**.

TIP

Saving a movie is equivalent to printing a document: You still have the original content to rebuild the movie, but the movie itself can't be edited.

NOTE

Opening a *project* opens the media in Movie Maker, where it can be edited. Opening a *movie* sets it up for playback in Media Player or other video display programs and devices.

4. If you wish to see your video, click **Preview**, use the player controls, and when you are done, click **OK**. Review the text, customization, and style alternatives to add a menu to your DVD to select among multiple videos.

5. When you are ready, click **Burn**. Put a blank DVD in your drive, and the process will begin. It will take a bit of time, depending on how long your movie is and the speed of your computer and DVD drive.

6. When the DVD is created, it will be ejected from the drive, and you'll be asked if you want to make another. Remove and label the disc using a soft felt-tip marker.

7. If you want to make another copy, click that option and insert another blank disc; otherwise, click **Close** and click **Close** again to close Windows DVD Maker. Click **Yes** to save your DVD project, enter a **Name**, and click **Save**.

EXPLORING WINDOWS MEDIA CENTER

With the right equipment, Windows Media Center allows you to view, record, and play back live TV. It also provides an enhanced playback and viewing experience with DVDs, CDs, and the music and photographic libraries you have on your computer. It connects you to Web services from Microsoft and other vendors. Windows Media Center is available in Windows 7 Home Premium, Professional, Enterprise, and Ultimate editions.

To effectively use and get the full benefit from Windows Media, you need all the recommended computer components discussed in the "Preparing to Make a Movie" QuickSteps, as well as a TV tuner card in your computer and a connection to TV media. The tuner cards are available for approximately $100 from several companies. Look for compatibility with Windows Media Center.

To use Media Center:

1. Click **Start**, click **All Programs**, and click **Windows Media Center**. The first time you do that, you will go through an initial setup.

2. Click **Continue** and then click **Express**. Windows will look at the hardware that is available on your computer. If you have a TV tuner card, you will then need to click **Live TV Set Up**, and Media Center will be configured for the type of TV signal you have (antenna, cable, or satellite).

3. Then you will be asked questions about your ZIP code so that you can receive an online TV guide tailored to your local area. When you are done with the setup, you will see the main Media Center window shown in Figure 7-12.

Continued . . .

PUBLISH TO THE INTERNET

If you want to publish your movie on the Internet:

1. In the Home tab Make Movie group, click **Publish** and click to choose the Internet service you want to use. You may need to download a plug-in.

2. Depending the service you select, you may have to register and enter an ID and password.

3. Follow the instructions from the service, entering such things as a title, description, and other information. Movie Maker will then make the movie (a slow process), and it will be uploaded to the Internet. You will get a message when the process is complete.

Figure 7-12: **The Windows Media Center brings live as well as recorded TV to your computer.**

QUICKFACTS

EXPLORING WINDOWS MEDIA CENTER (Continued)

At this point, you can use your mouse, the keyboard, or the TV remote control that came with your TV tuner card to navigate (move your mouse to see its controls) and watch TV, either in a window on your screen, as shown in Figure 7-13, or in the default full screen. If you don't have a tuner card, you can play recorded TV. The possibilities of what you can do are significant.

Figure 7-13: *You can watch TV in a window or have it take up the full screen.*

How to...

Chapter 8
Controlling Security

Controlling computer security is a complex subject because of the many different aspects of computing that need protection. In this chapter you'll see how to control who uses a computer, control what users do, and protect data stored in the computer.

Control Who Is a User

Controlling who uses a computer means identifying the users to the computer, giving them a secure way of signing on to the computer, and preventing everyone else from using it. This is achieved through the process of adding and managing users and passwords.

With Windows 7, like previous versions of Windows, the first user of a computer is, by default, an administrator; however, the Windows 7 administrator operates like a standard user until there is a need to be an administrator. Then a Windows 7 feature called *User Account Control* (UAC) pops up and asks if the administrator started the process. If so, click **Continue** to proceed. A non-administrative user in the same circumstance would have to enter an administrator's password to continue.

This book talks about setting up *local* user accounts, which are those that are set up on and use a local computer, as well as a workgroup local area network (LAN). If your computer is part of a domain (generally found in larger organizations—see Chapter 9 for a discussion of domains), it is important to use domain user accounts that are set up on a domain controller rather than local user accounts, since local user accounts are not recognized by the domain.

QUICK**FACTS**

UNDERSTANDING USER ACCOUNT CONTROL

Windows 7 has a feature called User Account Control, or UAC. UAC monitors what is happening on the computer, and if it sees something that could cause a problem, like installing a program, adding a new user, or changing a password, it interrupts that process and asks for physical user verification. When it does this, it also freezes all activity on the computer so that nothing can happen until verification is provided—either using the mouse or the keyboard. If the user has administrator privileges, this person is asked if he or she started the process and, if so, to click Continue. If the user doesn't have administrator privileges, he or she is asked for the administrator's password. By requiring a physical action, UAC ensures that an actual person is sitting at the computer and that malware is not attempting to modify it.

Continued ...

Even though you may initially be an administrator, *it is strongly recommended that your normal everyday account be as a standard user.* The reason for this is that if you are signed on as an administrator and a hacker or malevolent software (called "malware") enters your system at the same time, the hacker or software might gain administrator privileges through you. The best solution is to use a separate administrator account with a strong password just for installing software, working with users, and performing other tasks that require extensive administrator work.

Set Up Users

To add users to your computer, or even to change your user characteristics (as well as to perform most other tasks in this chapter), you must be logged on as an administrator, so you first need to accomplish that. Then you may want to change the characteristics of your account and add a Standard User account for yourself. Finally, if you have multiple people using your computer, you may want to set up separate user accounts and have each user sign in to his or her account.

LOG ON AS AN ADMINISTRATOR

The procedure for logging on as an administrator depends on what was done when Windows 7 was installed on your computer:

- If you are in an organization with people responsible for supporting the computers in the organization, you will most likely need to contact them to determine the procedure for logging on as an administrator.

- If you installed Windows 7 on your computer, or you bought a computer with it already installed and did nothing special to the default installation regarding administrator privileges, you should be the administrator and know the administrator's password (if you established one—it may be blank).

- If you did not do the installation or you got the computer with Windows 7 already installed and you are unsure about your administrator status or password, the instructions here will help you log on as an administrator. The first step is to determine the administrator status on your computer.

UNDERSTANDING USER ACCOUNT CONTROL *(Continued)*

If you have both Administrator and Standard User accounts, then, while you are using the Standard User account, you can simply enter the administrator's password when needed—you don't need to switch users. In addition, if a program requires you to be an administrator in order to run it, you can right-click the program and click **Run As Administrator**. If you are logged on as an administrator, that's all you have to do. If you are not logged on as an administrator, you will have to enter a password and click **Yes**.

All operations that require administrative privileges have a little shield icon beside them, as shown here:

Open
Troubleshoot compatibility
Open file location
Run as administrator
Scan with Panda Antivirus Pro 2009
Pin to Taskbar
Pin to Start Menu

For a while, especially if you are installing several programs, the UAC dialog boxes can be irritating. You can turn this off in the User Accounts control panel, but this is strongly discouraged. If you do turn it off while you are installing several programs, it is strongly recommended that you turn on again when you are finished.

TIP

If your personal account on your computer is currently set up as an Administrator account, it is strongly recommended that you create a new Standard User account and use that for your everyday computer use. Only use the Administrator account for installing software, changing and adding user information, and performing other tasks requiring an administrator.

1. Click **Start** and click **Control Panel**. In Category view, click **User Accounts And Family Safety**, and then click **User Accounts**. The User Accounts window opens, as shown in Figure 8-1.

   If your User Accounts window opens and shows you are a standard user, as does Figure 8-1, you need to proceed with these steps. If the window shows you are an administrator, you can skip these steps. To make changes to an account, see "Change Your Account" later in this chapter.

2. Click **Change Your Account Type**:

   ● If you are not an administrator but there is one on your computer, the User Account Control dialog box will appear and ask you to type the administrator's password. If you can, do that and skip to "Change Your Account" later in the chapter.

   ● If you are an administrator, the dialog box will ask if you started this action. If so, click **Continue** and skip to "Change Your Account" later in the chapter.

   ● If you are not an administrator and you don't know an administrator's password, try leaving the Password field blank and clicking **Yes**, which would be the password if someone didn't fill one in. If that doesn't work, you will need outside support to log on as an administrator.

*Figure 8-1: **Setting up users provides a way of protecting each user from the others and the computer from unauthorized use.***

CHANGE YOUR ACCOUNT

You can change an account name, the display picture, add or change a password, and possibly change the account type.

1. Click **Start** and click **Control Panel**. In Category view, click **User Accounts And Family Safety**, and then click **User Accounts**.
2. Click **Change Your Account Name**. If you are not already logged on as an administrator, the User Account Control dialog box will appear and ask you to type an administrator's password.
3. Type a new name, and click **Change Name**.

In a similar manner, you can change your display picture. If you are the only administrator, you will not be allowed to change your account type or delete your account. Changing and setting passwords are discussed in the "Setting Passwords" QuickSteps in this chapter.

SET UP ANOTHER USER

To set up another user account, possibly a Standard User account for your use:

1. Click **Start** and click **Control Panel**. In Category view, click **User Accounts And Family Safety**, and then click **User Accounts**. The User Accounts window opens.
2. Click **Manage Another Account**, and, if needed, type a password and click **Yes** to open the Manage Accounts window, as shown in Figure 8-2.
3. Click **Create A New Account**. Type a name of up to 20 characters. Note that it cannot contain just periods, spaces, or the @ symbol; it cannot contain " / \ [ ] : ; | = ,+ * ? < >; and leading spaces or periods are dropped.
4. Accept the default account type, **Standard User**, or click **Administrator** as the account type. You can see a summary of the privileges available to each user type.

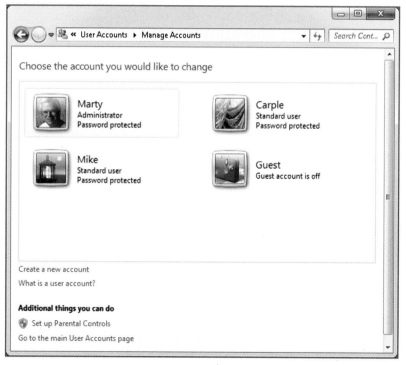

○ Standard user
Standard account users can use most software and change system settings that do not affect other users or the security of the computer.

○ Administrator
Administrators have complete access to the computer and can make any desired changes. Based on notification settings, administrators may be asked to provide their password or confirmation before making changes that affect other users.

*Figure 8-2: **User Accounts provides password and user account management.***

5. Click **Create Account**. You are returned to the Manage Accounts window. Changing other aspects of the account is described in later sections of this chapter.

Reset a Password

Windows 7 allows you to reset a password you have forgotten if you have previously created a password reset disk, which can be a USB flash drive, CD, or floppy disk.

CREATE A RESET DISK

1. Insert a USB flash drive in its socket, or insert a writable CD or a formatted and unused floppy disk into its respective drive. Close the AutoPlay window if it opens.

2. Click **Start** and click **Control Panel**. In Category view, click **User Accounts And Family Safety**, and then click **User Accounts**. The User Accounts window opens.

*Figure 8-3: **Creating, changing, or deleting a password will lose all items that are based on passwords, such as encrypted files, certificates, and other passwords.***

QUICKSTEPS

SETTING PASSWORDS (Continued)

This is the case every time you create, change, or delete a password.

3. Type the new password, click in the second text box, type the new password again to confirm it, click in the third text box, type a non-obvious hint to help you remember the password, and click **Create Password**.

4. Close the Change An Account window.

CHANGE A PASSWORD

It is a good idea to change your password periodically in case it has been compromised.

1. Click **Start** and click **Control Panel**. In Category view, click **User Accounts And Family Safety**, and then click **User Accounts**. The User Accounts window opens.

2. If it is not your account that you want to change, click **Manage Another Account**. If needed, type a password, click **Yes**, and click the account you want to change. In your account or in the other account that opens, click **Change Your/The Password**.

3. In your account, type the current password and click in the second text box. In either your or another's account, type a new password, click in the next text box, and type the new password again to confirm it. Click in the final text box, type a non-obvious hint to help you remember the password, and click **Change Password**.

4. Close the Change An Account window.

Continued . . .

---

3. Click **Create A Password Reset Disk** in the list of tasks on the left. If needed, type a password and click **Yes**.

4. The Forgotten Password Wizard starts. Click **Next**. Click the drive down arrow, and select the drive on which you want to create the password key. Click **Next**.

5. Type the current user account password, and again click **Next**. The disk will be created. When this process is done, click **Next**. Then click **Finish**. Remove and label the disk, and store it in a safe place.

6. Close the User Accounts window.

USE A RESET DISK

If you have forgotten your password and there isn't another person with administrator permissions on your computer who can reset it, you can use a reset disk you have previously created.

1. Start your computer. When you see the Welcome screen, click your user name. If you have forgotten your password, click the right arrow. You will be told that the user name or password is incorrect.

2. Click **OK** to return to the password entry, and look at your hint.

3. If the hint isn't of any help, click **Reset Password**. The Password Reset Wizard starts.

4. Click **Next**. Insert your reset disk in its socket or drive. Click the drive down arrow, select the drive the reset disk is in, and again click **Next**. Type a new password, confirm it, type a password hint, click **Next**, and click **Finish**. (You do not have to create a new reset disk with your new password; Windows updates the reset disk for you.) Remove the reset disk.

5. Enter your new password, and press **ENTER**.

CAUTION

If you or someone else changes your password, all passwords and encrypted files tied to the original password are permanently inaccessible with the new password. If you use a password reset disk to reset your password, you will retain access to all your original information.

NOTE

A CD, a floppy disk, or a USB flash drive can hold the password reset for only one user at a time, but it is just a file on the disk and can store other information if you want.

REMOVE A PASSWORD

If you move a computer to a location that doesn't need a password—for example, if it is not accessible to anyone else, or if you want to remove a password for some other reason—you can do so.

1. Click **Start** and click **Control Panel**. In Category view, click **User Accounts And Family Safety**, and then click **User Accounts**. The User Accounts window opens.

2. If it is not your account in which you want to remove the password, click **Manage Another Account**. If needed, type a password, click **Yes**, and click the account you want. In your account or in the other account that opens, click **Remove Your/The Password**.

3. If it is your account, type the current password, and, in any case, click **Remove Password**.

4. Close the Change An Account window.

TIP

For a password to be *strong*, it must be eight or more characters long; use both upper- and lowercase letters; and use a mixture of letters, numbers, and symbols, including spaces. It also should not be a recognizable word, name, or date.

Replace Passwords

The weakest link in the Windows 7 security scheme is the use of passwords. Users give their passwords to others or forget them, and passwords are often stolen or just "found." There is nothing to tie a password to an individual, which is handy for sharing, but also a security risk. Two potential means of replacing passwords are smart cards and biometric devices.

SMART CARDS

Smart cards are credit card–sized pieces of plastic that have a tamper-resistant electronic circuit embedded in them that permanently stores an ID, a password, and other information. Smart cards require a personal identification number (PIN), so they add a second layer (smart card plus PIN in place of a password) that is needed to log on to a system. Smart cards can also be used to encrypt something only you (or someone with your smart card and PIN) can open.

Windows 7 detects and supports smart cards, and lets them be used to log on to a computer or network, as well for other authentication needs.

Smart cards require a reader to be attached to the computer, either through a USB (Universal Serial Bus) port or a PCMCIA (Personal Computer Memory Card International Association) slot. With a smart card reader, users at the logon screen need to insert their card into the reader, click **Switch User**, and then, when prompted, enter their PIN. With a valid card and PIN, users are authenticated and allowed on the system in the same way as they would be by entering a valid user name and password.

Most smart card readers are usable with Windows 7. The drivers for these devices either are included with or are available for Windows 7, and installing them is not difficult; you need only follow the instructions that come with them.

With a smart card reader installed, set up new accounts (as described in "Set Up Users") and then, for both new and old accounts, open each user's Create Password window, and click **Smart Card Is Required For Interactive Logon**, which will appear when a smart card reader is present. You do not have to enter a password.

8

NOTE

In case you wondered, the PIN is encrypted and placed on the smart card when it is made. The PIN is not stored on the computer.

QUICKFACTS

CUSTOMIZING A USER ACCOUNT

Each user account can be unique, with a custom Start menu, desktop, color scheme, and screen saver. When programs are installed, you can choose whether they are for just the current user or for all users. When you set up a new user, it is as though you are setting up a new computer. The previous chapters of this book talk about the steps to set up a computer.

As you may have seen earlier in this chapter, a number of elements of the account itself can be changed, including the name, password, display picture, and account type. You can change the name and password in a manner almost identical to what you used to create them, as described in "Set Up Users" section and the "Setting Passwords" QuickSteps earlier in this chapter.

BIOMETRIC DEVICES

Smart cards do provide an added degree of security over passwords, but if someone obtains both the card and the PIN, he or she's home-free. The only way to be totally sure that the computer is actually talking to the authorized person is to require some form of physical identification.

This is the purpose of *biometric devices,* which identify people by physical traits, such as voice, handprint, fingerprint, face, or eyes. Often, these devices are used with a smart card to replace the PIN. Biometric devices are becoming more common, and Windows 7 will work with many of them. Devices are available for under $100, for a fingerprint scanner, to several thousand dollars for a face scanner. Many laptops have fingerprint scanners built in. Depending on your needs, you may want to keep these devices in mind.

Switch Among Users

When you have multiple users on a computer, one user can obviously log off and another log on; however, with the Welcome screen, you can use Fast User Switching (which is not available in the Starter Edition of Windows 7). This allows you to keep programs running and files open when you temporarily switch to another user. To use Fast User Switching:

1. Click **Start**, click the **Shut Down** right arrow, and click **Switch User**. The Welcome screen will appear. Let the other person log on.

2. When the other person has finished using the computer and has logged off (by clicking **Start**, clicking the **Shut Down** right arrow, and clicking **Log Off**), you can log on normally. When you do, you will see all your programs exactly as you left them.

Control What a User Does

User accounts identify people and allow them to log on to your computer. What they can do after that depends on the permissions they have. Windows 7 has two features that help you control what other users do on your computer: Parental Controls and the ability to turn Windows features on and off for a given user. In addition, Windows 7's NT File System (NTFS) allows the sharing of folders and drives as well as the assignment of permissions to use a file, a folder, a disk, a printer, and other devices. The permissions are given to individuals and to groups to which individuals can belong. So far, you've seen two groups: Administrators and Standard Users (also called just "Users,"), but there are others, and you can create more.

You can limit the sharing of files and folders to the *Public folder* within the Users folder on your computer. To do so, you must create or move the files and folders you want to share into the Public folder. The other option is to share directly the other folders on your computer. This is made easier by the *inheritance* attribute, where subfolders automatically inherit (take on) the permissions of their parent folder. Every object in Windows 7 NTFS, however, has its own set of *security descriptors* that are attached to it when it is created; with the proper permission, these security descriptors can be individually changed.

When permissions are appropriately set, other users on your computer can access and optionally change your files and folders. Also, with appropriate permissions and other settings (see Chapter 9 for a discussion on sharing across a network), people on other computers or even you on another computer on the local area network (LAN) of which your computer is a member, can access and optionally change your files and folders.

Depending on how your network has been set up (see Chapter 9), the disks, folders, and files on your computer may or may not be shared. You will see in the following sections how to share what is on your computer.

Set Parental Controls

If you have a child as one of the users on your computer and you are an administrator with a password, you can control what your child can do on your computer, including hours of usage, programs he or she can run, and access to the Internet. When your child encounters a blocked program, game, or Web site,

CAUTION

File sharing can be a valuable and useful capability, but it can also open up your computer to significant harm. It is important to think through what your needs are and how you want to do the file sharing to get the value without the harm.

NOTE

A child for whom you want to set up Parental Controls must have a Standard User account. To set up the Parental Controls, you must have an Administrator account with a password.

NOTE

For Parental Controls to work, the disk drives on which you want to control the use of games must use the NTFS file system. Parental Controls will not work with the older File Allocation Table (FAT) file system. While you are installing Parental Controls, if a drive with the FAT file system is detected, you will be told this. You can go ahead and install Parental Controls, but content on the FAT drive will not be controlled.

a notice is displayed, including a link the child can click to request access. You, as an administrator, can allow one-time access by entering your user ID and password.

1. Click **Start** and click **Control Panel**. In Category view, click **User Accounts And Family Safety**, and then click **Parental Controls**. If needed, type an administrator password and click **Yes**. The Parental Controls window opens.

2. Click the user for whom you want to set Parental Controls to open the individual User Controls window.

3. Click **On** under Parental Controls, as shown in Figure 8-4.

4. Click **Time Limits**, drag the hours to block or allow (you only need to select one or the other, and you can drag across multiple hours and days), and then click **OK**.

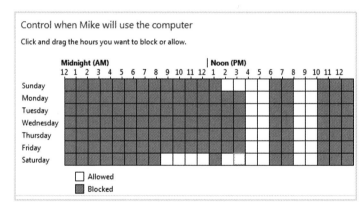

5. Click **Games** and choose if any games can be played. Click **Set Game Ratings**, choose if games with no rating can be played, click a rating level, choose the type of content you want blocked, and click **OK**. Click **Block Or Allow Specific Games**, click whether to block or allow specific games installed on the computer, and click **OK**. Click **OK** again to leave Game Controls.

6. Click **Allow And Block Specific Programs**, and choose whether to allow the use of all programs or only the ones you choose. If you choose to pick specific programs to allow, a list of all the programs on the computer is presented. Click those for which you want to allow access, and click **OK**.

7. Click **OK** to close the User Controls window.

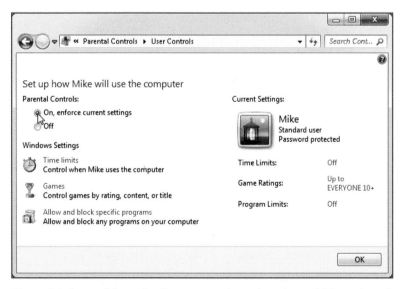

Figure 8-4: *Parental Controls allows you to determine what a child can do and see on your computer.*

NOTE

In addition to the parental controls that are described here, additional controls such as Web filtering and activity reporting are available for download and use at the bottom of the window that opens when you first open Parental Controls in step 1 of the "Set Parental Controls" section of this chapter.

Control What Parts of Windows Can Be Used

As an administrator, you can control what parts of Windows 7 each user can use.

1. Log on as the user for whom you want to set Windows feature usage.

2. Click **Start** and click **Control Panel**. In Category view, click **Programs** and then click **Programs And Features**.

3. Click **Turn Windows Features On Or Off** in the left column. If needed, type a password and click **Yes**. The Windows Features dialog box appears.

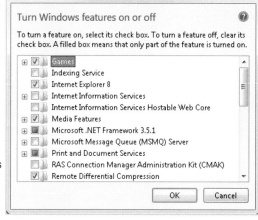

4. Click an unselected check box to turn a feature on, or click a selected check box to turn a feature off. Click the plus sign (+) where applicable to open the subfeatures and turn them on or off.

5. When you have selected the features the user will be allowed to use, click **OK**.

6. Close the Programs And Features window.

Set File and Folder Sharing

Files are shared by being in a shared folder or drive. Folders and drives are shared by their creator or owner or by an administrator. To share folders and drives, as well as printers and other devices, both locally and over a network, you must address three components of Windows 7 that allow you to control access to your computer and its components (see Figure 8-5):

- **The Windows Firewall**, which protects your computer and its contents from network access

Individual drive and folder sharing

The Network and Sharing Center

The Windows Firewall

Path to file, folder, and drive sharing

Figure 8-5: The sharing of your computer requires that you set up your firewall, the Network And Sharing Center, and the individual drives and folders to accomplish that.

Windows 7 QuickSteps *Controlling Security* 191

- **The Network And Sharing Center**, which is the primary means of controlling sharing in Windows 7

- **Sharing individual drives and folders**, which lets you determine if a drive, folder, or other device is shared; who has permission to access it; and what they can do with the contents

SET UP THE WINDOWS FIREWALL

Windows 7 includes the Windows Firewall, whose objective is to slow down and hopefully prevent anybody from accessing your computer without your permission, while at the same time allowing those who you want to use your computer to do so. The Windows Firewall is turned on by default. Check to see if it is; if it isn't, turn it on.

Help protect your computer with Windows Firewall

Windows Firewall can help prevent hackers or malicious software from gaining access to your computer through the Internet or a network.

How does a firewall help protect my computer?

What are network locations?

Home or work (private) networks	Connected ⌃

Networks at home or work where you know and trust the people and devices on the network

Windows Firewall state:	On
Incoming connections:	Block all connections to programs that are not on the list of allowed programs
Active home or work (private) networks:	Network
Notification state:	Notify me when Windows Firewall blocks a new program

Public networks	Not Connected ⌄

1. Click **Start** and click **Control Panel**. In Category view, click **System And Security**, and then click **Windows Firewall**. The Windows Firewall window opens and shows your firewall status.

2. If your firewall is not turned on, or if you want to turn it off, click **Turn Windows Firewall On Or Off** in the pane on the left. If needed, type a password and click **Yes**. The Windows Firewall Settings window opens. Click the respective option button to turn on your firewall (highly recommended) or to turn it off (not recommended). You can do this for both your local network and for the public network to which you are connected, which includes the Internet. Click **OK**.

3. To change the settings for what the firewall will and won't let through, click **Allow A Program Or Feature Through Windows Firewall** at the top of the left column. The Allowed Programs window opens, as shown in Figure 8-6.

4. In the Programs And Features list, select the services running on your computer that you want to allow people from the Internet to use. To share information across a LAN, click at least the following items:

- Core Networking

- File And Printer Sharing

TIP

In the Windows Firewall Allowed Programs window, you can determine what each option does by highlighting it and clicking **Details** at the bottom of the dialog box.

NOTE

You will probably have other programs selected, such as Internet Explorer and Windows Live Messenger, that can be used on the Internet.

TIP

If you have a specific program not on the Windows Firewall Allowed Programs And Features list, you can include that program by clicking **Allow Another Program** at the bottom of the Windows Firewall Allowed Programs window. Select the program from the list or browse to its location, and click **Add**.

QUICKSTEPS

TESTING AN INTERNET FIREWALL

You can test your firewall and see how well it is performing.

TEST FOR FILE SHARING

A Web site called ShieldsUP! has been set up by Gibson Research that will test and see how good your firewall is.

1. Click **Internet Explorer** on the taskbar. In the Address text box, type www.grc.com, and press **ENTER**. Click the **ShieldsUP!** logo.

2. Scroll down the page until you see the **ShieldsUP!** link, and click it. Read the page that opens, and click **Proceed**.

3. Read the next page that appears, and then click **File Sharing**. You should get a report similar to that shown in Figure 8-7. (Stay on the Gibson Research site.)

Continued . . .

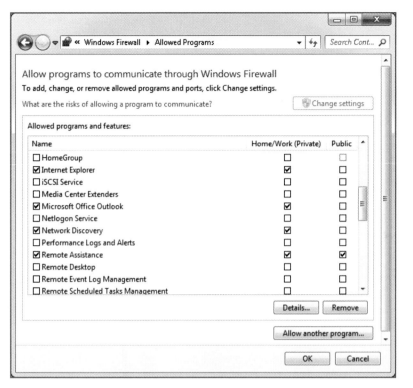

Figure 8-6: **The Windows 7 Firewall can be configured to allow certain programs and features to come through.**

- HomeGroup
- Network Discovery
- Windows Collaboration Computer Name Registration Service
- Windows Peer To Peer Collaboration Foundation

5. Click to select each program or feature you want to allow through the firewall. Click **OK** to close the Windows Firewall Allowed Programs window, and then click **Close** to close the Windows Firewall control panel.

⏰ QUICKSTEPS

TESTING AN INTERNET FIREWALL

(Continued)

The Windows 7 Firewall generally does pretty well on this test.

TEST FOR PORT VULNERABILITY

Gibson Research has a second test for specific port vulnerability. (In this case, "ports" are preassigned addresses that, when combined with your computer's address, allow a specific type of traffic, like email, into your computer).

1. While still on the Gibson Research site's ShieldsUP! page, scroll down and click **Common Ports**. Scroll down and look at the details. It is far better than Gibson would have you believe.

   On the computer in Figure 8-7, the test shows that all ports were either hidden or closed to outside connection, but in Gibson's opinion, all should be hidden. In my opinion, this is not a serious issue. Anyone who actually tried to exploit this vulnerability would have a hard time doing so with any success.

2. When you are done, close Internet Explorer.

Windows 7 Firewall is very good and one of the easiest to use. If you are still concerned about Internet security, however, there are both hardware and other software firewalls available. To start, consider the firewalls that come with antivirus software such as Norton Antivirus. You can also look at ZoneAlarm from Zone Labs (both free and paid-for software) at www.zonelabs.com and WatchGuard (various models of hardware) at www.watchguard.com.

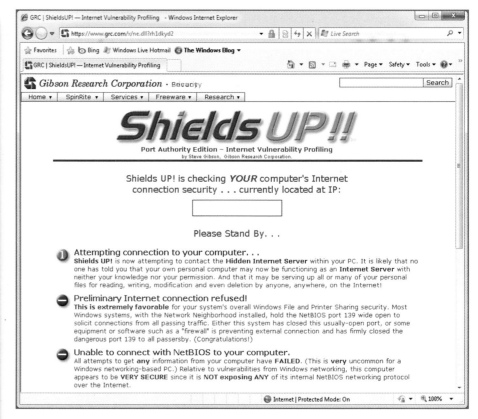

Figure 8-7: *The Windows 7 Firewall does well in the firewall tests.*

USE THE NETWORK AND SHARING CENTER

The second layer of file-sharing protection in Windows 7 is controlled with the Network And Sharing Center, shown in Figure 8-8, which allows you to turn on or off the primary components of sharing information among users on a computer and across a network.

The first time Windows 7 was run, a choice was made between a public and private network. The Network And Sharing Center allows you to change that. If you are primarily sharing your computer with other computers within an

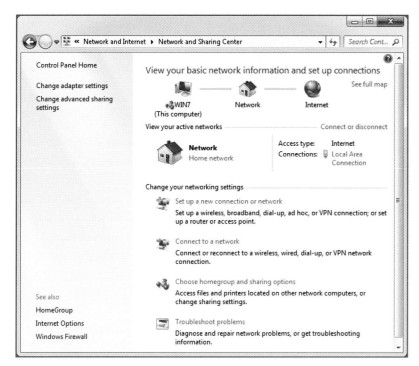

Figure 8-8: **The Network And Sharing Center is the primary means of sharing your computer.**

organization or a residence, you should select either Home or Work Network, where network sharing is relatively simple. If you are primarily using public wireless or cable Internet connections and allowing very little sharing of your computer, select Public, which makes it more difficult for someone to get into your computer.

1. Click **Start** and click **Control Panel**. In Category view, click **Network And Internet**, and then click **Network And Sharing Center**. The Network And Sharing Center window opens, as shown in Figure 8-8.

2. If you want to change the type of network (home, work, or public) you are connected to, click the current type of network to the right of the icon (in Figure 8-8, it is Home Network). The Set Network Location dialog box will appear.

3. Read the conditions that are expected in each network type, and then click the type that is correct for you. If needed, type a password and click **Yes**. Your choice will be confirmed. Click **Close**.

4. Each type of network has sharing settings that are automatically set. Home Network is the most open, with just about everything shared; Public Network is the other extreme. If you want to review the settings that have been made with your choice and possibly make changes, click **Change Advanced Sharing Settings**. The Advanced Sharing Settings window will open.

5. Review the settings that are shown. In a home or work network, you probably want and will have already set:

   - Turn On Network Discovery
   - Turn On File And Printer Sharing
   - Turn On Sharing So Anyone With Network Access Can Read And Write Files In Public Folders
   - Media Streaming Is On
   - Use 128-Bit Encryption
   - Turn Off Password Protection Sharing (with a Home Network)
   - Allow Windows To Manage Homegroup Connections (with a Home Network)

   For a public network, you probably want the opposite settings.

6. Make any changes that you feel you need, and then, if you made changes, click **Save Changes**. If needed, enter the password and click **Yes**. Otherwise, click **Cancel**.

7. When you have finished with the Network And Sharing Center, click **Close**.

HOMEGROUP FOLDER SHARING

The final layer of sharing settings is the determination of the disks and folders you want to share. Windows 7's HomeGroup makes sharing files and folders within the homegroup much easier. When Windows 7 is first installed or started, you are asked if you want a home, work, or public network. If you choose Home, which may also be a good idea for small businesses, a homegroup is either set up or joined, depending on whether a homegroup already exists. You are then shown a list of your libraries and asked if you want to share them. By default, your pictures, music, printers, and videos are shared for anyone to read, view, or use but not to change. Documents are not shared, but you can change this at the time of installation or at a later time. You can make these changes at the library level or at the disk and folder level. To do this at the library level:

NOTE

A *homegroup* is a group of networking computer users who want to easily share information and resources on their computers. Such a group can be in a residence or in a smaller organization. Only Windows 7 computers can join a homegroup.

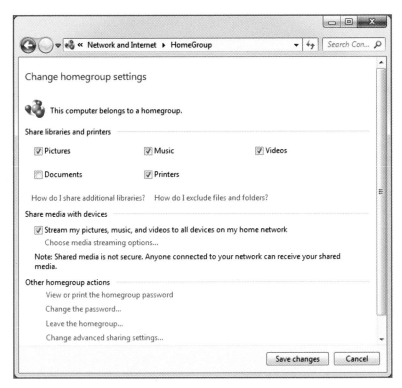

Figure 8-9: **The HomeGroup default is to share three of your libraries plus your printer within your homegroup.**

1. Click **Start** and click **Control Panel**. In Category view, click **Network And Internet**, and then click **HomeGroup**. The HomeGroup window opens.

   If this is the first time you are looking into HomeGroup, you'll be asked if you want to share any libraries. Click **Choose What You Want To Share**. The Share Libraries And Printers window will open, as shown in Figure 8-9.

   If you have previously reviewed HomeGroup, the Share Libraries And Printers window will open (see Figure 8-9).

2. Make any changes that you feel you need, and then, if you made changes, click **Save Changes**. If needed, enter the password and click **Yes**. Otherwise, click **Cancel**.

To go beyond the sharing of libraries within the homegroup, and even then only for someone to read, view, or use your libraries, you need to go to the individual drives and folders. You can change the sharing of libraries so that other users can change contents in addition to reading or viewing them. To do that:

1. Click **Start** and click **Computer**. In the folders (left) pane, click **Libraries** so the detail libraries (documents, music, pictures, or videos) are shown in the right pane.

2. Right-click the library whose sharing you want to change, and click **Share With**. The context menu and file-sharing submenu will appear.

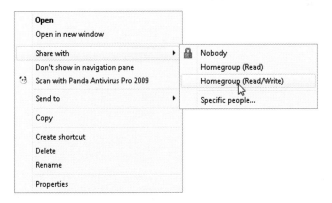

NOTE

Windows 7 Starter and Home Basic editions can only join a homegroup and can't establish one or change the sharing of one.

3. By default, the libraries are shared among the homegroup to be read only. You can allow homegroup members both read and write access to your libraries, or you can select specific people and give them specific permissions, as described in the next section, "Share Standard Folders with Specific People." Click the option you want, and, when you are finished, close the Windows Explorer window.

SHARE STANDARD FOLDERS WITH SPECIFIC PEOPLE

Standard folders are shared differently than disk drives and the Users folders, but are similar to sharing libraries, where you can share them with specific people. To share standard folders with specific people:

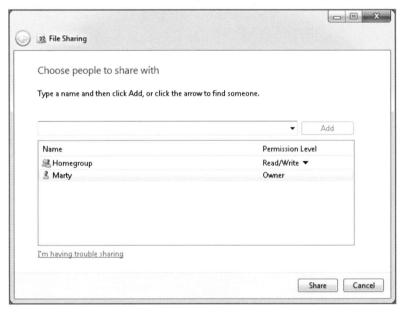

1. Click **Start** and click **Computer**. In the folders (left) pane, open the disk and folders necessary to see in the right pane the folder you want to share.

2. Right-click the folder and click **Share With**. The file-sharing menu will appear, as you saw in the last section.

3. Click **Specific People** to open the File Sharing dialog box. This shows you the current sharing of the folder, as you can see in Figure 8-10.

4. Click the down arrow on the right of the top text box to open a list of users and groups known to your computer. Click the user or group you want to give permission to use this disk or folder, possibly the Everyone group, and click **Add**. The user or group is added to the list in the lower part of the dialog box with the minimal permission level of Read.

Figure 8-10: **The sharing of standard folders with specific people takes you to a permissions dialog box.**

5. Click the **Permission Level** down arrow for your new user or group to open the alternative permission levels. Click the level you want for the addition:

   ● **Read** allows the user to view the files in the shared folder.

   ● **Read/Write** allows the user to view, add, change, and delete any of the files in the shared folder.

6. Click **Share** and, if needed, type a password and click **Yes**. Click **Done** to complete the process.

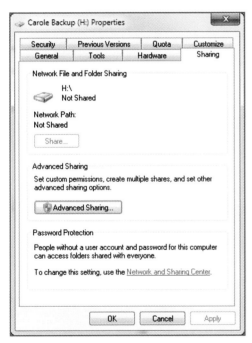

NOTE

When you share a folder, all folders and files within it are given the same sharing status due to inheritance. If that is not what you want for a particular folder, you must individually change the sharing status of the folders within it.

Figure 8-11: *Drives and special folders use a different sharing procedure.*

SHARE DRIVES AND SPECIAL FOLDERS

Disk drives and special folders—like the Users, Program Files, and Windows folders—have a more detailed sharing process.

1. Click **Start** and click **Computer**. Navigate to the drive or folder you want to share.

2. Right-click the drive or folder you want to share, click **Share With**, and click **Advanced Sharing**. The Properties dialog box will appear with the Sharing tab displayed, as shown in Figure 8-11.

3. Click **Advanced Sharing** and, if needed, type a password and click **Yes**.

4. Click **Share This Folder**, change the share name if desired, and click **Permissions**.

5. Select a listed user or group; or, if the one you want is not listed, click **Add**, click **Advanced**, click **Find Now**, double-click a user or group, and click **OK**.

6. With the user or group selected, click the permission level you want for that entity. The levels of permission are as follows:

   - **Read** allows the user or group to read but not change or delete a file or folder.

   - **Change** allows the user or group to read and change but not delete a file or folder.

   - **Full Control** allows the user or group to read, change, or delete a file or folder.

7. Click **OK** twice and close the Properties dialog box and Windows Explorer.

Use and Add Groups

Groups, or *group accounts,* are collections of user accounts that can have permissions, such as file sharing, granted to them. Most permissions are granted to groups, not individuals, and then individuals are made members of the groups. You need a set of groups that handles both the mix of people and the mix of permissions that you want to establish. A number of standard groups with preassigned permissions are built into Windows 7, but you can create your own groups, and you can assign users to any of these.

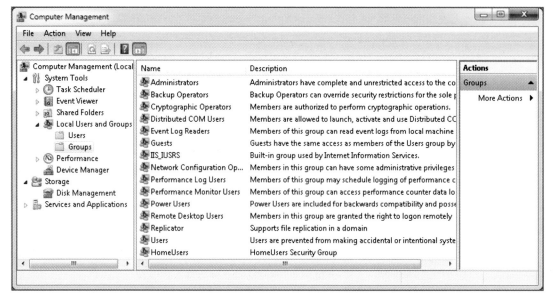

Figure 8-12: *There are a number of built-in groups to which users can be assigned.*

NOTE

"Standard Users" are called just "Users" in the list of groups.

OPEN EXISTING GROUPS

To open the groups in Windows 7 and see what permissions they contain:

1. Click **Start** and click **Control Panel**. In Category view, click **System And Security**, and then click **Administrative Tools**.

2. In the right pane, double-click **Computer Management**. If needed, type a password and click **Yes**.

3. In the left pane, click the triangle opposite **System Tools** to open it, click the triangle opposite **Local Users And Groups** to open that, and click **Groups**. The list of built-in groups is displayed, as shown in Figure 8-12.

4. Double-click a few groups to open the Properties dialog box for each and see the members they contain.

ADD USERS TO GROUPS

1. Right-click a group to which you want to add a user, and click **Add To Group**. Click **Add**. The Select Users dialog box will appear.

2. Either type a name in the text box and click **Check Names**, or click **Advanced** and then click **Find Now**. A list of users on that computer will be displayed. Select the user that you want to add (hold down CTRL to select several), and click **OK**.

3. When you are done, click **OK** twice.

ADD A GROUP

1. In the Computer Management window, in the list of groups in the middle (subject) pane, right-click in a white area so that no group is selected, and then click **New Group**. The New Group dialog box appears.

Figure 8-13: **Creating your own group lets you give it your own set of permissions.**

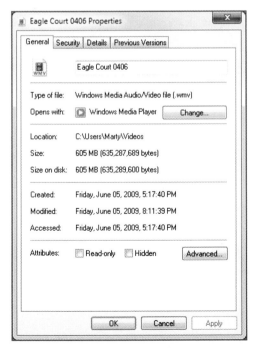

Figure 8-14: **Protecting files and folders is accomplished from the files' and folders' Properties dialog boxes.**

2. Enter a group name of up to 60 characters (Windows 7 lets you enter more, but if you ever want to use the group in Windows 2000 or NT systems, it will not work). It cannot contain just numbers, periods, or spaces; it can't contain " / \ [ ] : ; l = ,+ * ? < >; and leading spaces or periods are dropped.

3. Enter the description of what the group can uniquely do, and click **Add**. Then follow the instructions in "Add Users to Groups" except for clicking OK the final time in step 3.

4. When your group is the way you want it (see Figure 8-13), click **Create** and then click **Close**. The new group will appear in the list in the middle of the Computer Management window. Close the Computer Management window.

Protect Stored Data

Protecting stored data is another layer of protection. It works to make unusable whatever is found on the computer by someone who managed to break through the other layers of protection.

Protect Files and Folders

You can protect files and folders in two ways: hide them and encrypt them. Start by opening the Properties dialog box for the file or folder.

1. Click **Start** and click **Computer**. In the navigation pane, open the disk and folders necessary to locate in the right pane the file or folder you want to protect.

2. Right-click the file or folder you want to protect, and click **Properties**. The Properties dialog box will appear, as shown for a file in Figure 8-14 (there are slight differences among file and folder Properties dialog boxes).

HIDE FILES AND FOLDERS

Hiding files and folders lets you prevent them from being displayed by Windows Explorer. This assumes the person from whom you want to hide them does not know how to display hidden files or how to turn off the hidden attribute. To hide a file or folder, you must both turn on its hidden attribute and turn off the Display Hidden Files feature.

1. In the file or folder Properties dialog box, click **Hidden**, click **OK**, and click **OK** again to confirm the attribute change. If needed, type a password and click **Yes** (the object's icon becomes dimmed or disappears).

2. In the Windows Explorer window, click the **Organize** menu, click **Folder And Search Options**, click the **View** tab, and make sure **Don't Show Hidden Files, Folders, Or Drives** is selected. Click **OK** to close the Folder Options dialog box. Close and reopen the parent folder, and the file or folder you hid will disappear.

3. To restore the file or folder to view, click the **Organize** menu, click **Folder And Search Options**, click the **View** tab, click **Show Hidden Files, Folders, And Drives**, and click **OK**. Then, when you can see the file or folder, open its Properties dialog box, and deselect the **Hidden** attribute.

ENCRYPT FILES AND FOLDERS

File and folder encryption, called the *Encrypting File System (EFS)*, is built into Windows 7 using NTFS (it is not available in the Starter, Home Basic, or Home Premium editions). Once EFS is turned on for a file or a folder, only the person who encrypted the file or folder will be able to read it. However, you can back up the encryption key and use that to access the file or folder. For the person who encrypted the file, accessing it requires no additional steps, and the file is re-encrypted every time it is saved.

To encrypt a file or folder from Windows Explorer, starting with files:

1. From the General tab in the file's Properties dialog box, click **Advanced**. The Advanced Attributes dialog box appears.

2. Click **Encrypt Contents To Secure Data**, and click **OK** twice.

Encryption Warning

⚠ You are encrypting a file that is in an unencrypted folder. If this file is modified, the editing software might store a temporary, unencrypted, copy of the file. To ensure that files created in the parent folder are encrypted, encrypt the parent folder.

What do you want to do?

◉ Encrypt the file and its parent folder (recommended)

○ Encrypt the file only

☐ Always encrypt only the file   [OK]   [Cancel]

TIP

Because many applications save temporary and secondary files during normal execution, it is recommended that folders rather than files be the encrypting container. If an application is then told to store all files in that folder, where all files are automatically encrypted upon saving, security is improved.

CAUTION

If you encrypt a shared folder and select **This Folder, Subfolders, and Files**, any files or subfolders belonging to others will be encrypted with your key, and the owners will not be able to use what they created.

3. If you are encrypting a file, you will see an encryption warning that the file is not in an encrypted folder, which means that when you edit the file, temporary or backup files might be created that are not encrypted. Choose whether to encrypt only the file or to encrypt both the file and its parent folder, and then click **OK**.

4. If you are encrypting a folder, the Confirm Attribute Changes dialog box appears, asking if you want to apply the encryption to this folder only or to both the folder and its contents. If you click **This Folder Only**, *existing* files and folders in the folder will *not* be encrypted, while files and folders later created in or copied to the encrypted folder will be. If you click **This Folder, Subfolders, and Files**, all files and folders will be encrypted. Choose the setting that is correct for you, and click **OK**. If needed, type a password and click **Yes**.

5. Log off as the current user, and log on as another user. Click **Start**, click **Computer**, and open the drive and folders necessary to display in the right pane the file or folder you encrypted. You can see that the file exists, but when you try to open it, edit it, print it, or move it, you will get a message that access is denied.

6. To decrypt a file or folder, log on as yourself (given you're the person who encrypted it), reopen the file or folder Properties dialog box, click **Advanced**, deselect **Encrypt Contents To Secure Data**, and click **OK** twice (three times with folders).

BACK UP YOUR ENCRYPTION KEY

If you use file encryption, it is important to back up your file encryption key so that you do not lose the information you have, and you may be reminded of this. It is also important, of course, to keep the media that you back up on safe so that it can't be used. The key is part of a digital certificate, so this section refers to backing up the certificate.

Back up your file encryption key   🔦 ✕
This helps you avoid permanently losing access to your encrypted files.

1. Click **Start** and click **Control Panel**. In Category view, click **User Accounts And Family Safety**, and then click **User Accounts**. Your User Account window opens.

2. Click **Manage Your File Encryption Certificates** in the left column. If needed, type a password and click **Yes** to open the Encrypting File System dialog box.

3. Read about what you can do with this wizard, and click **Next**. By default, a certificate was automatically created when Windows was installed—that certificate or a more recent one will appear in the Certificate Details area, as shown in Figure 8-15. Click **Next**.

Encrypting File System

Select or create a file encryption certificate

Select an existing file encryption certificate or create a new one. If you have already encrypted files, you can update them to use this certificate.

◉ Use this certificate
If you are using a smart card, select the certificate on the smart card.

Certificate details:

Issued to: Marty
Issued by: Marty
Expires: 4/17/2109

[View certificate]
[Select certificate]

○ Create a new certificate

Why do I need a certificate for file encryption?

[Next] [Cancel]

Figure 8-15: *A security certificate is required to use file encryption.*

TIP

To use a backed up encryption key, insert the removable media with the key, open the drive in Windows Explorer, and browse to and double-click the file with the key. In the Certificate Import Wizard that opens, click **Next**, confirm that you have the right file, and click **Next**. Type the password used to back up the key, select how you want to use the key, and click **Next**. Select the certificate store you want, click **Next**, and click **Finish**.

4. Click **Browse** and navigate to the removable disk and folder you want to hold the certificate (it is not recommended to save the key on the same machine where the encryption is located). Type a filename and click **Save**.

5. Type a password and confirm it, and then click **Next**. Select the folders with encrypted files that you want the new certificate and key applied to, and click **Next**. Your files will be updated with the new key.

6. When you are told the files have been updated and where the key is stored, click **Close** and close the User Accounts window.

7. Store the removable disc or USB flash drive in a safe place.

Use Encrypted Files and Folders

If you are the person who encrypted a file or folder and you log on as yourself, you can use the file or folder exactly as you would if it hadn't been encrypted. The only way you know the files or folders are encrypted is that Windows Explorer shows them in green, as shown in Figure 8-16. If you log on as someone else, or if someone else logs on as anyone other than you, they will not be able to use the files or folders. Copying and moving encrypted files and folders, however, has a special set of rules:

- If you copy or move a file or folder into an encrypted folder, the item copied or moved will be encrypted.

- If you copy or move a file or folder to an unencrypted folder, the item moved remains as it was prior to being moved. If it was unencrypted, it remains so. If it was encrypted, it is still encrypted after being moved.

- Someone other than the owner who tries to copy or move encrypted files or folders to a different computer sees an error message that access is denied.

- If the owner copies or moves an encrypted file or folder to another file system, such as Windows NT 4 NTFS or Windows 98 FAT32, the encryption is removed, but a warning message is generated before the copy or move is complete.

- Backing up encrypted files or folders with Windows 7 Backup leaves the items encrypted.

UICKSTEPS

LOCKING A COMPUTER

By default, when your screen saver comes on and you return to use your system, you must go through the logon screen. If you have added a password to your account, you have to enter it to get back into the system, which is a means of preventing unauthorized access when you are away from your running computer. If you don't want to wait for your screen saver to come on, you can click **Start**, click the **Shut Down** right arrow, and click **Lock**; or you can press 🏁 (the Windows logo key)**+L** to immediately bring up the logon screen, from which your screen saver will open at the appropriate time.

Depending on your environment, having to go through the logon screen every time you come out of the screen saver may or may not be beneficial. To turn off or turn back on the screen saver protection:

1. Right-click the desktop and click **Personalize**. Click **Screen Saver**.

2. Select or deselect **On Resume, Display Logon Screen**, depending on whether you want to display the logon screen upon returning to your system (see Figure 8-17.)

3. Click **OK** to close the Screen Saver Settings dialog box, and close the Personalization window.

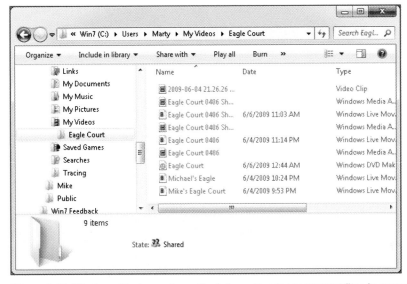

Figure 8-16: **Windows Explorer shows the information for encrypted files in green.**

Figure 8-17: **You can password-protect your system when you leave it unattended by having the logon screen appear when you return after using the screen saver.**

Chapter 9
Setting Up Networking

Networking is the ability to connect two or more computers and allow them to share information and resources, whether at home, in an organization, or around the world. The Internet, as was discussed in Chapter 4, is a form of networking. This chapter discusses a *local area network*, or *LAN*, which is generally confined to a single residence or building, or perhaps just a section of a building. (The Internet is a *wide area network*, or *WAN*.) You'll see what comprises a LAN, how to set it up, and how to use it.

Plan a Network

Windows 7 is a *network operating system*. This allows the interconnection of multiple computers for many purposes:

- **Exchanging information**, such as sending a file from one computer to another
- **Communicating**, for example, sending email among network users

- **Sharing information** by having common files accessed by network users
- **Sharing network resources**, such as printers and Internet connections

Networking is a system that includes the connection between computers that facilitates the transfer of information, as well as the scheme for controlling that transfer. The scheme makes sure that the information is transferred correctly and accurately. This is the function of the networking hardware and software in your computer and the protocols, or standards, they use.

Select a Network Architecture

Your network *architecture* is the combination of hardware, software, and standards that are used to perform networking. Today, the majority of LANs use the *Ethernet* standard, which determines the type of network hardware and software needed by the network, and *TCP/IP* (Transmission Control Protocol/ Internet Protocol), which determines how information is exchanged over the network. With this foundation, you can then choose between using a peer-to-peer LAN or a client-server LAN.

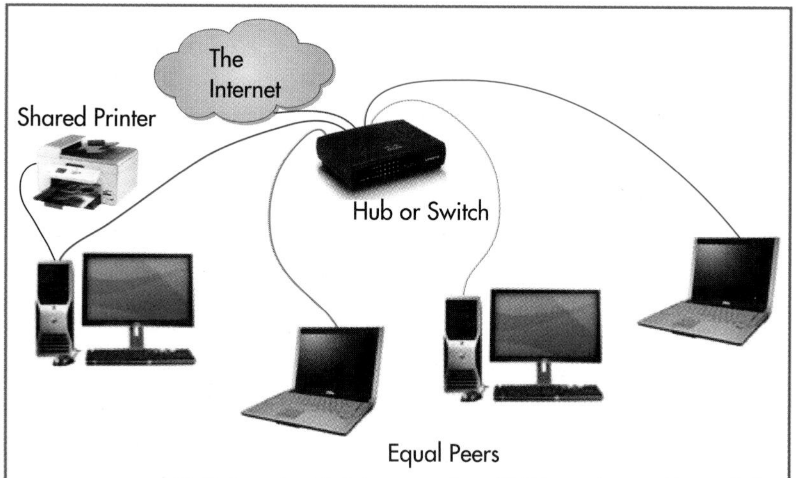

PEER-TO-PEER LANS

All computers in a *peer-to-peer LAN* are both servers and clients and, therefore, share in both providing and using resources. Any computer in the network may store information and provide resources, such as a printer, for the use of any other computer in the network. Peer-to-peer networking is an easy first step to networking, accomplished simply by joining computers together, as shown in Figure 9-1. It does not require the purchase of new computers or significant changes to the way an organization is using computers, yet resources can be shared (as is the printer in Figure 9-1), files and communications can be transferred, and common information can be accessed by all.

Computer equipment photos are courtesy of Dell, Inc., and are used by permission. Network equipment photos are courtesy of LinkSys by Cisco and are used by permission.

Figure 9-1: *In a peer-to-peer LAN, all computers are both servers and clients.*

Peer-to-peer LANs tend to be used in smaller organizations that do not need to share a large central resource, such as a database, or to have a high degree of security or central control. Each computer in a peer-to-peer LAN is autonomous and often networked with other computers simply to transfer files and share expensive equipment. Putting together a peer-to-peer LAN with existing computers is easy, and can be inexpensive (less than $40 per station).

CLIENT/SERVER LANS

The computers in a *client/server LAN* perform one of two functions: They are either servers or clients. *Servers* manage the network, centrally store information to be shared on the network, and provide the shared resources to the network. *Clients*, or *workstations*, are the users of the network and are standard desktop or laptop computers. To create a network, the clients and server(s) are connected together, with the possible addition of stand-alone network resources, such as printers, as shown in Figure 9-2.

The management functions provided by the server include network security, managing the permissions needed to implement security, communications among network users, and management of shared files on the network. Servers generally are more capable than clients in terms of having more memory, faster (and possibly more) processors, larger (and maybe more) disks, and more special peripherals, such as large, high-speed tape drives. Servers, generally, are dedicated to their function and are infrequently used for normal computer tasks, such as word processing.

Clients generally are less capable than servers and, infrequently, may not even have a disk. Clients usually are standard desktop and laptop computers that perform the normal functions of those types of machines in addition to being part of a network. Clients can also be "mini-servers" by sharing some or all of their disk drives or

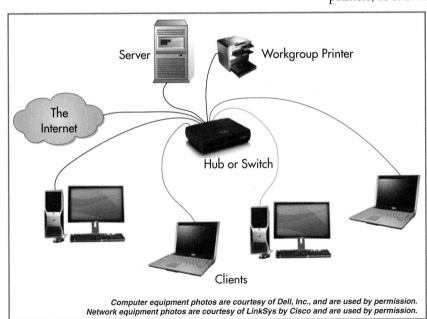

Computer equipment photos are courtesy of Dell, Inc., and are used by permission. Network equipment photos are courtesy of LinkSys by Cisco and are used by permission.

Figure 9-2: **In a client/server LAN, one or more computers are servers and the rest are clients.**

other resources. So the principal difference between peer-to-peer networks and client/server networks is the presence of a dedicated server.

Windows 7 and either Windows Server 2008 or Windows Server 2003 work together to form a client/server network operating environment, with Windows Server performing its function and Windows 7 being the client. Several Windows 7 computers can operate in a peer-to-peer network.

There are simple client/server networks, and there are client/server networks where one or more servers are set up as *domain controllers* and the entire network is considered a *domain*. In a large organization, a domain provides many benefits—most importantly, a central registry for all users so that one registration provides access to all the computers and resources in the domain. Domains, however, are complex and require significant expertise to set up and manage. This book, therefore, focuses on setting up and using a peer-to-peer network and on connecting to a client/server network.

Select a Network Standard

Windows 7 supports the two predominant networking standards: wired Ethernet and wireless. These, in turn, determine the type of hardware you need.

USE WIRED ETHERNET

The wired Ethernet standard comes in several forms based on speed and cable type. The most common, called 10/100/1000BaseT, provides a network that operates at the regular Ethernet speed of 10 Mbps, at the Fast Ethernet speed of 100 Mbps, or at the Gigabit Ethernet speed of 1000 Mbps.

A wired Ethernet 10/100/1000BaseT system, shown in Figure 9-3, has three major components:

- The **network interface card (NIC)** plugs into your computer or is built into it and connects it to the network.

- A **hub**, **switch**, or **router** joins several computers together to form the network:

    A **hub**, the simplest and oldest device, is where all computers are on the equivalent of a telephone party line (everybody can hear everybody else).

TIP

If you are using all Windows 7 computers in a peer-to-peer network, the Windows 7 HomeGroup (as described in Chapter 8) provides an easy setup and a number of file-sharing features that could be beneficial even to smaller organizations.

NOTE

In the name for the Ethernet standard, 10/100/1000BaseT, the "10/100/1000" indicates the alternative operating speeds in Mbps; the "Base" is for baseband, a type of transmission; and the "T" stands for the type of cabling (twisted-pair).

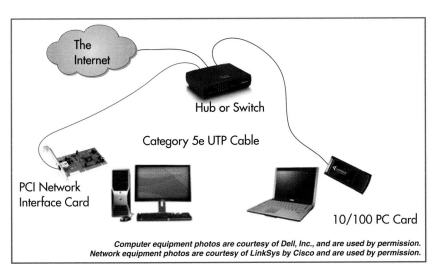

Figure 9-3: *A wired Ethernet network consists of a card in your computer, a hub or switch into which other computers are connected, and a cable connecting the two.*

Labels within figure:
The Internet
Hub or Switch
Category 5e UTP Cable
PCI Network Interface Card
10/100 PC Card

Computer equipment photos are courtesy of Dell, Inc., and are used by permission. Network equipment photos are courtesy of LinkSys by Cisco and are used by permission.

A **switch** is a newer device, about the same price as a hub and has virtually made them obsolete, where all computers are on the equivalent of a private telephone line.

A **router** joins two different networks, for example, the Internet to a local area network. Often, a router is combined with a hub or a switch, either in one device or in two devices, to join the Internet to several computers.

- An **unshielded twisted-pair (UTP)** telephone-like cable with a simple RJ-45 connector (similar to that for a telephone but larger) joins the NIC to the hub, switch, or router. This cable is called Category 5 or enhanced Category 5 ("Cat 5" or "Cat 5e," respectively).

Ethernet networks are easy to set up (see "Set Up a Network" later in this chapter), have become pervasive throughout organizations, and have an average cost for all components of less than $40 per computer on the network.

USE A WIRELESS LAN

Wireless LANs (WLANs) replace the cable used in a wired network with small radio transceivers (transmitter and receiver) at the computer and at the switch and/or router. There are several wireless standards, but the most common are 802.11b, 802.11g, and 802.11n. All three are WiFi-compliant (WiFi is a trademark for a set of wireless fidelity standards) and are compatible with one another.

- **802.11b** is the oldest and provides data transfer of *up to* 11 Mbps using a secure transmission scheme.

- **802.11g** came next, is currently the dominate standard, is *up to* five times faster than 802.11b (54 Mbps), but generally operates at 22 to 24 Mbps, and is built into many computers.

- **802.11n** is between three and seven times as fast as 802.11g, operating between 70 and 140 Mbps under normal conditions, and it can be as much as 10 times as fast (300 Mbps) under perfect conditions, which are difficult to achieve. 802.11n will operate proportionally faster at a longer distance than 802.11g, but all three standards are range-sensitive (the greater the distance between the computer and the wireless access point, the slower the speed).

Most public WiFi locations will handle 802.11b or g, while "n" is usually only available in private businesses and homes.

A WLAN has two components (see Figure 9-4):

- An **access point** is connected to the wired Ethernet network by being plugged into a hub, a switch, or a router. It uses a transceiver to communicate wirelessly with cards that are added to computers using the WLAN.
- An **adapter** plugs into or is built into your computer, and has a transceiver built in to communicate wirelessly with an access point within its range. There are PC adapters for use in notebook computers and PCI adapters for use in desktop computers.

If the access point is plugged into a hub or switch on a wired network, the wireless computers within the range of the access point operate on the network in exactly the same way as they would with a cable connection, except they are slower. A WLAN has some significant benefits over a normal wired LAN:

- You do not have the expense of cabling and the even higher expense of installing and maintaining cabling.
- Adding and removing users from the network is extremely easy.

QUICKSTEPS

SELECTING WIRED ETHERNET HARDWARE

Selecting networking hardware for wired Ethernet means selecting a NIC, a hub or switch, and cabling. For all hardware, a brand-name product giving you a company that stands behind what you are buying can be beneficial. Respected brands of networking gear include 3Com, Cisco and its subsidiary Linksys, D-Link, Netgear, and RealTek.

SELECT A NETWORK INTERFACE CARD

Most new computers come with a built-in 10/100 Ethernet NIC and some now include 1000 (Gigabit), so you may not need to add this. You already have a NIC if your computer has two telephone-style jacks, one slightly

Continued . . .

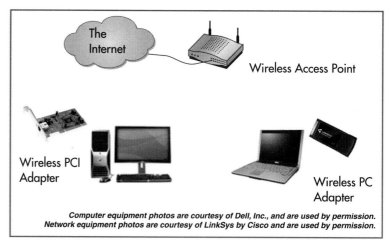

Computer equipment photos are courtesy of Dell, Inc., and are used by permission. Network equipment photos are courtesy of LinkSys by Cisco and are used by permission.

Figure 9-4: **A wireless network consists of an adapter that plugs into or is built into your computer and an access point that is connected to a wired network, the Internet, or both.**

⏰ **QUICKSTEPS** ▮

SELECTING WIRED ETHERNET HARDWARE *(Continued)*

larger than the other. The larger one is the connection to the NIC. The other jack is for the modem.

If you don't have a NIC, you can generally add one to your computer. For a desktop computer, you want a 10/100 or 10/100/1000 NIC for either the PCI (Peripheral Component Interconnect) bus or the USB (Universal Serial Bus). If you use a NIC that plugs into the PCI bus, you will need to open the computer case and plug it in. If you are uncomfortable doing that, most computer stores will do it for little more than the cost of the card ($25 to $50). You need to carry in only the computer itself, not the monitor, keyboard, or mouse. If you choose a USB NIC, it will cost slightly more, but it plugs into a socket on the outside of the case.[1]

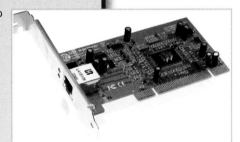

For a laptop computer, the NIC plugs in from the outside, so it is easy to add. It uses one of three connections (in all cases, you want a 10/100/1000 NIC):

- **PC Card** short for PCMCIA (Personal Computer Memory Card International Association), which goes into a slot on the side of laptops

- **Express card**, which also goes into a slot on the side of newer laptops

Continued . . .

[1]Network equipment photos are courtesy of LinkSys by Cisco and are used by permission.

- Users can move easily from office to office.
- Users can roam within an area, say, carrying their laptops to a meeting.
- Visitors can easily get on the network.

The downsides are (potentially) cost, speed, and security, but all of these are manageable. The cost per computer of a wired network, as was said previously, is less than $40 per computer. The cost per computer of a wireless network may be the same or less, considering that a wireless adapter is built into most laptops. The speed difference is more significant, not just because of the difference between a 54-Mbps or higher access point and a 100-Mbps network, but because of the net rate of dividing the 11- or 54-Mbps access point by the number of people trying to use it. Despite these drawbacks, there is a large movement to WLANs, and a number of systems are being sold for both offices and homes.

Set Up a Network

When you installed Windows 7, a basic set of networking services was installed and configured, using system defaults. This setup may, but doesn't always, provide an operable networking system. Look at these three areas to set up *basic networking,* which means that your computer can communicate with other computers in the network:

- Be sure the NIC is properly set up.
- Install the networking functions that you want to perform.
- Review your network security settings.

⏰ QUICKSTEPS

SELECTING WIRED ETHERNET HARDWARE *(Continued)*

- **USB connector**, which plugs into a USB port on the computer, either in laptops or desktops

SELECT CONNECTING DEVICES

There are two common connecting devices: hubs, which are like a party-line telephone system where everybody hears all the traffic; and switches, which are like a private-line telephone system. Switches once cost a lot more, so hubs were used. Today, switches and hubs are virtually the same price. A simple switch runs from under $20, for a 10/100 four-port one, to under $50 for an eight-port Gigabit switch. You need a port for each user on the system, plus one for your broadband (DSL or cable) Internet connection. The largest switches have 48 ports, but you can stack switches by plugging them into one another. You want at least an Ethernet 10/100 switch and possibly a Gigabit one with the number of ports that meet your needs.

SELECT CABLING

For 10/100 Ethernet networking, you need either Category 5 or Category 5e (for enhanced) cabling (these are called "Cat 5" or "Cat 5e," respectively) with RJ-45 male connectors on each end. Such cables come in various colors and lengths, up to 100 feet with the ends molded on, or in lengths up to 1,000 feet without the ends, where you need a crimping tool to add the ends. Cat 5e cable, which provides better transmission capability, is almost the same price as Cat 5, so I recommend it, and if you are going to use Gigabit Ethernet, you need Cat 5e.

📌 NOTE

In many of the steps in the following sections of this chapter, you will be interrupted and asked by User Account Control (UAC) for permission to continue. So long as it is something you started, you want to click **Continue** or enter an administrator's password. To keep the steps as simple as possible, we have left out the UAC instructions. Chapter 8 discusses UAC in more detail.

Set Up Network Interface Cards

If the computer you are setting up has a NIC that is both certified for Windows 7 and fully Plug and Play–compatible, then your NIC was installed by Windows Setup without incident and you don't need to read this section. Otherwise, this section examines how the NIC was installed and what you need to do to make it operational.

Assuming that a NIC *is* properly plugged into the computer, any of these things could be causing it to not operate:

- The NIC driver is not recognized by Windows 7; it is either missing or not properly installed.
- The NIC is not functioning properly.

Look at each of these possibilities in turn.

CHECK THE NIC AND ITS DRIVER

Check the status of your NIC and whether you have a driver installed. If you don't, you can install one.

TIP

If you want to network only two computers, you can do so without a hub or a switch, but you need a special *crossover* cable where the connections are reversed on each end. Most computer stores carry such a cable.

QUICKSTEPS

SELECTING WIRELESS HARDWARE

Selecting networking hardware for a wireless network means selecting a wireless adapter and a wireless access point. The same manufacturers as were listed for wired Ethernet hardware are recommended.

SELECT A WIRELESS SPEED

If you are installing a new wireless network, the up-to-54-Mbps 802.11g standard is the minimum, and you probably want to consider the up-to-300-Mbps 802.11n, although "n" is new and is two to three times more expensive.

SELECT A WIRELESS ADAPTER

Most laptops come with a built-in wireless adapter, so you may not need to buy one. For a desktop computer, you will need a PCI or USB wireless adapter for the speed you have chosen, and, with PCI, you will need to open up the computer to plug it in or have a store do it. For a laptop computer without the built-in capability, you need a PC Card, Express Card, or USB wireless adapter of the appropriate speed, which you can easily plug in (you need to check whether your laptop uses a PC Card

Continued . . .

1. Click **Start** and click **Control Panel**. In Category view, click **Network And Internet**, and then click **Network And Sharing Center**. The Network And Sharing Center window opens.

2. In the Network And Sharing Center, the top of which is shown in Figure 9-5, you can see if you are connected to a network by the double line between your computer and the network icon in the center and then if you are connected to the Internet by the double line between the network icon and the Internet icon on the right. In the middle-right area of the Network And Sharing Center, you see if you have a local area connection (wired) and/or a wireless connection. If your Network And Sharing Center looks like Figure 9-5, you have all these connections (you don't need both a local area connection and a wireless connection) and you can be assured your NIC is working, and you can skip to the next chapter.

3. If you do not see the connections shown in Figure 9-5, you need to start the process of figuring out why and getting it fixed. Click **Change Adapter Settings** in the left pane. The Network Connections window opens. If you have an icon in the window labeled "Local Area Connection" and/or "Wireless Network Connection," as shown here, you have the NIC driver properly installed and you can go on to the section "Enable Windows 7's Networking Functions."

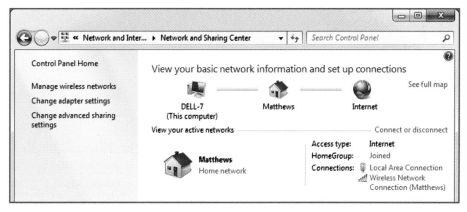

Figure 9-5: **The Network And Sharing Center will tell you if you are connected to a local area network, a wireless network, and to the Internet.**

UICKSTEPS

SELECTING WIRELESS HARDWARE

(Continued)

or Express Card adapter by looking at the information that came with your computer).

SELECT A WIRELESS ACCESS POINT

Wireless access points come in simple versions that plug into a wired Ethernet network, as well as more sophisticated versions, called "wireless broadband routers," that terminate a DSL, FiOS (fiber optic), or cable Internet connection. You have that choice and a choice of speeds when you choose a wireless access point.

4. If you do not have a Local Area Connection icon, you cannot create one by clicking Connect To A Network or Set Up A Connection Or Network. You must first install a Windows 7 driver for the NIC. Since it was not automatically installed by Windows 7, you will need to get one before proceeding. If a driver did not come with the NIC (most likely on a CD), you need to use another computer attached to the Internet to locate and download it.

5. On the other computer, bring up the manufacturer's Web site, locate and download the Windows 7 driver (you need to know the make and model of the NIC), copy it onto a disc or a USB flash drive, and then go back to the original computer.

6. Click **Start** and click **Control Panel**. In Category view, click **Hardware And Sound**, and then, under Devices And Printers, click **Device Manager**. The Device Manager window opens.

7. Double-click **Network Adapters** to display the network adapter in your computer. If you see your NIC and it doesn't have a problem icon (an exclamation point), Windows thinks that the NIC is installed and running properly. If you double-click the device, you should see the device status, "This device is working properly." If so, you may need to only install a new driver. Skip to step 14.

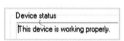

8. If you see your NIC with a problem icon, double-click the NIC. You will most likely see a device status message telling you that a driver was not installed. Skip to step 14.

9. If you don't see your NIC in the Device Manager window, click the **Action** menu, and click **Add Legacy Hardware**. The Add Hardware Wizard will open. Click **Next**. Click **Install The Hardware That I Manually Select From A List**—you don't want Windows to search for new hardware; if it was going to find it, it would have—and click **Next**.

10. Double-click **Network Adapters** in the Common Hardware Types list. A list of network adapters appears. If your NIC had been on the list, Windows Setup would have found it, so you need to insert and use the disk that you made prior to step 3 or the disk that came with the NIC.

11. Click **Have Disk**. Click **Browse**, locate the appropriate drive, and click **OK**. When it is displayed, select the driver for your adapter, and click **Next**. When told that the device will be installed, click **Next** again.

12. You may see a message stating that the driver you are about to install does not have a Microsoft digital signature. Click **Yes** to go ahead and install it anyway. The driver and its necessary supporting software will be installed.

13. Click **Finish**. The Network Connections window should now show the Local Area Connection icon. If you see this icon, go to the section "Enable Windows 7's Networking Functions."

14. If you saw your NIC in the Device Manager window, with or without a problem icon, you can install or reinstall a driver from there. Place the disk with the driver software in the drive. Right-click your NIC and click **Update Driver Software**, as shown in Figure 9-6.

15. Click **Browse My Computer For Driver Software**, click **Browse**, locate the drive and folder with the driver, and click **Next**. You will be told when the driver is installed. Click **Close** to close the Update Driver Software dialog box.

If you still do not have a Local Area Connection icon, or if some other problem occurred in the preceding process that does not point to an obvious solution, continue through the next section to see if a solution is presented.

DETERMINE IF A NIC IS FUNCTIONING

If installing a NIC driver did not cause the Local Area Connection icon to appear, it is likely that the NIC itself is not functioning properly. The easiest way to test that is to replace the NIC with a known good one, ideally one that is both Windows 7–certified and Plug and Play–compatible. It is wise to have a spare NIC; they are not expensive ($25 and under), and switching out a suspected bad one can quickly solve many problems.

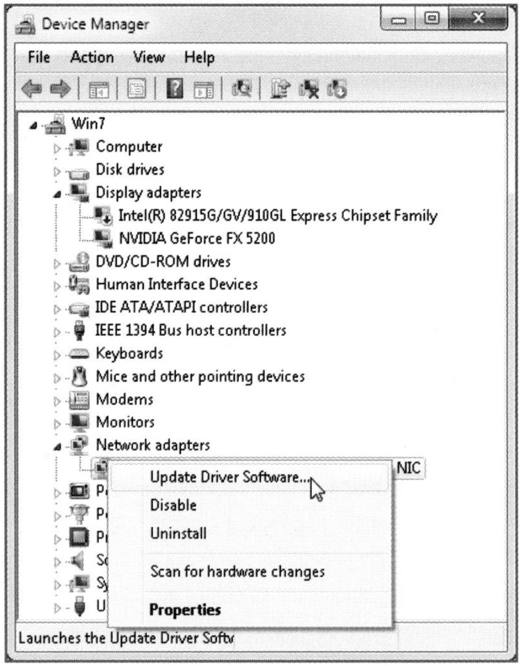

Figure 9-6: ***It is common to have to install device driver software for older hardware.***

> **NOTE**
>
> In this and the two following sections you can use the Have Disk button to install unique, non-Windows services for special purposes.

Enable Windows 7's Networking Functions

Windows 7's networking functions provide the software for a computer to access other computers and, separately, for other computers to access the computer you are working on. In other words, the two primary functions allow the computer to be a client (it accesses other computers) and to be a server (other computers access it). Make sure that these two services are enabled by following these steps.

1. Click **Start** and click **Control Panel**. In Category view, click **Network And Internet**, and then click **Network And Sharing Center**. The Network And Sharing Center window opens.
2. Click **Local Area Connection** in the middle-right area. The Local Area Connection Status dialog box appears, as shown in Figure 9-7. In the particular case shown here, the computer indicates it is connected to the network and that it is sending and receiving information, which indicates it is correctly set up.
3. Click **Properties**. The Local Area Connection Properties dialog box, shown in Figure 9-8, appears and displays the services and protocols that have been installed automatically.

   The minimum services needed for networking are Client For Microsoft Networks and File And Printer Sharing For Microsoft Networks, plus one protocol, Internet Protocol Version 4 (TCP/IPv4). By default, Windows 7 installs an additional service and three additional protocols.
4. Click **Install**. The Select Network Feature Type dialog box appears, in which you can add clients, services, and protocols.

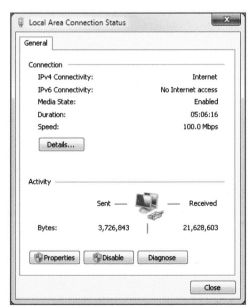

Figure 9-7: ***If your NIC is working correctly, you should see a lot of information being sent and received.***

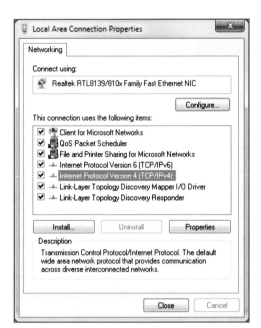

Figure 9-8: *Windows 7 automatically installs the networking services and protocols shown here.*

![NOTE]

NOTE

Windows 7's default installation of Internet Protocol Version 6 (TCP/IPv6) is done in preparation for a rapidly approaching future when TCP/IPv6 becomes the Internet and LAN standard. TCP/IPv6 provides for a greatly expanded address space, increased speed, and increased security.

INSTALL A CLIENT

1. Double-click **Client**. If you already have Client For Microsoft Networks installed, you will not have any services to install.

2. If Client For Microsoft Networks is not installed, select it and, in any case, click **OK**.

INSTALL A SERVICE

Windows 7 provides two services, both of which are automatically installed:

● **File And Printer Sharing For Microsoft Networks** handles the sharing of resources on your computer.

● **QoS (Quality of Service) Packet Scheduler** helps balance a network and alleviate bottlenecks when one part of the network is fast and another part is slow.

1. In the Select Network Feature Type dialog box, double-click **Service**. If you already have File And Printer Sharing For Microsoft Networks and QoS Packet Scheduler installed, you will not have any services to install.

2. If File And Printer Sharing For Microsoft Networks and QoS Packet Scheduler are not installed, select them and, in any case, click **OK**.

Configure a Networking Protocol

Networking protocols are a set of standards used to package and transmit information over a network. The protocol determines how the information is divided into packets, how it is addressed, and what is done to assure it is reliably transferred. The protocol is, therefore, very important to the success of networking, and its choice is a major one. Windows 7 offers three Internet protocols and two network-mapping protocols:

● **Internet Protocol Version 4 (TCP/IPv4)**, for use with the Internet and most LANs

● **Internet Protocol Version 6 (TCP/IPv6)**, the newest system for use with the widest variety of networks (many Internet service providers and the routers they provide for DSL and cable Internet service do not handle IPv6)

● **Reliable Multicast Protocol**, which is a special one-to-many protocol used in conferencing

- **Link-Layer Topology Discovery Mapper I/O Driver** that goes out and finds devices on the network

- **Link-Layer Topology Discovery Responde**
  Discovery Mapper

All of these protocols, except Reliable Multi
default. If the computer you are working or
Internet, it will require TCP/IPv4.

CHECK AND CHANGE PROTOCOLS

Check (and change if necessary) the protoc
settings that are being used.

1. In the Select Network Feature Type dialog
   Network Protocol dialog box appears listir

2. If you see any protocol you want installe
   protocol, double-click it too. Otherwise,
   Protocol and Select Network Feature T

3. Select the **Internet Protocol Version 4 (TCP/IPv4)** protocol in the Local Area Connection Properties dialog box, and click **Properties**. The Internet Protocol (TCP/IP) Properties dialog box appears, shown in Figure 9-9. Here you can choose either to use a dynamic IP (Internet Protocol) address automatically assigned by a server or DSL router, or to enter a static IP address in this dialog box.

*Figure 9-9: **If you use dynamic IP addresses that are automatically assigned, you don't have to worry about having two devices or computers with the same IP address.***

If you have a server or a DSL router that automatically assigns IP addresses, you need to leave the Obtain An IP Address Automatically option selected (it is selected by default).

ENTER YOUR OWN IP ADDRESS

1. If you are working on a computer that you know must have a static IP address, click **Use The Following IP Address** and enter an IP address. The IP address that you use should be from the block of IP addresses that an ISP or other authority has assigned to your organization.

2. If you entered a static IP address, you must also enter a subnet mask. This mask tells the IP which part of an IP address to consider a network address and which part to consider a computer, or *host,* address. If your organization was assigned a block of IP addresses, it was also given a subnet mask. If you used the APIPA range of addresses, use 255.255.0.0 as the subnet mask.

OBTAIN AN IP ADDRESS AUTOMATICALLY

1. If you don't have a specific reason to use a static IP address, click **Obtain An IP Address Automatically**, and use the addresses from either a server or DSL router on the network or APIPA.

2. Click **OK** to close the Internet Protocol Version 4 (TCP/IPv4) Properties dialog box, click **Close** to close the Local Area Connection Properties dialog box, click **Close** to close the Local Area Connection Status dialog box, and close all open dialog boxes and windows.

3. Click **Start**, click the **Shut Down** right arrow, and click **Restart**. This is required to utilize your network settings.

VERIFY YOUR CONNECTION

1. When the computer restarts, reopen the Local Area Connection Status dialog box (click **Start** and click **Control Panel**; in Category view, click **Network And Internet** and then click **Network And Sharing Center**). Click **Local Area Connection** in the middle-right area to open the Local Area Connection Status dialog box. You should see activity on both the Sent and Received sides.

2. If you do not see both sending and receiving activity, click **Start**, click in the **Search Programs And Files** text box, enter a computer name in your same subnet in the form *computername*\, and press **ENTER**. Windows Explorer will open and you should see the drives on the computer you entered, as shown in Figure 9-10. If you see this, the

9

10

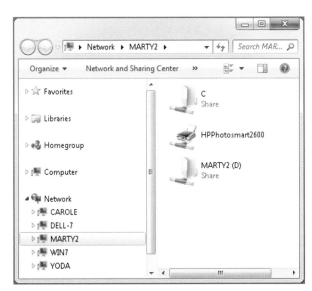

Figure 9-10: ***When networking is functioning properly, you'll be able to see shared resources on other computers in your network.***

TIP

If your organization doesn't plan to directly access an outside network like the Internet or you have a router between your network and the Internet, the static IP address can be from the block of APIPA numbers or from several other blocks of private IP addresses. (See the "Getting a Block of IP Addresses" QuickSteps.)

QUICKSTEPS

GETTING A BLOCK OF IP ADDRESSES

The block of IP addresses you use with the Internet Protocol depends on whether the computers to be assigned the addresses will be private or public.

GET PRIVATE IP ADDRESSES

If the computers will be operating only on an internal network, where they are separated from the public network by a router or bridge, they are *private* and need only organizational uniqueness. Four blocks of IP addresses have been set aside and can be used by any organization for its private, internal needs without any coordination with any other organization, but these blocks should not be used for directly connecting to the Internet. These private-use blocks of IP addresses are:

- 10.0.0.0 through 10.255.255.255
- 169.254.0.0 through 169.254.255.255 (the APIPA range)
- 172.16.0.0 through 172.31.255.255
- 192.168.0.0 through 192.168.255.255

GET PUBLIC IP ADDRESSES

If your computer(s) will be interfacing directly with the Internet, they are *public* and thus need a globally unique IP number. If you want a block of public IP addresses, you must request it from one of several organizations, depending on the size of the block that you want. At the local level, for a moderate-sized block of IP addresses, your local ISP can assign it to you. For a larger block, a regional ISP may be able to handle the request.

Continued . . .

computer is networked. If this doesn't work, you need to double-check all the possible settings previously described:

- If you are using APIPA, make sure that the computer you are trying to contact is also using that range of numbers, either as a static assigned address or with automatic assignment.
- If all the settings are correct, check the cabling by making a simple connection of just several computers.
- If you do a direct connection between two computers, remember that you need a special crossover cable with the transmitting and receiving wires reversed.
- If all else fails, replace the NIC.
- It could also be that network security is getting in your way of seeing the drives and resources on the other computer. See "Review Network Security" later in this chapter.

With a good NIC, good cabling, the correct settings, and network security properly handled, you'll be able to network.

Test a Network Setup and Connection

You can use several command-line utilities to test a TCP/IP installation. The more useful of these commands are the following:

- **Ipconfig** is used to determine if a network configuration has been initialized and if an IP address is assigned. If an IP address and valid subnet mask are returned, the configuration is initialized and there are no duplicates for the IP address. If a subnet mask of 0.0.0.0 is returned, the IP address is a duplicate.
- **Hostname** is used to determine the computer name of the local computer.
- **Ping** is used to query either the local computer or another computer on the network to see whether it responds. If the local computer responds, you know that TCP/IP is bound to the local NIC and that both are operating correctly. If the other computer responds, you know that TCP/IP and the NICs in both computers are operating correctly and that the connection between the computers is operable. Figure 9-11 shows the testing results on my system.

1. Click **Start**, click **All Programs**, click **Accessories**, and click **Command Prompt**. The Command Prompt window opens.

GETTING A BLOCK OF
IP ADDRESSES *(Continued)*

If not, you have to go to one of three regional Internet registries:

- American Registry for Internet Numbers (ARIN), at www.arin.net, which covers North and South America, the Caribbean, and sub-Saharan Africa

- Réseaux IP Européens (RIPE), at www.ripe.net, which covers Europe, the Middle East, and northern Africa

- Asia Pacific Network Information Centre (APNIC), at www.apnic.net, which covers Asia and the Pacific

CAUTION

Remember that private ranges work only with other computers in their own subnets and with IP addresses from the same range. You can tell what the subnet is from the subnet mask. For example, with a subnet mask of 255.255.255.0, all computers in the network must have IP addresses with the same first three groups of numbers and vary only in the last group. Thus, computers with the numbers 192.168.104.001 and 192.168.104.002 are in the same subnet.

Figure 9-11: **You can test a network with TCP/IP utilities such as Ipconfig, Hostname, and Ping.**

2. Type ipconfig and press **ENTER**. The IP address and subnet mask of the current computer should be returned. If this did not happen, there is a problem with the current configuration.

3. Type hostname and press **ENTER**. The computer name of the local computer should be returned.

4. Type ping, type the name of another computer on your network, and press **ENTER**. You should get four replies from the other computer.

NOTE

The 127.0.0.1 IP address is a special address set aside to refer to the computer on which it is entered.

5. If Ping did not work with a remote computer, try it on the current computer by typing ping 127.0.0.1 and pressing **ENTER**. Again, you should get four replies, this time from the current computer. If you didn't get a reply here, you have a problem with either the network setup or the NIC. If you did get a reply here, but not in step 4, then there is a problem either in the other computer or in the cable and devices connecting them.

6. Type exit and press **ENTER** to close the Command Prompt window.

If you do find a problem here, go on to the next section on network security, and then review earlier sections on setting up network hardware, functions, and protocols to isolate and fix the problem.

Review Network Security

Chapter 8 discusses network security in depth. This section provides a brief synopsis of the specific steps you need to take to share your computer across a LAN so that other computers similarly set up can see your computer and access the drives, folders, and printers. You will be able to see and access other computers that do the same thing. The steps to take in the appropriate order are described next. The specific steps to open the required windows and dialog boxes, as well as the specific settings to use, were provided in Chapter 8.

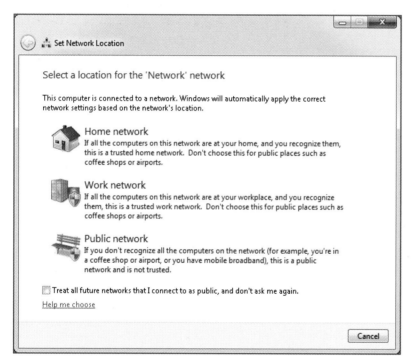

Figure 9-12: Decide if the network you use is private or public.

1. When you complete the installation of Windows 7, or the first time you turn on a new computer with Windows 7 already installed, you are asked if the network you want to be a part of will be at home, at work, or in some public location, as shown in Figure 9-12. Both Home and Work are considered private locations where you want your computer to be seen and shared. You can change this later on (see step 2).

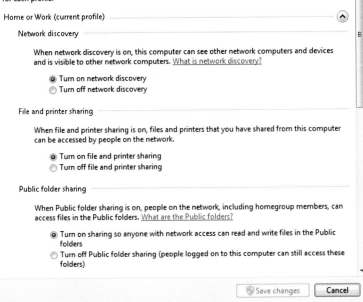

Figure 9-13: *Turn on the sharing of your computer.*

2. If you want to share your computer's resources, such as files, folders, disk drives, and printers, you need to turn on that capability (it is turned off by default in a Work and Public network, but partially turned on in a homegroup Home network). This is done in the Advanced Sharing Settings window, shown in Figure 9-13, for both the private and public aspects of this computer.

3. To share individual drives, folders, and printers, you must turn on that capability for the most senior drive or folder you want to share (also known as the parent). Subsidiary folders and the files within those folders will inherit the sharing aspect of the parent unless you individually change that sharing. Only in a homegroup can you share the full C: (or system) drive. Sharing a drive, folder, or printer is done through the object's Properties dialog box, shown in Figure 9-14.

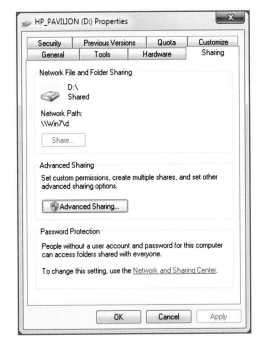

Figure 9-14: *Share the specific objects you want others to be able to use.*

4. Finally, you must set up the Windows Firewall to allow the network and its sharing aspects to come through even though you have Windows Firewall turned on (which is highly recommended). Setting up the firewall to allow networking is done in the Windows Firewall Allowed Programs window, shown in Figure 9-15.

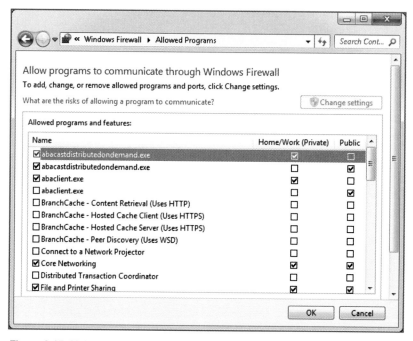

Figure 9-15: *Make sure Windows Firewall allows networking.*

Chapter 10

Using Networking

Networking brings a vastly enlarged world of computing to you, giving you access to all the computers, printers, and other devices to which you are connected and have permission to access. Using a network and its resources is no more difficult than accessing the hard disk or printer that is directly connected to your computer. Your network connection can be either wired or wireless, and you'll notice no difference, except for the hardware and the possibility that wireless is slower.

In this chapter you'll see how to access other computers and printers over a local area network (LAN), how to let others access your computer and resources, and how to access your computer remotely—across a LAN, through a telephone connection, or over the Internet.

Access Network Resources

Begin by looking at the network available to you through your computer. Then access a disk and retrieve files and folders from another computer, use a network printer, and access the Internet over the network.

Explore a Network

Whether you have just installed a small home network or have just plugged into a large company network, the first thing you'll probably want to do is explore it—see what you can see. You can do that from Windows Explorer.

1. Click **Start**, click **Computer**, scroll down the navigation pane, and click **Network** to open it. The network resources will be displayed, as you see in Figure 10-1.

2. Double-click one of the shared computers on your network. It will open and display the drives, printers, and other resources (such as tape drives and removable disks) on that computer.

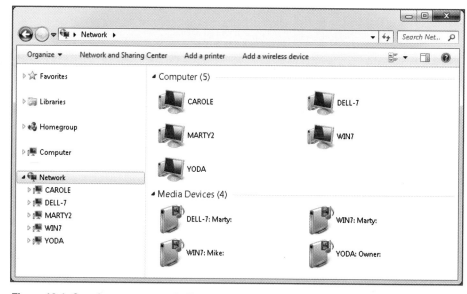

Figure 10-1: Opening your network displays the computers that are shared, as well as media being shared (the top two and fourth icons are used to share media).

NOTE

If the computer you are trying to access is not in a homegroup and has password-protected sharing enabled, which is done in its Network And Sharing Center, you will need to enter a user name and password to access that computer.

TIP

The shared folders, disks, and other resources that appear when you open your network are the result of your computer having searched your workgroup or domain for shared resources. When you first set up networking, you won't see anything until resources have been shared by other computers and your computer has had time to find them.

3. In the navigation pane, click the triangle next to one of the drives to open it, and then click one or more of the folders to see the files available to you (see Figure 10-2).

4. Click **Back** one or more times, and then open other computers, drives, and folders to more fully explore your network.

5. Click **Close** to close Windows Explorer.

Permanently Connect to a Network Resource

If you use a specific network drive or folder a lot, you may want to connect to it permanently so that you can use it as if it were a drive on your computer. This permanent connection is called a "mapped network drive." Note that it is only "permanent" until you decide to disconnect from the drive. See "Disconnect a Mapped Drive" later in this chapter.

CONNECT TO A MAPPED NETWORK DRIVE

To set up a mapped network drive:

1. Click **Start**, click **Computer**, scroll down the navigation pane, and click **Network** to open it. The network resources will be displayed, as you saw in Figure 10-1.

In the navigation pane, click the triangle opposite **Network**, and click the computer that contains the drive you want to connect to permanently. You should see the drive in the subject pane.

2. Right-click the drive in the subject pane, and click **Map Network Drive** (see Figure 10-3). The Map Network Drive dialog box will appear.

3. Select the drive letter you want to use for the mapped drive or the specific folder, if that is applicable, choose whether you want to reconnect to the drive every time you log on to your computer, and whether you need to use different credentials— whether you want to log on to that resource using a different user name and password.

4. Click **Finish**. The drive will open in a separate window. Close that window.

Name	Date modified	Type	Size
Firefox Setup 3.0.5	1/10/2009 6:16 PM	Application	7,343 KB
jsvalidation	8/19/2008 12:38 PM	Compressed (zippe...	6 KB
js-validator	8/19/2008 12:33 PM	Compressed (zippe...	13 KB
phpmysqllogin-0.1b	8/18/2008 7:06 PM	Compressed (zippe...	13 KB
RegCure License	8/18/2008 7:24 PM	MHTML Document	197 KB
SourceForge-4_4-DL6	12/30/2007 2:35 PM	Compressed (zippe...	760,082 KB
xampp-win32-1.7.0-installer	1/10/2009 2:00 PM	Application	39,805 KB

Figure 10-2: If the computers on your network have been shared, you should be able to see the folders, files, and other resources that are available to you.

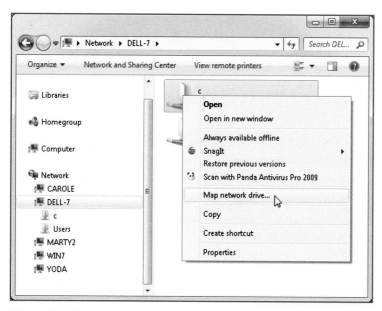

Figure 10-3: *Mapping a network drive gives you a permanent connection to that device.*

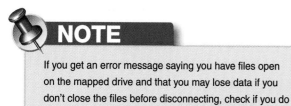

NOTE

If you get an error message saying you have files open on the mapped drive and that you may lose data if you don't close the files before disconnecting, check if you do have files open, and if so, close them. Then once you are sure nothing is open, click **Yes** to disconnect.

5. In the navigation pane of the original Windows Explorer window, click the triangle to the left of **Network** to close it. Then, if it isn't already displayed, click **Computer** to open that view. Both in the navigation pane and in the subject pane, you should see the new network drive, as shown in Figure 10-4.

6. Close Windows Explorer.

DISCONNECT A MAPPED DRIVE

1. Click **Start**, click **Computer**, and, if needed, scroll down the navigation pane so you can see your mapped drive(s).

2. In the navigation pane, right-click the mapped network drive, and click **Disconnect**. The drive will disappear from the navigation and subject panes.

Connect Outside Your Workgroup or Domain

If you want to connect to another computer or network resource outside of your workgroup or domain, you will not see that

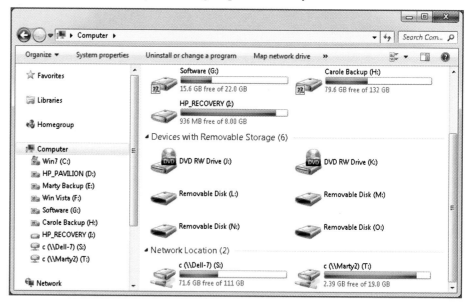

Figure 10-4: *You have the same access to a mapped network drive across a network as you do to any drive on your computer.*

10

NOTE

In order to connect to a network, one has to first be created. If that hasn't been done, return to Chapter 9 and follow the instructions there.

QUICKSTEPS

USING NETWORK ADDRESSES

Network addressing uses the *Uniform Naming Convention,* or UNC, to identify files, folders, and other resources on any computer on the network.

IDENTIFYING A NETWORK RESOURCE

A network resource, which is a folder or disk on a computer on the network, is identified by:

*computername**drivename:**pathname**folder name*

For example, on a computer named "Marty2," a folder named "2010 Budgets" on the D: drive in the Budgeting folder would have the full network address of:

\\Marty2\D:\Budgeting\2010 Budgets

IDENTIFYING A NETWORK PRINTER

Identifying a network printer is similar to identifying any other network resource. It takes the form of:

*computername**printername*

For example, a printer named HP4500 on Server 1 would have the UNC of:

\\Server1\HP4500.

computer or resource when you open Network view. You must use a different procedure to connect to it.

1. Click **Start** and click **Computer**. Scroll down and click **Network**. The Network window opens, as you saw in Figure 10-1.

2. Click **Network And Sharing Center** on the toolbar. The Network And Sharing Center window will open.

3. Click **Connect To A Network**. A list of the networks you can connect to is displayed. Click the network you want, and click **Connect**.

4. If requested, enter a user name and a password, and click **OK**. Given the appropriate permissions, you'll see and be able to open the computers in the other network.

5. Close the Network And Sharing Center and Windows Explorer.

Copy Network Files and Information

Once you have opened a network resource, it is easy to copy information from the resource to your local hard disk.

1. Click **Start** and click **Computer**. If needed, scroll through the navigation pane, and click the triangle opposite **Network** to open it. Then open the computer, drive, and folder(s) in order to see the files that you want to copy in the subject pane.

2. In the navigation pane on your local computer, click the triangle opposite the drive and, if needed, open the folder to display the folder you want to hold the information from the network.

3. In the subject pane, click the first file or folder you want to copy, and then hold down **CTRL**, clicking the remaining files and/or folders you want. When all are selected, drag them to the folder in the navigation pane in which you want them, as you can see in Figure 10-5.

4. Close Windows Explorer.

Print on Network Printers

Like using other network resources, using a network printer is not much different from using a local printer. To locate a network printer, see the "Finding or Adding a Network Printer" QuickSteps.

FINDING OR ADDING A NETWORK PRINTER

There are two ways to find a network printer: by using Find Printer in the Print dialog boxes of some programs and by using Add A Printer in the Printers And Faxes dialog box.

USE FIND PRINTER

Recent versions of Microsoft Office products and other applications have included a Find Printer button to search for and locate network printers. This is the same as the printer search capability, which uses the Windows domain's Active Directory service. To use this, you must be in a domain and not in a workgroup.

1. In an Office 2007 application, click the **Office Button**, click **Print**, and click **Find Printer**. If your network is not part of an Active Directory domain, you will get a message to that effect. Otherwise, the Find Printers dialog box will appear and begin a search for a printer.

2. A list of printers will be displayed. When you have located the printer you want, right-click that printer and click **Connect**.

3. Close the Search Results window.

USE ADD A PRINTER

Add A Printer is the most common way to locate a network printer, and is available to both workgroup and domain users.

1. Click **Start**, click **Control Panel**, and, in Category view, click **View Devices And Printers** under Hardware And Sound. The Devices And Printers window opens.

Continued . . .

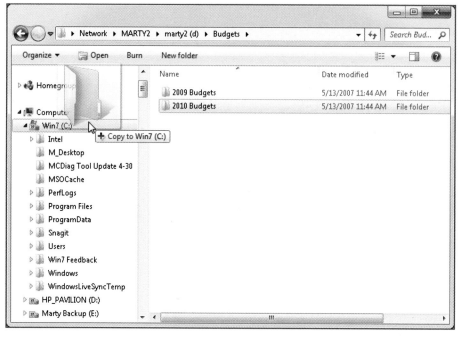

Figure 10-5: You can locate and copy files and folders across the network.

To use a network printer that has been previously found, either automatically or manually—from Microsoft Word 2007, for example:

1. Click the **Office Button**, and click **Print** to open the Print dialog box.

2. Under Printer, click the **Name** down arrow, and choose the network printer you want to use.

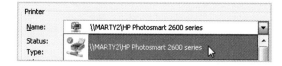

3. Make any needed adjustments to the printer settings, and click **OK** to complete the printing.

QUICKSTEPS

FINDING OR ADDING A NETWORK PRINTER *(Continued)*

2. Click **Add A Printer**. Click **Add A Network, Wireless, Or Bluetooth Printer**. A list of printers will be presented to you (see Figure 10-6). Select one and click **Next**.

3. If you don't see a list of printers, click **The Printer That I Want Isn't Listed**. Click **Select A Shared Printer By Name**, click **Browse**, double-click the computer that has the printer you want, and then double-click the printer. You should see the printer you want in the Add Printer dialog box, as shown in Figure 10-7.

4. Click **Next**. A permanent connection will be made to the printer. Click **Install Driver** if you are asked to do so. Click **Next**.

5. If desired, click the **Set As The Default Printer** check box. Click **Print A Test Page**. When a test page prints, click **Close** and then click **Finish**. If a test page does not print, click **Get Help With Printing**, and follow the suggestions.

6. Close Control Panel.

TIP

You can copy information among any computers on the network, not just from a network computer to your local computer, *if* you have the necessary permissions.

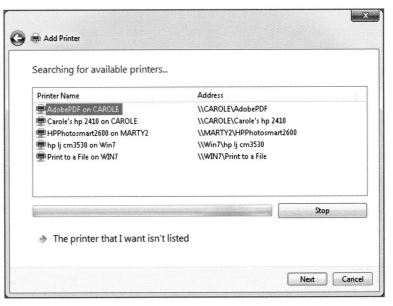

Figure 10-6: *The automatic search for a printer may not find the printer you are looking for if you are not on an Active Directory domain.*

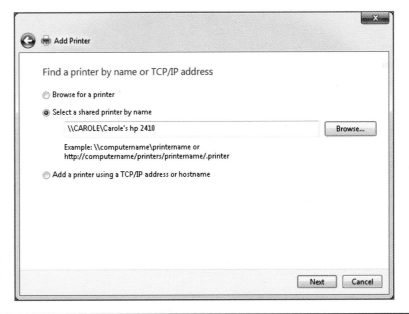

Figure 10-7: *If you know of a network computer to which a printer has been attached and it has been shared, you can connect to it easily.*

Access a Network Internet Connection

If the network you are on has an Internet connection, you are automatically connected to it and can use it directly, unless it requires a user name and password. In most instances, you simply have to open your browser (click the **Internet Explorer** icon on the taskbar) or your email program (click **Start**, click **All Programs**, click **Windows Live**, and click **Windows Live Mail**), and you are on and using the Internet. See Chapter 4 for more information.

Let Others Access Your Resources

The other side of the networking equation is sharing the resources on your computer to allow others to use them. This includes sharing your files, folders, and disks, as well as sharing your printers. The mechanics of setting up your computer to share its resources is discussed in depth in Chapters 8 and 9 (in particular, see Chapter 8). Here we'll look at how that is used once it is turned on.

Share Files and Folders

You can share files and folders by putting them into a shared folder. By default, your computer has a series of folders within Libraries that can be shared; however, the folders aren't shared by default unless you are in a homegroup. You can also create more shared folders (see Chapters 8 and 9).

1. Click **Start**, click **Computer**, and open the disk and folder(s) needed to locate and display the files and/or folders you want to share in the subject pane.

2. In the navigation pane, click the triangle opposite **Libraries**, **Documents**, **Public Documents** to display the public folders.

3. Drag the files and/or folders you want to share from the subject pane to one of the Libraries folders in the navigation pane, as shown in Figure 10-8.

4. Close Windows Explorer.

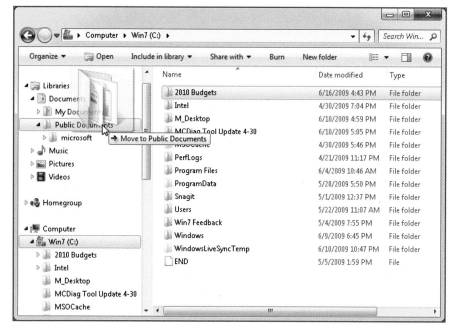

Figure 10-8: You can share a file by putting it into one of the public Libraries folders.

Work Remotely

Windows 7 allows you to work remotely from another computer—for example, from a remote computer (like your laptop) to a computer or server in your office—using Windows 7's Remote Desktop Connection. The objective is to transfer information and utilize resources from a distance using a LAN connection. Using Remote Desktop Connection requires both a Remote Desktop host and a Remote Desktop client.

Set Up a Remote Desktop Connection

Remote Desktop Connection enables you to literally take control of another computer and do everything on it as if you were sitting in front of that computer. Remote Desktop Connection is run over a LAN, where the computer you are sitting at is the *client* and the computer you are accessing is the *host*. To set up the host, you must first establish user accounts and then enable a LAN-based host.

SET UP REMOTE DESKTOP ACCOUNTS

To use Remote Desktop Connection, the host must have user accounts established for that purpose and the user accounts must have a password. Therefore, the first step in setting up the account is to set up one or more such accounts on the host.

1. Click **Start** and click **Control Panel**. In Category view, click **User Accounts And Family Safety**, and then click **User Accounts**.

2. Click **Manage Another Account**, click **Create A New Account**, enter the name for the account (this example uses "Remote"), select the type of account you want, and click **Create Account**.

3. Click the new account, click **Create A Password**, enter the password, press TAB, type the password again, press TAB twice, enter a hint if you wish (anyone can see the hint), and click **Create Password**. Close the Change An Account window.

4. Click **Start** and click **Control Panel**. In Category view, click **System And Security**, scroll to the bottom, and click **Administrative Tools**.

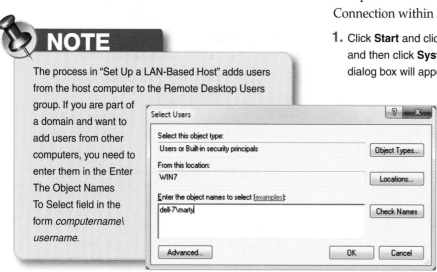

Figure 10-9: User accounts must be members of the Remote Desktop Users group in order to use Remote Desktop Connection.

5. In the subject pane, double-click **Computer Management**. In the Computer Management window that opens, in the left column, if it isn't already open, click the triangle opposite **System Tools** to open it, click the triangle opposite **Local Users And Groups** to open it, and click **Users**. In the list of users in the subject pane, shown in Figure 10-9, double-click the new user you just created.

6. In the user's Properties dialog box that appears, click the **Member Of** tab, and click **Add**. In the Select Groups dialog box, click **Advanced** and then click **Find Now** to search for groups. Click **Remote Desktop Users**, click **OK** three times, and close the Computer Management, Administrative Tools, and Control Panel windows.

SET UP A LAN-BASED HOST

Set up the host for using Remote Desktop Connection within a LAN.

1. Click **Start** and click **Control Panel**. In Category view, click **System And Security**, and then click **System**. Click **Remote Settings** on the left. The System Properties dialog box will appear with the Remote tab displayed.

2. In the bottom Remote Desktop panel, click **Allow Connections From Computers Running Any Version Of Remote Desktop**, as shown in Figure 10-10.

3. Click **Select Users**. Users that you added to the Remote Desktop Users group are displayed.

4. If you want to add more users, click **Add**, click **Advanced**, and click **Find Now**. Select the users you want to include by holding down **CTRL** while clicking them, and then click **OK** four times to close all open dialog boxes. Close Control Panel.

NOTE

The process in "Set Up a LAN-Based Host" adds users from the host computer to the Remote Desktop Users group. If you are part of a domain and want to add users from other computers, you need to enter them in the Enter The Object Names To Select field in the form *computername\ username*.

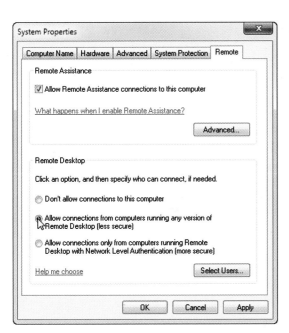

Figure 10-10: *Remote Desktop Connection is not turned on by default.*

SET UP A REMOTE DESKTOP CLIENT

The Remote Desktop Connection client is probably already installed on the computer you will be using for the client, since it is part of the default Windows 7 installation. Verify this, and, if it is not installed, do so.

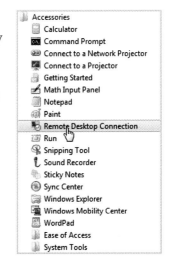

Click **Start**, click **All Programs**, click **Accessories**, and click **Remote Desktop Connection**.

If you see the Remote Desktop Connection dialog box, you need to do nothing further here.

If you do not see Remote Desktop Connection, you'll need to reinstall Windows 7.

Connect to a Remote Desktop over a LAN

When you are sitting at the client computer connected to a LAN, to which the host is also connected, you can connect to the Remote Desktop host.

1. Click **Start**, click **All Programs**, click **Accessories**, and click **Remote Desktop Connection**. The Remote Desktop Connection dialog box appears.

2. Enter the name or IP address of the computer to which you want to connect in the form *computer name.*

3. After you have entered the computer name, click **Connect**. The Windows Security dialog box appears. If asked, enter the user name and password for the Remote Desktop host computer (this was the "Remote" user you created earlier), and click **OK**.

   If you see a message that someone is currently logged on to the remote host, decide if you can disconnect them, and click the appropriate choice. (See "Use a Remote Desktop Connection.")

   If you get a message that the remote computer does not have a security certificate from a trusted certifying authority, click **Yes** to go ahead and connect. (You may have created your own certificate in Chapter 8.)

The Remote Desktop toolbar appears in the top center of the screen with the name of the computer that is hosting you.

Figure 10-11: *When the remote desktop is reduced from full-screen size, the Remote Desktop toolbar, the Connection Bar, disappears.*

Use a Remote Desktop Connection

Once you are connected to the host computer, you can perform almost any action that you could if you were sitting in front of that computer—you can run programs, access data, and more. In addition, the Remote Desktop toolbar, called the Connection Bar, allows you to close the Remote Desktop window without logging out so that your programs will keep running, to minimize the window so that you can see the computer you are sitting at (see Figure 10-11), and to maximize the window. In addition, there is a pushpin icon that determines whether the Connection Bar is always on the desktop or if it is only there when you move the mouse to the upper-center portion of the screen.

Remote Desktop Connection also gives you the ability to transfer information between the host computer and the client computer you are using. This means that you can:

- Print to a local printer connected to the client (this is enabled by default)
- Work with files on both the remote host and the client computers in the same window (this is not enabled by default)
- Cut and paste between both computers and documents on either one (this is enabled by default)

The local client resources that are available in a Remote Desktop session are controlled by the Remote Desktop Connection dialog box options.

TIP

If your LAN has particularly heavy traffic and is slow, you might want to lower the screen size and colors.

Figure 10-12: You can control what client devices are available with Remote Desktop.

1. From the Remote Desktop, click **Start**, click **All Programs**, click **Accessories**, and click **Remote Desktop Connection**. The Remote Desktop Connection dialog box appears. Click **Options**, and the box expands to give you a number of controls for Remote Desktop.

2. Click the **Display** tab. The default for a LAN is to use Full Screen mode and up to the maximum color level your computer can use, as well as to display the Connection Bar.

3. Click the **Local Resources** tab. As you can see in Figure 10-12, you can determine your audio settings, which include bringing sound to the client, and if you want the ability to use shortcut keys. Also:

   ● If you want to print on the printer attached to the local client, keep the default Printers selection.

   ● If you want to transfer information using the Cut and Paste commands between the two computers, the Clipboard should be selected.

   ● If you want to transfer information by dragging between disk drives, click **More** and click **Drives** to select them all; or click the plus sign (+) next to **Drives**, and select individual drives.

   ● If you intend to use a Plug And Play device on the local client, click that option.

4. If you want to start a program when you open the Remote Desktop Connection, click the **Programs** tab, click the relevant check box, and enter the path and filename of the program and the starting folder to use.

5. Click the **Experience** tab, and select the connection speed you are using. This will determine which of the items below the drop-down list box are selected. You can change the individual items if you want.

6. Click the **Advanced** tab. Look at the choices for authentication, and select the one that is correct for you. If you have to go through a Remote Desktop (RD) Gateway (generally in larger organizations), click **Settings**, select the option that is correct for you, type any needed information, and click **OK**.

7. Click the **General** tab. If you will use several settings, save the ones you just made by clicking **Save As**, entering a name, and clicking **Save**.

8. If you are not already connected, enter your password and click **Connect**. Otherwise, close the Remote Desktop Connection dialog box.

9. When you are done using Remote Desktop, you may leave it in any of three ways:

- Click **Close** on the Connection Bar. This leaves you logged on, and any programs you have will remain running. If you restart Remote Desktop Connection with the host computer and no one else has logged on locally, you will return to the same session you left.

- Click **Start** and click **Log Off**. This terminates your Remote Desktop session and all programs are stopped. If you restart Remote Desktop Connection with the host computer and no one else has logged on locally, you will begin a new session.

- Click **Start**, click the **Shut Down** right arrow, and click **Disconnect**. This is the same as clicking the Close button on the Connection Bar.

Set Up and Use a Wireless Network

Wireless networks have become a popular way to create small networks in homes and small businesses for the simple reason that you don't have to run cables everywhere. With a wireless access point connected to the Internet, any wireless-enabled computer within approximately 150 feet (46 m) of the access point indoors can connect to the Internet and communicate with any other network-connected or wireless-enabled computer. If the access point is also connected to a wired network, all the members of the wired network are available to the wireless computers. Chapter 9 talked about the hardware requirements needed to do this. Here we will talk about what is needed to set up and use a wireless network in Windows 7 and make it secure.

Set Up a Wireless Connection

The first task is to make a connection with a wireless access point and then set it up so its use is secure. If you have a recent computer with wireless capability that is turned on (there may be a small switch on your computer to do that) and are near a wireless access point, your computer may automatically connect. If you click on the network connection in the notification area, you will get a message you are connected. In any case, continue from here to set up and secure the connection.

NOTE

The effective range of a wireless access point is highly dependent on which protocol (802.11b, 802.11g, or 802.11n) you are using ("n" is better than "b" or "g"), the types of walls you have to go through (wood and plaster are better than concrete or metal), and on your device—see http://reviews.cnet.com and search on "wireless access points."

1. Click **Start** and click **Control Panel**. In Category view, click **Network And Internet**, and then click **Network And Sharing Center**. If you are already connected, you will see your connection both graphically and textually, as shown in Figure 10-13. Skip to step 6.

2. If you don't see a wireless connection already established, click **Set Up A Connection Or Network**. Click **Set Up A New Network**, and click **Next**. Your system will search for a wireless adapter in your computer and then for a wireless access point.

3. When a wireless network is found, you are asked to name your network. Type a name and click **Next**. Type a "passphrase" or password of at least eight characters, and click **Next**.

4. Choose the file and printer sharing option you want, or keep your current settings, and click **Next**.

5. Insert a USB flash drive on which you can save your settings, and click **Next**. This drive can be used to transfer these settings to other computers and wireless devices. Click **Close**.

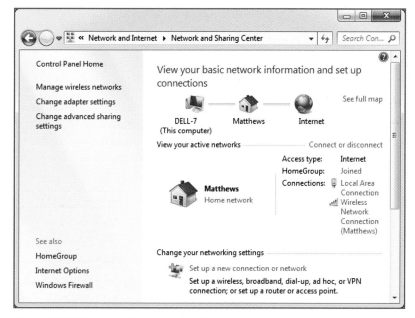

Figure 10-13: You want the connection between your computer and a wireless access point to be secure so that someone within range of your access point cannot use it.

6. In the Network And Sharing Center window (as in Figure 10-13), look at the type of wireless network you have—Private or Public—and determine the type your situation requires. If you need to change the type, click **Customize**, click the type you want, change the icon if desired, click **Next**, and click **Close**.

Manage Wireless Network Sharing

When you use a wireless connection, you most likely do not want other network users to access your computer. That is the default setting, but check and make sure that is the way your connection is set up.

1. From the Network And Sharing Center, click **Change Adapter Settings** in the Tasks list. The Network Connections window opens, displaying the connections available on the computer.

2. Double-click **Wireless Network Connection** to open the Wireless Network Connection Status dialog box, shown in Figure 10-14.

3. Click **Properties**, click the **Sharing** tab, and look at your connection-sharing settings. In most circumstances where you are using a public WiFi hotspot, you want these check boxes *not* selected, which is the default in a public network. In a home network, the setup shown here is the default. The primary instance in which you would want this enabled would be in a secure organizational setting.

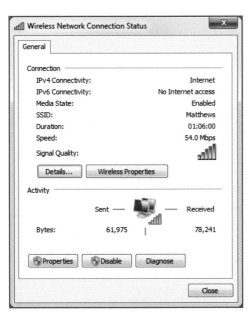

Figure 10-14: A wireless network is particularly susceptible to intrusion and needs to be protected.

10

IMPLEMENTING WINDOWS DEFENDER

Windows Defender guards your computer against spyware and other unwanted programs. It watches what is happening on your computer and looks for programs that are trying to install themselves or change important Windows settings, both without your approval. Windows Defender does this on a real-time basis, as well as letting you manually start a scan of your computer. It uses a Microsoft database called the SpyNet Community that tracks, with the user's approval, what programs people think might be dangerous.

REVIEW WINDOWS DEFENDER SETTINGS

By default, Windows Defender is running on your computer and you must take some action to turn it off, if that is what you want, although this is not recommended. To open, review, and possibly change the Windows Defender setting:

1. Click **Start**, click **Control Panel**, click the **Category** down arrow, click **Large Icons**, scroll to the bottom, and click **Windows Defender**. Windows Defender appears.

2. Click **Tools** on the toolbar, and click **Options** to display the many settings you can change to have Defender run the way you want, as shown in Figure 10-16.

3. Click each of the options on the left, and for each, scroll through the settings and make any changes that meet your needs.

4. When you have finished, click **Save** to return to the Tools And Settings window and check out the other options there.

Continued . . .

4. When you have assured yourself that the settings are the way you want them, click **OK**, click **Close** in the Status dialog box, and close the Network Connections window.

Use a Wireless Network

Once you have a wireless network up and running the way you want, you can use it in the same way you use a wired network.

1. Click the **Internet Explorer** icon on the taskbar to open Internet Explorer, and explore the Internet in the same way you would with a wired network, as shown in Figure 10-15.

2. Close Internet Explorer and open your email program, which you can use in the same way as with a wired network connection.

3. Close your mail program, and try any other networking program you use.

Figure 10-15: You can use a wireless network connection in the same way you used a wired one.

QUICKSTEPS

IMPLEMENTING WINDOWS DEFENDER *(Continued)*

DO A MANUAL SCAN

If you suspect that software you don't want has gotten on your computer, you can run a manual scan to see what Windows Defender finds.

1. While in Windows Defender, click **Scan** on the toolbar. The scanning will immediately start. When it completes, you will be told what was found and given the scan statistics, as shown in Figure 10-17.

2. When you have finished, click **Close** and close the Control Panel.

CAUTION

Windows Defender is not designed or recommended as a replacement for antivirus software. It is meant solely to get rid of spyware and unwanted programs. You should also have an antivirus program, most of which also get rid of spyware.

Figure 10-16: *Windows Defender provides some protection against spyware and unwanted programs.*

Figure 10-17: *Windows Defender can do a quick manual scan anytime you want it.*

Index

Numbers

10/100/1000BaseT Ethernet, 210
802.11* wireless standards, 211
10.0.0.0 IP address, 222
127.0.0.1 IP address, 224
169.254.0.0 IP address, 220
172.16.0.0 IP address, 222
192.168.0.0 IP address, 222

Symbols

! (exclamation) point in shield, 18
" (quotation marks), using with search criteria, 76

A

A: drive, 51
access point, using with WLANs, 212
accessory programs. *See also* programs
    Calculator, 114
    Character Map, 114–115
    Notepad, 115
    Paint, 115
account picture, changing, 33
accounts. *See* user accounts
Action Center, using, 5, 117
adapter, using with WLANs, 212
address bar
    described, 9, 47
    location of, 9, 46
    using for navigation, 54
administrator, logging on as, 182–183
Aero Peek feature, using, 14–15, 35
Aero Shake feature, using, 15
Aero Snaps feature, using, 15–16
All Programs menu, starting programs on, 8
ALT key. *See* keyboard shortcuts
APIPA (Automatic Private IP Addressing), 220

APNIC (Asia Pacific Network Information Centre), 223
application icons, using jump lists with, 16
applications. *See* programs; software
archiving attribute, 61
ARIN (American Registry for Internet Numbers), 223
Attach, using with email, 94
audio. *See also* Media Player
    playing, 85
    mixing in movies, 176
automatic programs, controlling, 112. *See also* programs
Automatic Updates, 115–116
AutoPlay dialog box, displaying, 139

B

Back button
    function of, 47
    location of, 46
    using on Internet, 75
backed up encryption key, using, 204
background picture, selecting, 25
backing up
    file encryption key, 203–204
    files and folders, 62–64
Bcc text box, using with email, 88
biometric devices, using, 188
bits, defined, 68
broadband connection, setting up, 72
browser navigation, using, 75
browsers
    choosing in UK and Europe, 72
    starting, 74
Burn
    choosing in Media Player, 161
    choosing in Movie Maker, 178
Burn List, correcting, 168

burning
    files to disc, 65–66
    music to CDs, 167–168

C

C: drive
    avoiding indexing of, 113
    disk associated with, 51
    opening, 52
Calculator accessory program, 114
calendar in Windows Live Mail
    adding events to, 95
    opening, 94
camcorder, importing video from, 171–172
camera images, importing, 138–139
cameras, installing, 134–137
card games, playing, 19–21
Category view, 40
Cc text box, using with email, 88
CD drive, label for, 51
CDs
    burning music to, 167–168
    copying, 164–165
    copyright concerns, 165
    installing software from, 122
    playing, 160–161
    ripping, 164–165
    viewing copying process, 164–165
    writing files and folders to, 64–66
cell phone wireless connection, 70–71
Change permission, setting, 199
Character Map accessory program, 114–115
check box, example of, 12
children, setting Parental Controls for, 189–190
classic menus, turning on, 11
ClearType, adjusting, 28
"click Start," explained, 6

taskbar
areas of, 33
closing programs from, 109
hiding, 34
location of, 2, 4
moving and sizing, 33–34
pinning icons to, 34–35
programs pinned to, 5, 33
removing pinned icons from, 35
starting programs from, 8
switching programs on, 107–108
ungrouping tasks in, 110
unlocking, 34
using, 4
using small icons, 34
taskbar buttons, customizing, 34–35
taskbar previews, using, 16–17
taskbar properties
closing, 35–36
opening, 34
TCP/IPv4 and TCP/IPv6, 219–220
telephone connections
dial-up, 68
DSL (digital subscriber line), 68–69
fiber optic, 69–70
text, copying from Internet, 84
text box, example of, 12
text file printer, creating, 149–150
text size, changing, 25–26
themes, reviewing, 25
thumbnails
displaying for open web pages, 78
displaying for open windows, 16–17
viewing in Photo Gallery, 141
time and date, setting, 4, 36–38
title bar
contents of, 11
described, 9
location of, 9, 12

titles, adding to movies, 175–176
Toggle Keys option, 39
toolbars
described, 9, 46–48
example of, 9
transitions, adding to movies, 175
Trim, clicking in Video group, 174
Turn Shuffle On, using, 166
TV cable service connection, 70

U

UAC (User Account Control) QuickFacts, 182–183
UK (United Kingdom), choosing browsers in, 72
updates. *See* Windows Update
USB flash drive, using disc as, 65
user account type, changing, 183
user accounts. *See also* group accounts
customizing, 188
domain, 182
renaming, 184
setting up, 184–185
user-related folders, opening, 7
users
adding to groups, 200
Administrator, 182–183
logging on as administrator, 182–183
Standard, 182–183
as Standard Users, 200
switching among, 188

V

video
importing from camcorder, 171–173
playing on web pages, 85–86
synchronizing with photos, 142
video clips, trimming, 174–175

video DVDs, playing, 170
visualizations, displaying in Media Player, 168
volume, controlling in Media Player, 162

W

Web Browser Ballot, 72
Web History in IE8
deleting and setting, 81
using, 81
Web mail, using, 93
web pages. *See also* pages
copying from Internet, 84–85
printing, 150
seeing thumbnails of, 78
Web sites
adding to Favorites, 76
adding to Favorites bar, 81
browsing and viewing in IE8, 85
APNIC (Asia Pacific Network Information Centre), 223
ARIN (American Registry for Internet Numbers), 223
categorizing for security, 82
categorizing into zones, 81–82
entering directly, 74
Google's Gmail, 93
RIPE (Réseaux IP Européens), 223
saving, 76
Windows Live Essentials, 86
Windows Live Hotmail, 93
Yahoo! Mail, 93
WiFi standard, 211
window layout, changing, 11
windows
versus dialog boxes, 10–11
hiding and unhiding, 15
resizing and positioning, 15–16

Y

Z